THE LIFE OF NUNS

The Life of Nuns

Love, Politics, and Religion in Medieval German Convents

Henrike Lähnemann and Eva Schlotheuber

https://www.openbookpublishers.com
©2024 Henrike Lähnemann and Eva Schlotheuber

This work is licensed under an Attribution-NonCommercial 4.0 International (CC BY-NC 4.0). This licence allows you to share, copy, distribute and transmit the text; to adapt the text for non-commercial purposes of the text providing attribution is made to the author (but not in any way that suggests that they endorse you or your use of the work). Attribution should include the following information:

Henrike Lähnemann and Eva Schlotheuber, *The Life of Nuns: Love, Politics, and Religion in Medieval German Convents*. Cambridge, UK: Open Book Publishers, 2024, https://doi.org/10.11647/OBP.0397

Copyright and permissions for the reuse of the images included in this publication may differ from the above. This information is provided in the captions and in the list of illustrations.

Further details about CC BY-NC licences are available at https://creativecommons.org/licenses/by-nc/4.0/

All external links were active at the time of publication unless otherwise stated and have been archived via the Internet Archive Wayback Machine at https://archive.org/web

Any digital material and resources associated with this volume will be available at https://doi.org/10.11647/OBP.0397#resources

ISBN Paperback: 978-1-80511-266-2
ISBN Hardback: 978-1-80511-267-9
ISBN Digital (PDF): 978-1-80511-268-6
ISBN Digital ebook (EPUB): 978-1-80511-269-3
ISBN HTML: 978-1-80511-271-6
DOI: 10.11647/OBP.0397

Cover image: *Apparition of the crucified Christ from the vision of Dorothea von Meding in 1562*, painted in 1623, on the nuns' choir in Kloster Lüne. Photo by Sabine Wehking. ©Kloster Lüne

Cover design by Jeevanjot Kaur Nagpal

Contents

Prologue: Voices from the Past	1
I. Enclosure	9
1. The Nuns' Flight	10
2. The Convent Living Space	19
3. The Ebstorf World Map	31
II. Education	37
1. The Convent as School	37
2. The Convent as Cultural and Educational Space	43
3. The Heiningen Philosophy Tapestry	52
III. Nuns, Family, and Community	59
1. Life History and Family Influence	59
2. The Family and the Convent Community	64
3. Representation and Status	72
IV. Love and Friendship	81
1. Friendship Beyond Convent Walls	81
2. The Idea of Friendship	93
3. Christ Embracing John the Evangelist as Spiritual Bridehood	96
V. Music and Reform	103
1. Secular Songs while Breaking Flax	103
2. Convent Reform	106
3. Music Instruction in Kloster Ebstorf	118
VI. Reformation	127
1. The Papal Legate Arrives in Town	128
2. Convents during the Reformation	139
3. A Vision of the Reformation	149

VII. Illness and Dying	155
1. Death in the Community	156
2. Medicinal Knowledge and the Rituals of Dying	163
3. This World and the Next in the Wienhausen Nuns' Choir	169
VIII. Appendix	177
1. Convent Histories	177
2. Schematic Representations of Convent Life	179
3. Glossary of Terms	181
4. List of Illustrations	187
5. Sources and Secondary Literature	189
Index	193

Prologue: Voices from the Past

In the Middle Ages, half of all those who entered religious houses were women. Why, then, do we hear so little about them? From the German lands, only a few names are familiar: Hildegard of Bingen, of course. Perhaps also Roswitha of Gandersheim and Mechthild of Magdeburg. In recent years, they have had books or exhibitions dedicated to them. Yet the great group of learned, feisty, devout, capable, and enterprising nuns from countless generations has faded into oblivion, their voices unheard. Nevertheless, in the Middle Ages women who lived in *convents[1] were by no means unremarkable or unremarked – quite the opposite. The title of the original German version of this book[2] plays on the word 'unerhört', meaning both 'unheard' in the sense of not noticed by research and 'unheard of' in the sense of outspoken, even outrageous. The nuns' communities were often powerful institutions, and the nuns saw themselves as occupying a highly influential position, since their way of life made them into 'brides of Christ', the now and future spouses of the 'king of kings'. Such a position meant they had his ear as no one else did. The conviction that Christ heard and listened to them permeated medieval society and bestowed upon them a special status, one which manifested itself not just politically and economically, but also socially and culturally – and which allowed these women to become effective and influential in hitherto unprecedented ways.

To be unheard-of and unheard is a fate first suffered by these nuns in the modern era; thus every act of rendering them visible – and

---

1 Explanations of asterisked key terms can be found in the Appendix. The term 'convent' is used throughout for the German 'Frauenkloster' (female monastic community); the word 'Kloster' is retained when referring to the convent as geographic place, as in 'Heilig Kreuz Kloster' or 'Kloster Lüne' for the convent dedicated to The Holy Cross or the convent situated at Lüne.
2 Henrike Lähnemann and Eva Schlotheuber, *Unerhörte Frauen. Die Netzwerke der Nonnen im Mittelalter*, Berlin 2023.

audible – constitutes a minor revolution. In her book on entering the convent, education and the world of nuns in the late Middle Ages,[3] Eva Schlotheuber has edited and contextualized a small parchment manuscript which, through daily use, had grown to a considerable girth: the convent diary of a nun from the convent dedicated to the Holy Cross (Heilig Kreuz Kloster) near Braunschweig, an eloquent and important 'witness statement' in which, for over twenty years, a Cistercian nun described her life in the convent just outside the town gates of Braunschweig. For her part, Henrike Lähnemann brought together, from libraries across the globe, the devotional manuals of the *Cistercian nuns from Kloster Medingen and edited their liturgy from the Manual of the Provost in order to open the door into the world of images and devotion inhabited by the nuns.[4] For background information, both authors drew on a unique source which had, up to then, languished amongst the medieval manuscripts in the convent archive at Kloster Lüne: the community's unedited collection of letters. They copied nearly 1,800 of these, written between 1460 and 1560, into three voluminous books of which the first volume, together with short summaries and a comprehensive introduction in both German and English, is available open access.[5] These are moving testimonies from the late Middle Ages and Reformation, when the nuns resolutely resisted the introduction of Lutheran practices into the convent. In their letters, the women debate a broad spectrum of themes stemming from their work days, high days and holidays – from lobbying for additional rights for their convent to theological debates to letters dispensing consolation and advice.

The German Reformation was a hugely complex and regionally diverse process. While Protestant historiography traditionally told the story of a clear break marked by Martin Luther's publication of the *Ninety-Five Theses* in 1517, the reality in the multitude of small German principalities, many of which changed sides several times, was much more complex. Dissolution during the Reformation was a fate only about half of the convents experienced in the areas that converted to

---

3   Eva Schlotheuber, *Klostereintritt und Bildung. Die Lebenswelt der Nonnen im späten Mittelalter*, Tübingen 2004.
4   Ulrike Hascher-Burger and Henrike Lähnemann, *Liturgie und Reform. Das Handbuch des Medinger Propsts*, Tübingen 2013.
5   Links to these and other recommended reading are available at the end of the volume.

Protestantism.[6] Those in the territory of Lüneburg, among them Kloster Lüne, continued to exist as a Protestant community in its original buildings. In 2022, the convent celebrated 850 years of uninterrupted existence. A community of women under an *abbess still lives in these premises. The construction of the buildings is reported in the letters, and its archive has preserved the medieval sources to this day. The women of Kloster Lüne can be seen in the image on the front cover, a detail from a painting which captures the vision of a Lüne conventual in the sixteenth century. It still hangs on the wall of the nuns' choir at Kloster Lüne. Other convents, such as the home of the Cistercian diarist, were initially dissolved but deemed indispensable after all and refounded a short while later, as a Protestant foundation for women from high-ranking families.

The diarist does not mention her name in her work. At no place in her entertaining record of convent life, which stretches over two decades, does she provide any clue to her identity. She lived as a nun in the Cistercian Heilig Kreuz Kloster towards the end of the fifteenth century and, like two thirds of the community, probably died of the disease in 1507. Her chronicle breaks off abruptly with the description of the plague, which started within the town, slowly spreading to the convent and claiming its first fatalities there. The handwritten diary, preserved in the form of a compact volume, is twice as thick as it is wide. In 1848, the book, part of the estate of the collector Carl Friedrich von Vechelde, who came from Braunschweig, was sold to the Herzog August Bibliothek in Wolfenbüttel and is preserved there under the shelfmark Cod. Guelf. 1159 Novi. Since the von Vechelde family had several of its members in the convent, the diary notes by the anonymous Cistercian nun may have been handed down in the family over the centuries. Unfortunately, the beginning of the manuscript, where the writer of the diary may have said something about herself, is lost. Her journal notes begin in 1484 and, given the noticeable effort and care behind its creation, the journal was clearly an important personal item for her. She procured her own writing material in the thriftiest but most laborious way possible: she scraped off the text of an old parchment prayer book to write on it again and cut further scraps of parchment to the right size or even sewed

---

6   Marjorie Elizabeth Plummer, *Stripping the Veil. Convent Reform, Protestant Nuns, and Female Devotional Life in Sixteenth Century Germany*, Oxford 2022.

smaller pieces together to have sufficient material for her writing. In some places, she supplemented her stock of parchment and paper by using the reverse side of old letters. Her position in the convent can only be established in as far as she does not appear to have held any of the leading monastic offices and officiated neither as *prioress nor as *cellarer nor as *teacher of the girls (*magistra puellarum*). This means that the writer of the diary is one of the rare voices which report on life behind the convent walls from the internal perspective of the convent: she uninhibitedly discusses matters that either appeared problematic to the nuns or simply went wrong. For her, there is nothing which needs defending or glossing over; and in places her judgement on the various office-holders who steered the fortunes of the convent is shot through with quite startling criticism.

Around the year 1500, the duties which fell to the author of the diary probably included participating in the organisation and supervision of the celebratory dinners which took place in the convent in the company of the nuns' relatives whenever new members were admitted to the community. In 1499, she describes just such a dinner, to which families from the minor aristocracy were invited, and concludes her description with the words: 'I have written this down so that I may conduct myself somewhat more cautiously should I be entrusted with the care for a similar dinner in the future'.[7] In other words, she notes down the events of her life in the convent not least for herself. Her lowly position in the convent leaves its mark on her narrative perspective: her comments have a certain unfiltered quality. She writes in Latin, perhaps also to practise that language, on whose orthography and syntax she did not always have the firmest grasp. In some places, she lapses suddenly into the local dialect of Middle Low German, namely, whenever the subject matter becomes emotional, she wishes to reproduce the words of relatives and lay people, or the appropriate Latin expression does not occur to her. Her narrative style is captivating: lively, refreshing, and humorous.

While the writer may have kept a diary as a source of reassurance for herself in difficult situations, she also envisages future generations of nuns in the Heilig Kreuz Kloster as the intended readers of her record.

---

7   *Hoc ideo exaravi, ut si in futuro simile mihi aliquid procurare convivium vel prandium occurrerit, caucius mihi habere valeam*, fol. 131v. Folio numbers for quotations from the diary correspond to those in the edition by Eva Schlotheuber.

She wishes to pass on what the convent has done wrong, whether from lack of awareness or lack of thought, so that these things might be avoided in future: 'I have written this so that those who come after me do not believe every word they hear'.[8] Such were her words of caution to her readers when the provost and convent were forced into a shamefaced admission that they had been fooled by swindlers who had promised them a sizeable endowment from nobles living a considerable distance away. Similarly, in her view the individual nuns who rashly ran away when fire broke out one night on the Rennelberg, the little hill on which the convent was built, would have been better advised to hold their ground, for with a little more faith in God their abandoning of enclosure – especially running around in their nightclothes like vagabonds – could have been avoided.

Building on the tales told by the writer of the journal, we deal with larger, interlinked themes: the nature of life in the convent (Chapter I); what we know about the education there (Chapter II); the nuns' relationship to their families and how the convent economy functioned (Chapter III); the specific shape that love and friendship took within the convents (Chapter IV); the role played by music and what it meant to be reformed (Chapter V); how the women's communities coped with the upheavals of the Reformation (Chapter VI); how illnesses were healed and how death was dealt with in the convents (Chapter VII). The Appendix includes a glossary with a systematic compilation and explanation of concepts marked by asterisks in the text, as well as overviews and suggestions for further reading.

The book is based on material from the German lands – partly because that is the area of the expertise of the authors, but even more so because the surviving documents here are rich in a way which is unparalleled, particularly in England, where the dissolution of the monasteries eradicated the greater part of the material heritage of the convents. Wall paintings in the nuns' choirs, painted sculptures with their dresses for different occasions, illuminated prayer books, and elaborate tapestries would have existed in noble foundations for religious women across the British Isles but have been at best converted, but mostly destroyed. By contrast, in the Cistercian convent of Wienhausen alone, more than 2,000

---

8 *hec scripsi, ut postere non credant omni verbo*, fol. 96v.

objects – among them the oldest spectacles in the world – were found untouched under the floorboards in the 1960s, having fallen through the cracks of time.

Within this corpus of objects and texts, a large number of the sources stem from the fifteenth century. These are fascinating decades in which written testimonies increase sharply in number. Just as the nun from the Heilig Kreuz Kloster recycles a parchment prayer book to make writing space for her notes, many other written documents from convents also bear witness to creativity when dealing with precious writing material. At the end of the fourteenth century, the first paper mill in Germany commenced operations in Nuremberg and the number of those able to read and write increased, above all in the cities and, due to the efforts for reform, in the monastic houses, developments which led to a marked rise in text production. The traditional designation of 'late medieval' is problematic if 'late' represents a value judgement. The stories and records left by the nuns do not speak of decline and discontinuation followed by the dawning of a new age in the sixteenth century, whether with the Reformation or the rebirth ('Renaissance') of Antiquity, one understood in secular terms. Rather, from the perspective of contemporaries, the fifteenth century manifested itself as an age of radical departures and the discovery of new horizons.

We always look back on the past with our own eyes, but we can expand our perspective through that of women from earlier generations if we allow their voices to be heard – whether we are dealing with Hildegard of Bingen and her community in the twelfth century or the anonymous Cistercian nun from the Heilig Kreuz Kloster and her sister nuns in the fifteenth. They are the main protagonists in their own story. We would like to make as many as possible of the forgotten voices audible again. For that reason, we decided to start each chapter with an account from the convent diary of our Cistercian nun from Braunschweig – first-hand reports on lice, Lebkuchen, and attestations of love for Christ.

The rich heritage of the convents also includes their musical and material culture, aspects we similarly wish to incorporate into this book – from their large tapestries to their sculptures to their medieval architecture, of which more has been preserved in Germany than in most other European countries. Hence every chapter is supplemented by medieval works of art from convents: illustrative examples which shed light on a given theme from the perspective of the nuns.

This book has grown out of many years of collaboration and was jointly conceived. Eva Schlotheuber contributed the initial stories and was responsible for the classificatory chapters, while Henrike Lähnemann took this further and was responsible for elucidating the narratives represented in the images. Kristin Rotter of the publishers Propyläen proposed the original project; she accompanied it with enthusiasm, as did Martina Backes, Berndt Hamm, Thomas Noll, Friedel Helga Roolfs, Philipp Stenzig, Sabine Wehking, and Christine Wulf. We also profited from feedback after publication at readings, by reviewers, and by letters. This helped us reshape the volume when Alessandra Tosi encouraged us to bring the book across the Channel, and got her team at Open Book Publishers on board. Particular thanks are owed to Anne Simon who worked with us a number of times through the whole book to turn it into a readable account that opens up the world of Northern Germany to an Anglophone readership, Charlotte Pattenden, prioress of Kloster Lüne, who offered her professional expertise as copy-editor, and Andrew Dunning, curator of medieval manuscripts at the Bodleian Library. Wolfgang Brandis, archivist of the Lüneburg convents, provided the majority of the original illustrations and clarified image copyright with the individual convents. As with the German edition, the abbesses and their convents heartened us from the very beginning with their interest in their own history.

I. Enclosure

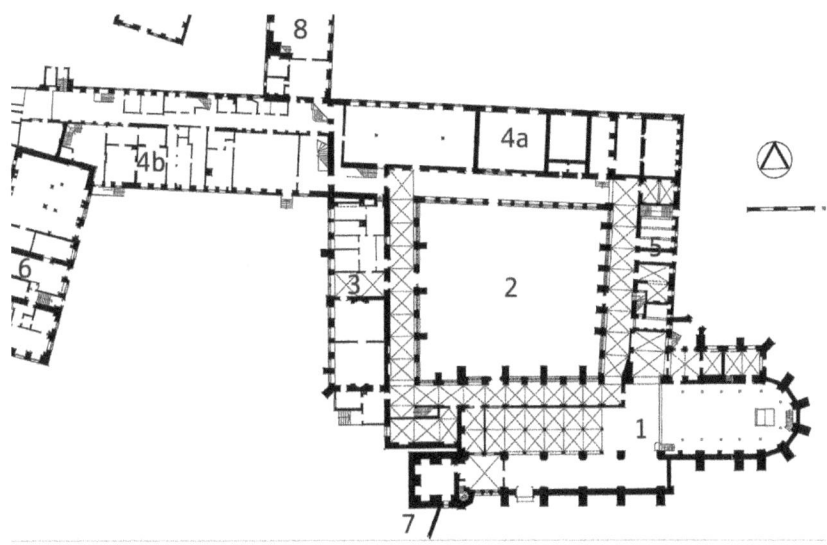

Fig. 1 Floor plan of the monastic buildings at Ebstorf. 1 Church. 2 Cloisters. 3 Abbess's House. 4 Dormitory on the first floor. 5 Bell. 6 Clergy. 7 Lodge. 8 Kitchen. ©Klosterkammer Hannover

Monastic houses are built around the concept of enclosure, the cloistered life away from the world as can be seen still in the floor plans for example of the Lüneburg convents. In its basic features, the plan of the Benedictine convent of Ebstorf (Figure 1) goes back to the time of the world map (Figure 8), on which the convent is represented by a stylized house with a cross on top (Figure 9). The centre of the plan is occupied by the convent church with its choir orientated towards the east and the nuns' choir spanning the western half of the church, above a vaulted lower church for the laity. The nuns could access their choir from the cloister to the north of the church, around which lay the chapter house, refectory, and the other communal rooms. The congregation could access the lower church from the south side. The cloister had stained-glass windows and figured keystones (Figure 25). The gatehouse was to the south-west of the church. Not shown here are the farm buildings which lay outside the complex of connected buildings.

1. The Nuns' Flight

Characteristic features of the nuns' particular way of life become apparent at precisely the moment when this order is disturbed, when war breaks out and the nuns are forced to flee, just as the author of the diary from the Heilig Kreuz Kloster reports for the year 1492.

Suddenly in the Midst of War: The Great Braunschweig Civic Feud

On 12 August 1492 the young Duke Henry the Younger sent written challenges into the town of Braunschweig. Braunschweig's town councillors had refused to pay homage to the new duke, who did not wish to confirm their ancient rights and freedoms. The Cistercian Heilig Kreuz Kloster, marked as 'Convent s. Crucis' on the Rennelberg, a hill to the northwest of the town, lay between the ducal residence in Wolfenbüttel and the town of Braunschweig, just outside the town walls.[1]

The nuns were in turmoil. What were they to do? Stay and hope the duke would spare them, or leave convent and enclosure and flee to Braunschweig? War loomed on the horizon, and the town councillors urged the nuns to flee. Not just the council's messengers but also townswomen came to the convent and painted a colourful picture of the duke's atrocities – the nun reports in direct Low German speech their pleas: 'Dear children, where do you intend to stay? The duke is closer to us than you yourselves believe', with another one adding: 'Run, run, dear children, run, he already stands with his army before the *Krüppelholz* (stunted wood)'. Time and again they came out to the convent and pressed the women: 'Dear children, are you still here? The duke is already inside the lines of fortification and wanted to take the

---

1 Map of Braunschweig around 1400, produced for the edition of town charters by Ludwig Hänselmann and Heinrich Mack, *Urkundenbuch der Stadt Braunschweig* 1, Berlin 1905.

cows from the old town. Alas, alas! If we had you inside the town, we would know that you were kept safe, that you would not be robbed of the noble treasure of your virginity'.[2] Still, the nuns hesitated – violating enclosure was a serious step.

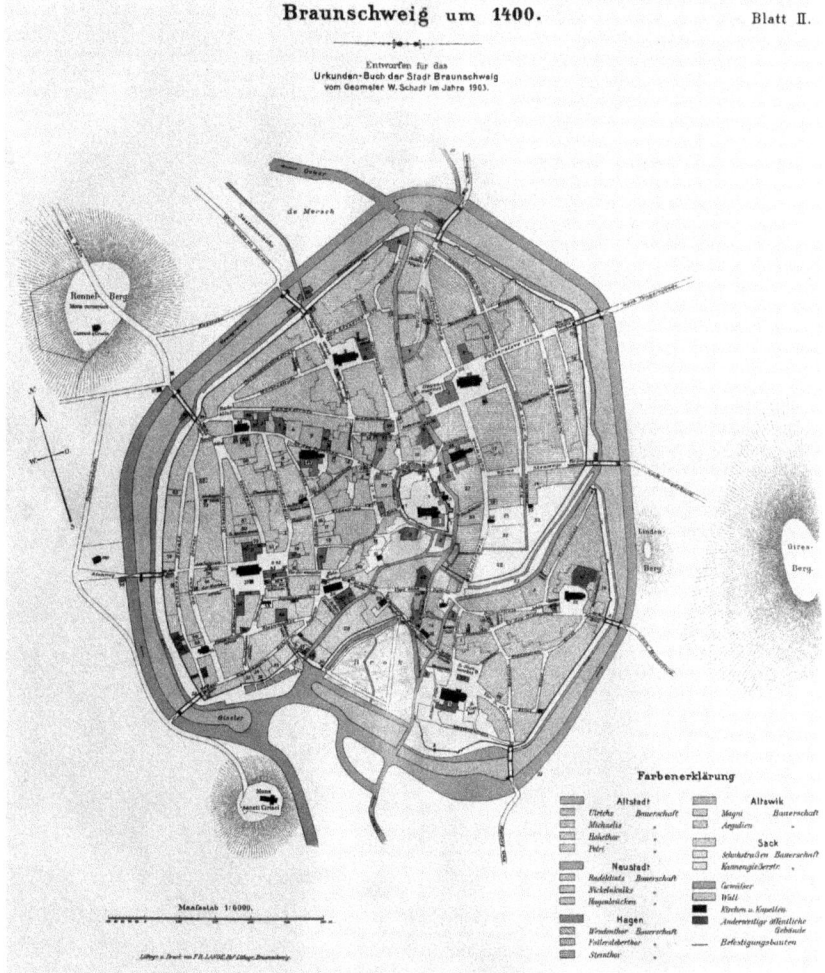

Fig. 2 Map of Braunschweig around 1400. ©W. Schadt, 1903.

---

2 'Leven kynder, wor wil gy bliven? De hertege is uns neger, wan gy sulvest loven', hec una, et continuo venit altera dicens: 'Lopet, lopet, leven kynder, lopet, he holt rede vor deme Kroppelholte', et altera: 'Leven kynder, sint gy hyr noch? De hertege is rede bynnen der lantwere unde wolde der olden stat koyge neme. Ach ach, hedde we gick in der stat, so wuste we gick wolde wart, dat gy des eddelen scattes iuwer iunckfruwenschopp nichten worden berovet', fol. 78r.

Their fear and uncertainty speak to us vividly through the diary of the nun from the Heilig Kreuz Kloster, who does not reveal her name but recounts many of these moving events. The nuns did not hesitate without reason. They knew full well that the Braunschweig town councillors were parties in the dispute. In her diary, the Cistercian nun shrewdly notes that the nuns were more exercised by the horrific nature of the reports than by the actual danger. They also knew it was an easy matter to bombard the town from their well-fortified convent. For that reason, the council had a considerable interest in the nuns' moving into the town so that they could billet town soldiers in the convent before the duke arrived and seized it. Suddenly, the nuns from the Heilig Kreuz Kloster found themselves at the heart of the conflict; furthermore, they occupied the centre ground between the two parties not just spatially but also socially. Within the convent walls, the daughters of the Braunschweig *patriciate, that is, of the urban upper bourgeoisie, lived harmoniously side by side with the daughters of noble families from the surrounding area. That had not happened by chance. The Cistercian Heilig Kreuz Kloster had been founded as an act of atonement and owed its establishment to a feud which had broken out in 1227 between the traditional chivalric nobility and the up-and-coming town of Braunschweig. At that time, the *ministeriales* had taken advantage of a tournament outside the town walls to launch a surprise attack on the town by armed knights. The citizens of Braunschweig had known how to hold their own and had subsequently forced the nobles to found a convent on the Rennelberg, their former jousting field, in atonement for their act of violence (see Figure 2 for the position of the hill). The endowment of a convent just outside the town gates brought with it many advantages. It freed the citizens of Braunschweig from the presence of the knights and their tournaments directly before the gates, particularly since tournaments could always also be used as preparation for military campaigns. Instead, an enclosed site was created where the daughters of the citizens of Braunschweig and the surrounding nobility could together lead a spiritual life and hence, in their way, serve to safeguard the peace between the rival social classes.

This solution succeeded for centuries, but old antagonisms resurfaced with the Great Braunschweig Civic Feud in August 1492. In this tricky situation, the nuns were at a loss; as the conflict came to a head, they packed up all their worldly goods, their bedding, their good cloaks and veils and sent everything off by messenger to their relatives, where it was out of harm's way. Town mercenaries were already loitering around the convent day and night, but – as the author of the diary bitterly remarks – less for their protection than to hold the location for the town. While they were, admittedly, not permitted to enter the *enclosure, the women's inner domain, they ran amok in the courtyard, the kitchens, and the storerooms. In the process, they gave the nuns' provost such a fright that he told the women he intended to leave the convent and seek safety in the town. If they wished to remain, that was their responsibility. This did not improve the situation.

Some nuns recommended sending letters to those noble families with connections to the convent who also exercised influence in the ducal council in order to ask them to spare the nuns and the convent. This discreet diplomacy bore fruit inasmuch as the addressees of the letters promised to intervene with the duke on the nuns' behalf to the best of their ability. Yet they warned that, due to the readiness on the part of the various armies to use violence, the women's protection could not be guaranteed. The nuns were in a real dilemma, since they could not achieve certainty by this means either. Hence the Cistercian nun adds to her diary something we rarely hear: unvarnished criticism of the way the Mother Superior Abbess Mechthild von Vechelde, only recently elected, exercised her office. The author of the diary complains that in those fearful days, they had been like lost sheep – and precisely because their shepherdess, the abbess, had been as if paralysed by fear and panic and was completely at a loss to know what to do. For that reason, she had made promises which subsequently had to be rectified amidst expressions of remorse.

It was no longer possible to think of an orderly daily routine. On the feast of the Assumption of the Virgin (15 August), they once more undertook a communal procession through the convent, cloisters, and cemetery. When they looked through the bars on their windows the following morning, they saw terrifyingly armed knights, heard shots, and heard the bells ringing. Then, during the night, messengers came from the council who more or less ordered them to leave the convent. Their departure had been decided. In the morning, the nuns gathered punctually in the church on the chiming of the bell in order to place themselves and the convent into the hands of God. Our Cistercian nun relates that they wept and wailed so much that they were hardly able to sing. Together they intoned the *antiphon 'O cross, more splendid than all the stars', which they knew so well.[3] This was followed by five recitations of the *paternoster before they entrusted themselves to God and their patron the Holy Cross and, amidst a veil of tears, left the choir.

For their departure, they lined up in the normal processional order: at its head the provost and his clerics; followed by Abbess Mechthild von Vechelde, at whose side a townswoman from Braunschweig was placed as an escort; then Prioress Remborg Kalm and the oldest nuns, the *seniores*; then the *subprioress and, finally, all the nuns who had already been consecrated as well as the novices, the girls with their *magistra*. These were followed by the *lay sisters; and two or three men and the remaining women brought up the rear. A similar procession is depicted in the panel painting from Medingen which shows the move from the old to the new convent place (Figure 16). They all solemnly walked together to the Grauer Hof,[4] the farmyard and economic centre of the Cistercian monks in Braunschweig.

Exile

The Grauer Hof at the south end of the 'plank way',[5] the central medieval street in Braunschweig, belonged to the Cistercians in Riddagshausen, who stored and sold the grain produced by their farms there.

---

3   *O crux splendidior* (Cantus Index 004019). Liturgical chants are given with the numbers from the *Online Catalogue for Mass and Office Chants* (cantusindex.org).
4   'Grey Yard', named after the grey habits of the monks, see Letter A on the early modern map of Braunschweig. Translation of the full title: 'Plan of the Town of Braunschweig on which can be seen the location of all ducal and public buildings, mills, bridges, streets and alleys, similarly the inflow and outflow of the River Oker with its canals', in: Jürgen Mertens, *Die neuere Geschichte der Stadt Braunschweig in Karten, Plänen und Ansichten*, Braunschweig 1981, sheet 31.
5   Called 'Bohlweg' (or 'Bollewech' on the early modern map of Braunschweig) because it was constructed from wooden planks ('Bohlen').

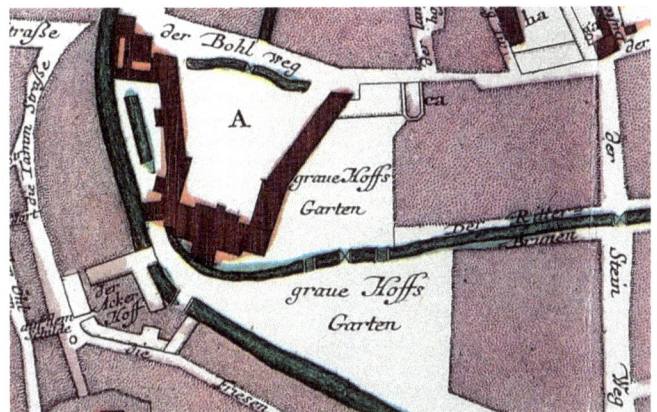

Fig. 3 Map view of the Grauer Hof in Braunschweig. Albrecht Heinrich Carl Conradi *c*. 1755. ©Stadt Braunschweig.

A monk from Riddagshausen received the group and led them in. Initially he showed them only a single room. It rapidly became clear to the provost and his clerics that they could not remain there with the women because there was not enough space to accommodate both groups. Hence, in tears, the latter bade the provost goodbye for this first night. Together the nuns read *compline in the room into which they had been led by the monk and, exhausted, fell asleep perched in the window niches or with their heads leant against the walls. The next morning, things assumed a very different complexion. The monk returned and showed them a chapel in which they could celebrate divine office; two rooms which were suitable for a communal dormitory; and for the abbess, a room of her own. The room in which they had passed the first night was transformed into a refectory, and there was even a heated chamber with hot-air heating from a stone oven, so-called hypocaust heating, and eleven seats which could be warmed by hot air. Now, in the light of day, they discovered in the middle of the Grauer Hof complex a large courtyard with trees and a small pond for which the provost procured them some fish. Ultimately, a solution was also found for all the other duties which made up their daily religious routine: the nuns took communion in a room by the entrance to the chapel, but always with the doors closed. They equipped a small chamber above the chapel, the gallery (*priche*), as their space for confession. It was so cramped that they were obliged to kneel in front of their father confessor, without a screen between them. They also used the room in front of the chapel as a place for the sermons normally preached to them by their father confessor, the provost, or sometimes even by a cleric invited from outside the convent. The daily reading (*collatio*) after *vespers took place there as well and on Thursdays the washing of feet. In the chapel itself, they sang the seven *hours together every day, celebrating the divine office as they always had.

There was a clear hierarchy amongst the rooms in monasteries and convents, one dictated by their sacred function and significance, and very important to the nuns and monks. At the heart of monastic life was the daily assembly in the *chapter house, the meeting of the monastic chapter. In exile, the nuns chose the room in front of the church for this purpose, but because it could not be securely locked and since it was a place where topics meant exclusively for the nuns were dealt with – such as breaches of the rules and other sensitive issues – it was not an ideal environment.

During the period of exile, communal processions which in the convent could take place in the sheltered space of the cloisters, had to be cancelled completely. The Braunschweig town councillors certainly kept an eye on the nuns in their enforced place of refuge. As a precaution, they ordered the monk from Riddagshausen to return to his monastery after a few days. The provost and his clergy, who celebrated mass for the nuns and were their spiritual advisors, as well as the cook, the baker, and some other servants, remained with them, albeit in separate accommodation. However – the diarist adds critically – they were not as securely separated by locks and bolts as they should have been. Each group in the monastic community had its own household, which had to be reorganized here. The cook for the priests and the *familia*, i.e. the nuns' secular servants, and the lay sisters all cooked together and warmed themselves at one fire; the priests and scholars and rest of the *familia* at another. The spatial separation of the different social groups in the community, men and women, was thus established on a makeshift basis. This was necessary for a monastic life in strict enclosure such as lived by the Cistercian nuns of the Heilig Kreuz Kloster. Separation was the basis for their way of life and the prerequisite for their most important task, namely, divine service and the performance of the *liturgy. In the nuns' own understanding of themselves, the quality of their prayers and worship depended upon the quality of their spiritual life in enclosure, upon the regular fulfilment of their duties and their inner turning towards God. Ensuring this in exile was a great challenge, one which the community now had to face together – and it was not possible to find a good solution for everything.

Enclosure had been carefully protected by the structural organization of medieval monasteries, but now the community had to improvise. For the celebration of mass, the priests, along with the scholars and everyone else who took part in the mass, had to pass through the rooms where the women resided. Thus, the Cistercian nun writes worriedly, they could hear and see everything that was otherwise hidden from them and all the more secret things, even if they physically turned away. The provost had impressed upon the male clergy that they should keep as far away from the women as possible; and the abbess ordered the nuns that no one was allowed to leave the premises assigned to them without special permission, except the chapel mistresses for the preparation of the liturgy, the cellar mistress, and the lay sisters for their various jobs and tasks. According to the diarist, the majority of the men and the women carefully observed the prohibitions, 'but some were curious and stood at the windows or went under some pretext into the kitchen and the weaving mill, where the priests, scholars and servants quite frequently exchanged a few words with the lay sisters, because they wanted to see and be seen, hear, and be heard'.[6] She concludes this delicate subject by observing: 'However, with God's help and through the Virgin Mary's intervention, and although some were rather careless and went without witnesses or a companion to places forbidden to us', fortunately nothing bad happened, although there were rumours. Here the diarist addresses her readers directly: 'Of this I write nothing further for now, but I admonish those who will read this in the future so that they take note and understand and take care of themselves and theirs not to run into similar dangers'.[7]

Even personal hygiene was not easy in the new situation. There was

---

6 *sed tamen alique ex nostris curiositate agitate frequenter stabant ante fenestras, et si quando poterant sibi negocium ad sorores conversas, et ibant in coquinam vel textrinum vel ubi solebant sacerdotes et scolares vel de familia aliquando cum conversis aliqua verba conferre volentes illos videre seu ab illis videri, audire vel audiri*, fol. 88v.

7 *De hiis non scribam ad presens plura, sed hortor has, que lecture sunt, ut notent et intelligant et sibi et suis provideant, ne in simile periculum corruant*, fol. 89v.

a small apple orchard in the courtyard, where the women installed a large barrel as a bathtub and, as the diarist joyfully notes, had their bathhouse without a roof and a stove, 'which we liked very much, even in winter in the cold air'. Of course, the courtyard was damp, and the women suspected it was a breeding ground for pests. One day, when an old and already slightly infirm sister sat in the cell block for an hour or two and looked at her coat, she discovered it was 'alive': it was crawling with worms and lice. Initially she said nothing and hid it as best she could, but then the same thing happened to other sisters, and they could no longer conceal it because the lice bit so fiercely. When they collected the clothes to wash them, it turned out that most of the community was infested with this plague of lice.

In the meantime, the duke laid siege to the town and tried to starve it into submission. It became increasingly difficult to obtain food, with the result that the women in Braunschweig who could no longer support themselves and their families through their work painted their faces black to avoid detection and at night walked as far as Peine and Hildesheim to procure food, which they then sold in the town at double the price. The abbess also bought from them for the community of the Heilig Kreuz Kloster because there was nothing else. A Braunschweig chronicle also mentions these women, who successfully undermined the duke's attempt to starve the town. Under the heading 'Of the Enemies of Women' it says the duke was so incensed by their actions that he sent letters of feud against the women into the town so that he could declare them combatants, i.e. enemies in war, and could fight them. While famine was breaking out in the city, the lay sisters and clerics ran back to the Heilig Kreuz Kloster on numerous occasions and brought everything they could carry and use from there into the town. In the process, the scholars found in various places in the convent and in the cells the braids which had been cut off the girls when they had entered the religious estate, a practice comparable to the shaving of the tonsure in monks. They had hidden them in every conceivable nook and cranny in their cells. According to the diarist, because the scholars were honourable, nothing bad had happened to them. She continues: 'But they told the lay sisters how stupid and careless we were, that we did not keep our braids in a safer place, especially when we left the convent, not knowing what kind of people we would encounter and how much danger to our virginity could arise from that'.[8] What the scholars and lay sisters could not take with them, such as the devotional pictures on the walls and some other, less valuable items, was stolen by town women and others who roamed through the place and took everything holy they could find, 'which filled our hearts with very great sorrow'.[9]

On the occasion of the nuns' exile, the diarist's stories reveal for the first time the everyday life and spiritual interaction that were otherwise hidden from the eyes of contemporaries. Because she also reports everyday occurrences in what was for them a highly unusual, threatening situation, she also gives later readers a special, and vivid, insight into a life otherwise shielded and protected by walls and secure enclosure.

2. The Convent Living Space

A medieval convent was a complex organism which included women and men, different social groups, and many people who were tied to the women's community with varying degrees of closeness. All these groups had specific tasks and their own needs, for which they required their own living spaces. The organizational form of medieval women's religious houses, like that of men's, had developed over centuries. Their space was oriented towards the church as the sacred centre where all involved parties gathered. In the sacral hierarchy, second place was occupied by the area which comprised the enclosure of the women; and then the sphere of the lay sisters and brothers, who, because of their countless tasks in the convent yard and the fields, lived a 'semi'-spiritual life between the convent and the world, so to speak. The complex structure that was the 'convent' had constantly to be adapted to the respective local conditions and its occupants.

---

8 *sed dixerunt conversis, quod valde stultum eis videretur actum a nobis, quod non cum diliencia crines nostros servassemus, precipue cum exeuntes de locis nostris ignorassemus, quales intraturi erant, et quod non advertissemus, quanta dampna et pericula virginitatis nostre possunt inde venire*, fol. 103v.

9 *quod cordi nostro dolorem permagnum intulit*, fol. 104r.

Convent and Enclosure: On Terminology

What becomes particularly clear in the account of the forced flight to Braunschweig is the significance of enclosure for a convent: the state of being closed off from the world can be taken as the very definition of a monastic house, particularly for women. The German word 'Kloster' (which existed in medieval English as *closter*) derives from the Latin *claustrum*, past participle of the verb *claudere* (to close), which in medieval Latin took the popular form *clostrum*. In German, the term refers to monastic houses in general, which can be specified as for men ('Männerkloster') or women ('Frauenkloster'). The English term 'cloister(s)' which came from the same root via Old French *cloistre* into English, more specifically just means the inner part of a monastic community, particularly a 'covered walk or arcade connected with a monastery, college, or large church, serving as a way of communication between different parts of the group of buildings, and sometimes as a place of exercise or study; often running round the open court of a quadrangle, with a plain wall on the one side, and a series of windows or an open colonnade on the other'.[10] The term 'monastery' from post-classical Latin *monasterium* ('monk's cell, monastery'), which is a loan word from Byzantine Greek (μοναστήριον) of the same meaning, derived from the Hellenistic Greek verb for 'living alone' (μονάζειν). It was taken over into the vernaculars as 'Münster' (in German, as in 'Freiburger Münster', the Cathedral including the 'Münsterbauhütte', the medieval workshop still attached to it) or 'Minster' (in English, as York Minster); even though the nuns sometimes refer to their institution as *monasterium*, in English it traditionally just referred to religious institutions for men even though the latest edition of the *Oxford English Dictionary* now allows more flexibility. OED2 defines 'monastery' as 'A place of residence of a community of persons living secluded from the world under religious vows; a monastic establishment. Chiefly, and now almost exclusively, applied to a house for monks; but applicable also to the house of any religious order, male or female.' OED3 allows more flexibility with 'A place of residence for a community living under religious vows, *esp.* the residence of a community of monks.' Still, for

---

10   *Oxford English Dictionary*, s.v. 'cloister (n.)', July 2023, https://doi.org/10.1093/OED/5794023973.

the German 'Frauenkloster', in this book the term 'convent' is used, even though this means a doubling of use: both for the community of nuns and for the institution they inhabit. The word 'enclosure' like 'Kloster' comes from *claudere*, with the added prefix 'in' after the Old French verb *enclore* which also gave English the word 'inclusive'.[11] The walls surrounding the convent limit the women's sphere of activity to the inside, but also offer protection from the outside. The outer world was meant to be closed off so that an inner one could open up. Accordingly, the convent life of the old orders – such as the Benedictine and Cistercian nuns – served contemplation and meditation. Later Protestant historiography perceived only the function of confinement: the novels of the nineteenth century are full of figures of poor imprisoned girls who long for their romantic liberator from the dungeon that was the convent and who are trapped within its walls against their will by the clerics and the abbess. One of the most frequent word combinations in German is 'to lock up in a convent/monastery'.[12] In English, this is apparent in the derogatory undertones which 'nunnery' acquired over the early modern period, 'get thee to a nunnery' in *Hamlet* III.i, even playing with the anti-Catholic Tudor meaning of 'brothel'. The Middle Ages, however, viewed the religious space very differently.

The exile of the nuns of the Heilig Kreuz Kloster shows how difficult it is for the community to leave this shelter. In the Lüne letters, too, the women themselves consistently use positive images when they speak of enclosure. It is their space. It is the 'vineyard of the Lord', fenced in against wild boars; or the 'rose garden', where, like the bride in the Song of Songs, the women can walk with Jesus as their sweetheart. On the Wichmannsburg *Antependium, for example, a richly embroidered altar cloth produced by the nuns of Kloster Medingen and used in the parish church of Wichmannsburg that belonged to the convent, a woman sits at the foot of the cross in a rose garden enclosed by a woven fence, gathering flowers in a cloth, with a Middle Low German caption that links the delight of gathering flowers and seeing her beloved, i.e. Christ, as part of the garden experience.

---

11   The equivalent *Klausur* in German is a direct later derivation from the same verb form as 'Kloster', namely *claustrum*, *Digitales Wörterbuch der deutschen Sprache*, https://www.dwds.de/wb/Klausur, consulted 19 04 2024.

12   *ins Kloster einsperren*, *Digitales Wörterbuch der deutschen Sprache*, https://www.dwds.de/wb/Kloster, consulted 19 04 2024.

Fig. 4 Wichmannsburg Antependium, Kloster Medingen, late 15th century. Photograph: Christian Tepper. ©Landeshauptstadt Hannover.

Nuns' Choir, Chapter House, Refectory, Dormitory: On the Architecture of the Convent

Because protection was derived from this very seclusion, the channels of communication were particularly important. Naturally, close contacts to and well-established spaces for communication with the outside world were needed. The convent area was usually only permeable for this world in three places: first, at the convent gate, which for the nuns symbolized the narrow gate leading to the kingdom of heaven; second, at the communication grille, where the nuns could converse with their relatives from the city at visiting times; third, in the convent church, which, however, was also divided into distinct areas according to the sacral hierarchy: the east was the place for the clergy; while the west was, in many cases, divided into a lower church for the local congregation and above them the *nuns' choir.

As can still be seen today in Wienhausen in Lower Saxony, for example, the nuns' choir could take on the dimensions of a small church, equipped with choir stalls and altars for worship. At west end, the seat of the abbess is located; on the south and north side, the nuns sit in the stalls, with lower benches for the novices who would only join in at certain times (for further images of the architecture from the inside and seen from outside see Chapter VII.3).

Fig. 5 Nuns' choir at Wienhausen, looking towards west. Photograph: Ulrich Loeper ©Kloster Wienhausen.

Since the nuns met in the nuns' choir for matins at night or early in the morning, the distances had to be short. The nuns usually reached it via their own corridor, directly connecting the dormitory on the upper floor of the cloister with the nuns' choir. The significance of the nuns' choir as a sacred space is clear from the fact that the lay sisters were only allowed to enter it on special feast days. Moreover, they were not allowed to use the path through the nuns' choir as a shortcut to reach the church more quickly.

Another area reserved for the choir nuns was the chapter house, even though the provost could join them for important events. As the report from the Braunschweig exile of the nuns from the Heilig Kreuz Kloster makes clear, it formed the centre of communications within the community because the daily assemblies took place there. During their exile, improvisation was necessary, and the nuns rededicated a room not originally intended for this purpose; otherwise, the chapter house was often an area of the convent which boasted specifically designed architecture and was decorated, like the church, with columns and ornaments to emphasize the importance of this representative community space. Here reports were given, the course of the liturgy on feast days was discussed, plans were deliberated and decisions taken for the future.

For this purpose, the lay sisters had their own area, the workhouse, where they performed manual work. It had to have good light and was situated somewhat outside the narrower area of enclosure, the architectural backbone of which was the *cloister. Accordingly, the lay sisters' dormitory was located in a wing further away from the church and closer to the work area.

The kitchen was the realm of the *celleraria*, who supervised the lay sisters, who then served the food in the refectory. In the refectory, the nuns sat at long tables with the abbess presiding over them while the *lectrix*, the 'reader' designated for that occasion, read spiritual works out aloud to them. We know from Kloster Lüne that an important part of the conventual reform (which is discussed in detail in Chapter V) was the return to communal meals. An experienced housekeeper (*celleraria*) was sent from Kloster Ebstorf especially for this purpose, one who knew how to provide for all those living in the convent throughout the year. This can also be seen on a panel from Kloster Medingen depicting the reform; on the left it shows the *celleraria* seasoning the stew cooked by a lay sister in the large cauldron (Figure 26, Chapter V.2).

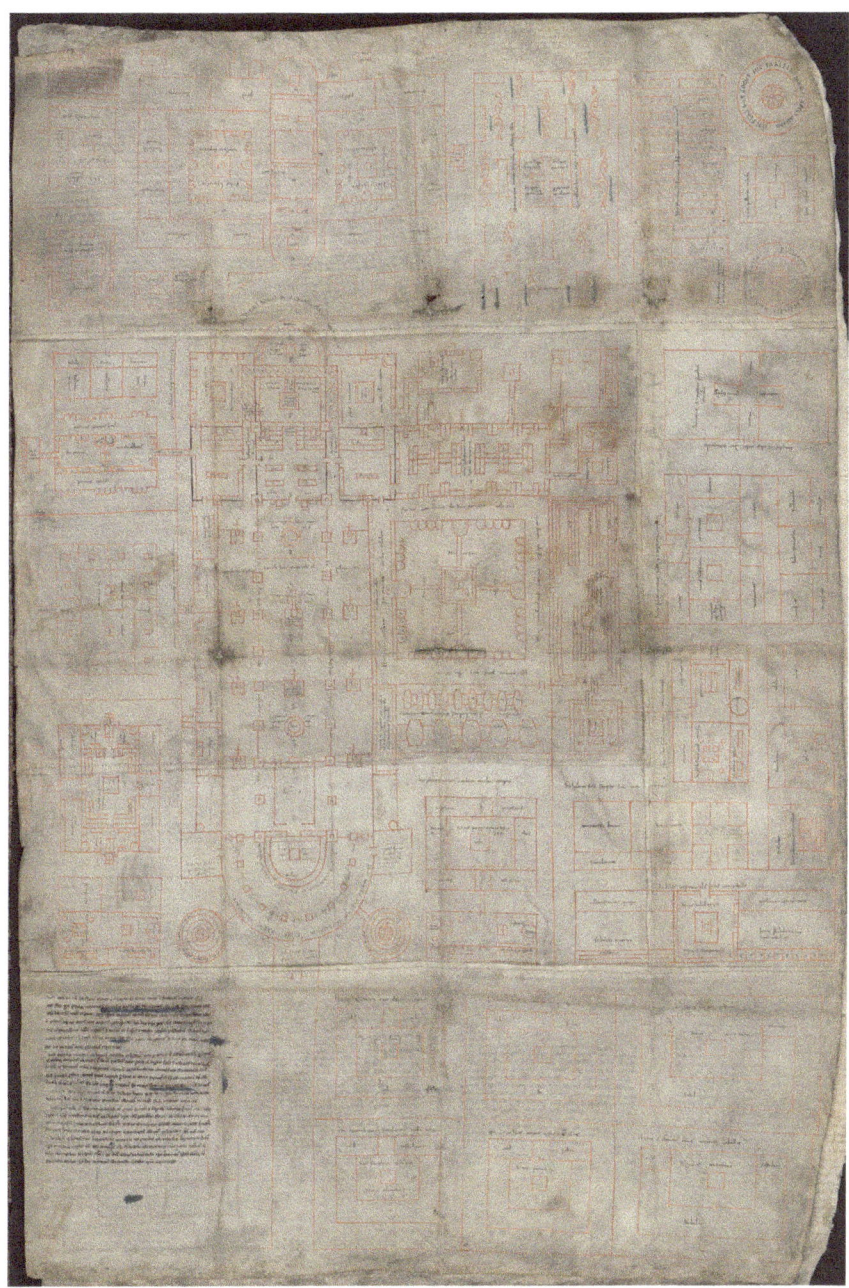

Fig. 6 Plan of St Gall, Reichenau, early 9th century. Stiftsbibliothek St. Gallen, Ms. 1092. Public domain.

On the whole, the basic layout found in a men's monastery also applies to women's convents. It is best known from the Plan of St Gall, the earliest surviving visual representation of any architecture complex, which outlines forty different areas for praying, living, eating, healing, entertaining guests, and managing the monastic economy.[13]

This ideal plan was implemented in religious institutions for women even more rarely than for male communities, whether completely or even to a considerable extent. Unlike monasteries, convents were more frequently founded by rededicating existing buildings, which were then extended piecemeal and as needed. Within the convent walls, one thus often finds a loose conglomeration of buildings rather than the precisely encircled complexes of e.g. Cistercian foundations for men which followed clear building regulations. This complexity, illustrating the growth of the female community over the centuries and the adaptation to new demands on the organization of their space, makes architectural complexes like Kloster Lüne so attractive. Here a Baroque house stands side-by-side with red-brick Gothic, and an ultramodern textile restoration workshop gets a dedicated space above a purpose-built textile museum.

Hours, Masses, Church Year: On Monastic Structures of Time

The nuns' daily routine was determined by structuring time into multiple layers. True to the words of the Psalm 113:3, 'From the rising of the sun to its setting, praise be to the name of the Lord' and to Psalm 119:164, 'seven times a day I praise you', the prayer times, also called the *canonical hours after the Latin word *hora* for hour, were spread across the day from sunrise to sunset and even beyond, since the nuns, like the Wise Virgins from Christ's parable,[14] wished to be properly prepared to meet their bridegroom at midnight. In the convent, the day was structured by the seven hours during which, above all, the psalms were recited. The table in the Appendix (Chapter VIII.2) provides an overview of the resulting daily structure. The day began after sunset, a tradition which to this day has been preserved for Christmas with

---

13   Drawn c. 820–830 on five sewn-together parchment leaves (overall size 112 cm × 77.5 cm). *Zoomable version available at the website reconstructing the medieval library of St Gall.*
14   Matthew 25:1–4.

Christmas Eve. In the evening, compline concluded the day's work and matins began the new day. Nocturns, the night prayers, were celebrated at matins in the early hours of the morning so that the night's rest was not interrupted.

 The day had different lengths in summer and winter since it was not based on modern time but on sunrise and sunset. At dawn, the nuns rose for the second time for prime, followed by the chapter office, for which the entire convent went to the chapter house in the east wing of the enclosure. The so-called 'chapter' took its name from the reading of a chapter from the rule of the order and was the most important gathering point for the community. The chapter was presided over by the abbess of the convent; and the nuns sat on her right and left according to their 'professed age', i.e. the date of their *profession – a seniority rule still observed in the seating plan for the Protestant convents. At chapter, the abbess or prioress gave addresses on spiritual matters to the community; violations of the rule were punished, the daily schedule was discussed, and the particular tasks for the day were distributed. In addition, the deceased members of the convent, lay sisters and brothers or benefactors were remembered. Afterwards, one to two hours were free for the work which was waiting to be done before the convent gathered again for terce, the third hour, after which, at about 10 o'clock, followed the conventual mass, which the nuns attended in the nuns' choir. Only then, at around 11 a.m., came the first meal of the day, the *prandium*, which orders leading a communal life took together in the refectory. At the communal meals, a sister undertook the table readings, which included exegetical writings by the church fathers, explanations of the liturgy or exemplary stories, as well as descriptions of the lives of exemplary saints. Sext was sometimes recited before the meal, sometimes after it; then the nuns had none in the early afternoon, followed by time for work or rest. Vespers concluded the working day. At around 5 or 6 p.m., the convent gathered again for dinner in the refectory. Before the night's rest, which began with the onset of darkness, there was often an evening reading (*collatio*) in the north wing of the cloister, usually with a fortifying drink, before the day was placed in God's hands with the Canticle of Simeon during compline.

 The prayer books of the nuns from Kloster Medingen clearly illustrate how every step of the daily routine is symbolically charged. When rising in the morning, the nun is supposed to think of Christ's resurrection from the dead; when putting on her robe, of Christ one day clothing her with the robe of eternal life; when going to the nuns' choir, of Christ's entry into Jerusalem etc. A layer of spiritual meaning is superimposed on the structures of convent life, one which elevates everyday life symbolically, interpreting it in terms of the history of salvation. In the eyes of both the nuns and the monks themselves, as well of the broader community outside the convent, their 'service' to God was central to the salvation of humanity. They could thus be seen as experts in the immaterial for the semantic space beyond the material world: for that reason, they always located themselves within larger contexts of space and time.

This is particularly apparent in the division of the year, determined by the events of the history of salvation recurring within the liturgy. At Christmas, the devotional texts instructed the nuns to help the Virgin Mary swaddling and caring for the Christ child (quite literally, in the case of the devotional cradles sometimes used in convents or clothing the doll-like statues from Brabant). In Passiontide, they were called to suffer with him by contemplating his wounded limbs (see Figure 24 for the larger-than-life figure of Christ of the Holy Sepulchre from Kloster Wienhausen), thus enabling them to encounter the risen Christ once more on Easter along with Mary Magdalene. The extent to which the Liturgy of the Hours allowed the nuns to participate directly in biblical events is particularly evident at Easter, when Christ is equated with Sunday, the course of which is followed from hour to hour. In this, they are emulating the passage of time, from the Resurrection at sunrise to the evening, when Christ is invited to stay with the two disciples encountered on the road to Emmaus.

The church year is structured in such a way as to repeat the history of salvation, made audible and tangible in the liturgy by the nuns who simultaneously insert themselves into events that encompassed time and space. Since their enclosure meant that they were forbidden to go on pilgrimages, they visualized Rome or Jerusalem as a spiritual pilgrimage within their own cloister and the church. Conceptual designs such as that of the Ebstorf World Map (Figure 8) rendered concrete the imagined order of time and space. The Liturgy of the Hours was conducted by the nuns themselves, with the singing of the psalms alternating between both sides of the choir stalls and led by the precentrix and her deputy. High mass and feast-day masses, on the other hand, were public affairs for which, if the convent church was also the parish church, the local congregation attended the service. In these cases, the nuns could hear and therefore follow the proceedings at the high altar in the east from their gallery. To this day, a candelabrum in the shape of a garland with a Madonna in an aureole hangs above the nuns' choir in Kloster Lüne.[15] It has two faces: one looks down on the nuns from close by, while the other is visible from a distance to the clergy in the east choir. A renovation note from 1649 shows that it continued to be in use after the Reformation.

Fig. 7 Candelabrum from the nuns' choir. Photograph: Wolfgang Brandis ©Kloster Lüne.

---

15 Inv. Nr. LÜN Ae 2 (DI 76, Lüneburger Klöster, A1, Nr. 41 (Sabine Wehking), in: www.inschriften.net, urn:nbn:de:0238–di076g013a1004108

Some convent churches included a Holy Sepulchre, or alternatively, the altar doubled as the Tomb of Christ, which could be approached together with the Three Marys (see Figure 24 for the Wienhausen entombed Christ). While the priests chanted about Christ's descent into limbo to free the Old Testament patriarchs, the arrival of Christ's advance could be followed in the liturgy as if in real time. At Christmas, the altar then became the manger from which the priest could lift the host representing the Christ Child. More on this can be found in the chapter on the sacred and social space of the convent (Chapter V.2).

In addition to the division of the day and the structure of the church year, there were also special feast days, especially for the saints. Each *psalter, the basic manuscript of the psalms which the nuns used daily, begins with a calendar of feasts and commemorative days, both those of the convent in general and those of the individual scribe or user. Each women's convent had its own canopy of saints which determined which feasts were particularly highlighted. The English expression 'a red-letter day' for special events comes from the medieval practice of highlighting particularly important feasts in red.

In addition to saints' days on which the patron saints of the convent were celebrated, for example, there were numerous days of personal celebration and commemoration. Widespread throughout the late Middle Ages was the assigning of an apostle who, like the guardian angel, personally watched over those entrusted to his care. This 'personal apostle', who was responsible for the protection of an individual nun and for whose veneration she was responsible, especially on his feast day, is also occasionally noted in the manuscripts. It was even more important to record precisely who had died and their date of death in order to remember them in prayers and masses. The community of both the living and the dead transcended the boundaries of time through *memoria*, an active form of remembrance which was renewed every year.

3. The Ebstorf World Map

The Ebstorf World Map is an example of the macro- and microcosm of the convent and the positive connotations of enclosure. Moreover, it is more closely connected to nuns than one might think: it is a large, round map that was created in the Benedictine convent of Ebstorf in the 14th century. It was destroyed by a fire in Hanover during World War II, but full-scale reproductions on parchment were made before the war.

Fig. 8 The Ebstorf World Map. 14th century. Facsimile Kloster Ebstorf Ebs Cb 009.
©Kloster Ebstorf.

A World Map from the Middle Ages

Originally, the Ebstorf World Map consisted of 30 sheets of goatskin parchment on which a circle 3.5 metres in diameter was drawn, a so-called 'wheel map', as noted in the upper left margin:

> The orb (*orbis* = ring) is named after the roundness (*rotunditas*) of the circle because it is like a wheel (*rota*). For the Ocean flows around it in a circle. It is divided into three parts, that is, into Asia, Europe, and Africa. Asia alone covers one half of the earth; Europe and Africa together occupy the other half and are divided by the Mediterranean Sea. Asia takes its name from a woman who ruled the east in ancient times. It is laid out like this on three sides: it is bounded in the east by the rising of the sun; in the south by the ocean; in the west by our (= the Mediterranean) Sea; and in the north by the Maeotian Sea or Marshes and the River Don. Asia includes a multitude of provinces, regions and islands. Europe is named after the daughter of King Agenor; Africa after a descendant of Abraham and Keturah called Afer. There are countries, islands and provinces. You will find a few of their names and their locations on the drawn map if you look more closely.[16]

In the top right-hand corner, we find an explanation of the multiple uses of such a map, whose origins are traced back to Antiquity:

> The term *mappa* refers to a form. Hence *mappa mundi* means the form of the world. Which Julius Caesar, having sent legates throughout the expanse of the whole globe, first established. Regions, provinces, islands, cities, coasts, marshes, stretches of ocean, mountains, rivers: he compiled a complete overview of everything on one sheet; which indeed provides not insignificant usefulness to readers, direction to travellers, and the most delightful contemplation of the course of things.[17]

---

16 *Orbis a rotunditate circuli dictus, quia est ut rota. Undique enim Oceanus circumfluens in circulo. Est triphariam divisus, id est in Asiam, Europam, Africam. Sola Asia medietatem orbis, due tenent alteram partem Europa et Africa, quas intersecat velut subterraneum Mediterraneum mare. Asia ex nomine cuiusdam mulieris est appellata, quae apud antiquos imperium tenuit orientis. Haec a tertia parte disposita est: ab oriente ortu solis, a meridie Oceano, ab occiduo nostro mare finitur, a septentrione Maeotide lacu sei paludi et Tanai fluvio terminatur. Habet multas provincias, regiones et insulas. Europa Agenoris regis filia dicta est, que idem nomen sortita est. Africam appellari dicunt ab uno ex posteris Abrache de Cethura, qui vocatus est Afer. Habent et ipse regiones insulas privinciasque, quarum nomina pauca et situs in figura mundi inveniens, si inspicere procures.* Kugler I, p. 20.

17 *Mappa dicitur forma. Inde mappa mundi id est forma mundi. Quam Julius Cesar missis legatis per totius orbis amplitudinem primus instituit; regiones, provincias, insulas, civitates, syrtes, paludes, equora, montes, flumina quasi sub unius pagine visione coadunavit; que scilicet non parvam prestat legentibus utilitatem, viantibus directionem rerumque viarum gratissime speculationis dilectionem.* Kugler I, p. 21.

Unlike most of today's maps, the Ebstorf map of the world does not have north at the top but east. The upper half forms Asia, the lower-left quarter Europe, and the lower-right quarter Africa. Like the convent, the inhabited world is enclosed twice: geographically by water, the world sea; spiritually by Christ, whose head 'orients' the map at the east end and who marks the north-south axis with his hands; his feet peep out at the bottom, illustrating the west end. The two-dimensional wheel shape applies only to the surface of the earth. The fact that the world is a sphere had been known since Antiquity and throughout the Middle Ages, this knowledge is demonstrated by the shape of the globe in Christ's hand in numerous depictions.

As in the normal arrangement of the T and O map, Jerusalem is positioned at the hub of the wheel, around which literally everything revolves. A square, golden wall with twelve towers encloses the scene of Christ's resurrection, in which he rises from the grave depicted in the same way as many works of art, for example on the nuns' choir in Wienhausen. Therefore, the city is at one and the same time the biblical Jerusalem, where Christ was crucified and rose from the dead; the contemporary Jerusalem, to which the pilgrimages and crusades set out; and the heavenly Jerusalem, entry to which is promised to the wise virgins: Jerusalem, the golden, in all its manifold splendour. Here the structures of space and time overlap; long-remembered history is captured in the image as the history of the world and salvation, one into which the nuns integrate themselves because they contribute to the salvation of the world through their way of life. On the map, Adam and Eve are found in the Garden of Eden, right next to the face of Christ; Alexander the Great is depicted on his journey to India in the very top left; and the fabulous creatures of the far south are represented on the right edge, with their feet pointing towards the ocean which surrounds the world. On the lower-left-hand edge of the world, however, at about the level of Christ's right shin, the nuns of Kloster Ebstorf inscribe themselves into the map.

Ebstorf and Its Surroundings

Fig. 9 Lower Saxony on the Ebstorf World Map. Photograph: Wolfgang Brandis ©Kloster Ebstorf.

On the map, North Germany (Figure 9) consists of a sequence of architectural symbols connected rather than separated by bodies of water: shipment on the rivers Elbe and Ilmenau, then onwards via the North Sea and the Baltic into the trading network of the Hanseatic League, constituted the most important long-distance transport system in northern Germany in the late Middle Ages. The towns of Braunschweig and Lüneburg stand out prominently. Braunschweig, the point of reference for the nuns of the Heilig Kreuz Kloster, bears the Guelph lion as a crest, just as it did on the city wall; the lion had stood in the Castle Square[18] at Dankwarderode Castle since the reign of Duke Henry the Lion in the 12th century. Lüneburg, the town that contributed to the prosperity of the convents in Lüne, Medingen, Wienhausen, Isenhagen, Walsrode and, of course, Ebstorf with the income from its saltworks, can be recognized from the round object with the inscription *luna*: the town traced its name back to the Roman moon goddess Luna. Also visible are the bishoprics in the region: Bremen, Verden and Hildesheim, each as towers. The convent of Ebstorf is embedded in this regional structure of duchies, cities and dioceses as a small symbol with three rectangular fields directly below it: these are martyrs' graves, the presence of which further served to make the convent a holy site.

A World View as a Map

The World Map is a combined narrative of history and space and can be read in several dimensions, inviting both study and wonder. This results in differing densities of development and emphasis for the different regions. Even if, for example, it is possible to plan a concrete itinerary through Franconia with the map points of Nuremberg, Forchheim and Bamberg along the blue veins of the rivers Main and Regnitz, the edges of the world perform a completely different function. The Sciapods, Cyclopes and Blemmyes, or headless creatures, are drawn with vivid detail in the south on the right edge, as are the man-eaters in the Caucasus, as well as Alexander the Great on his journey to India at the outer reaches of Asia on the top left. On the one hand, these fantastic beings constitute imaginative world travel and adventure novels but, on the other, these pictures and texts also invite us to marvel at the diversity of God's creation, who has ordered everything according to measure and number (Wisdom 11:20).

---

18 *Burgplatz*, no. 4 on the map of Braunschweig around 1400 (Figure 2).

The nuns who recorded remarkable geographical and historical facts through texts and images on goatskins made more systematic sense of the globe from reports, encyclopedias, and world chronicles than was possible even compared to merchants or pilgrims. They might have been able to travel as far as Mount Ararat but, despite being eyewitnesses to the actual physical surroundings, likely perceived less of the allegorical and historical significance of the place than the nuns. The latter had, in fact, their own understanding of space and time. For example, for them Noah's Ark was more important than the actual appearance of the place, since the Ark stood for God's covenant with humanity.

Most of the space in the marginal notes is taken up by exotic animals and their significance: lions, panthers, salamanders, Scitalis snakes, hydra, basilisk. This was not the product of fantasy, but derived from the most important encyclopaedist of the Middle Ages, Isidore of Seville (d. 636): 'Whoever wants to know more, let him read Isidore', as a note on the map says. The animals not only broaden the zoological horizon, but are bearers of meaning and, as the annotations show, bear witness not least to the nuns' knowledge of the bible: the oversized camel is placed next to the gates of Jerusalem in such a way that it simultaneously refers to the biblical verse that says a camel goes more easily through the eye of a needle than a wealthy man into the kingdom of heaven (Matthew 19:24; Mark 10:25; Luke 18:25).

In the fifteenth century Erhart Groß wrote instructions for the Dominican sisters of St Katherine in Nuremberg on how they could travel to Jerusalem in spirit with the help of a map, a compass and the Lord's Prayer but without leaving their cells. They were to read off the distance on the map using a compass to measure miles and pray one Lord's Prayer per mile; then, when they had prayed their way to Jerusalem, they would receive the same indulgences as were offered to pilgrims. The Ebstorf map does not have an exact mileage scale by which the distance could be measured, but the viewer can nevertheless seek a spiritual pilgrimage route along which she can pause at several symbols, such as the various saints buried and venerated in the towns along the way.

Even if some maps could be 'measured' with dividers and other instruments, unlike modern road maps this material does not become obsolete. In the Ebstorf map the nuns brought the world into their enclosure in a representation that transcended time and retained its validity.

II. Education

The nuns gave the girls entering the convent a demanding education, which lasted several years and included scholarly Latin, theology and music for the choir services; knowledge of economic and organizational matters pertaining to convent administration; as well as handicrafts and the production and decoration of books. Their instruction offered more than mere 'professional training'. As the example of the Ebstorf World Map in the previous chapter shows, knowledge was always also a carrier of spiritual and intellectual meaning. The allegorical interpretation of their environment and religious tasks was an important part of their education in the convent school and one that created meaning. The individual phases in a nun's training were intertwined with the various steps involved in entering the convent on the way to becoming a choir nun with a seat and voice in the chapter. They were linked by rites of passage – such as the investiture of, profession by and crowning of the nuns – which both structured and motivated the course of their education.

1. The Convent as School

Educational Trip to the Neighbouring Convent

At the beginning of 1487, the nuns of the Heilig Kreuz Kloster received a visit from the Cistercian convent of Derneburg. The abbess of Derneburg, Sophie von Schulenburg, had fallen ill and travelled to the sisters at the Heilig Kreuz Kloster in order to obtain medicine more easily in the nearby town of Braunschweig. The guest from Derneburg made a deep impression on the Cistercian nuns of Braunschweig. Almost all the nuns, young and old, visited Sophie and enjoyed talking to her, fascinated by her education and wisdom. The learned abbess made such an impression, especially on the younger nuns, that some of them asked their own abbess, Elisabeth Pawel, to be allowed to go to Derneburg for a year to receive better instruction in theology and, above all, Latin.

By the 15th century, Derneburg already had an eventful history behind it. Towards the end of the 14th century, the convent there, originally founded in 1143 as a house of *Augustinian canonesses, had, like so many other monasteries and convents, become impoverished when after the Black Death of 1348 the old farming methods no longer yielded enough, not least due to a lack of labour. The late medieval monastic reform attempted to combat these crises with greater discipline in the nuns' conduct of their lives and in their theological education, but above all with a new approach to the management of the convent economy. A functioning economy was the prerequisite for the entire convent to be provided for throughout the year, both from its own lands and from other income, and for the women not to be forced to return to their families in the months of famine during the spring or when they were ill. When the Augustinian canon and reformer Johannes Busch wished to introduce a life governed by the rules of the Order as well as strict enclosure in the Derneburg convent, the nuns resisted. Johannes Busch only narrowly escaped an 'assassination attempt' when the nuns locked him into their cellar rooms. Now the patience of the Bishop of Hildesheim with the canonesses in Derneburg was at an end. He had the unruly women distributed amongst other convents and in 1442 filled Derneburg with highly educated Cistercian nuns from Wöltingerode, who were faithful to the reforms.

The monastic communities which had accepted reform constituted, as it were, a new religious movement characterized not only by greater discipline, but above all by a new, inward-looking piety (Chapter V). The reformed nuns and monks probably saw themselves as a spiritual elite and established their own networks among themselves. The reform was therefore often associated with an intensified education of the rising generation, improved instruction in Latin and the rebuilding of monastic libraries. On the other hand, the Cistercian nuns of the Heilig Kreuz Kloster had eluded the 'grasp' of the monastic reformers and therefore their community stood somewhat apart from the major upheavals, from the discourse on the new forms of religious life and from the wide-ranging literary networks of the reform monasteries. Now, when the abbess of Derneburg, Sophie von Schulenburg came to visit, they were abruptly confronted by the result of a more profound education and an internalized understanding of their spiritual life and it fascinated them. Sophie's counterpart, the abbess of the Heilig Kreuz Kloster Elisabeth Pawel, saw a great opportunity in the desire of the younger nuns to go to Derneburg in order to become better acquainted with the new way of life. Although concerns were raised in the convent that this might harm the reputation of the Heilig Kreuz Kloster, the abbess placed two younger nuns from her convent, one of them named Dorte Damman, in the care of her fellow abbess. This decision remained controversial.

The convent reacted indignantly to the permission granted arbitrarily by the abbess because Elisabeth Pawel had not sought beforehand the advice of the elders and the sisters who held convent offices. This shows the extent to which the abbess's decision-making powers were constrained by internal power structures and her dependence on gaining acceptance within the convent itself for her decisions to be acted upon and respected. Elisabeth Pawel had good reasons to give her permission without consultation, because she had obviously feared that the sisters in office and the elders would have misgivings if word went round that 'remedial tutoring' was needed at the Heilig Kreuz Kloster. The good reputation of a convent was crucial, not least for the economic survival of its community: it determined how much families were inclined to make endowments, to choose the convent as their burial place and to give their daughters to the convent.

Abbess Elisabeth's unauthorized decision had consequences: there was much 'grumbling' in the convent and a split, since some liked her actions while others did not. On the day the two girls left the Heilig Kreuz Kloster for Derneburg, the abbess came to chapter and announced that anyone who continued to grumble or to say anything at all on this topic would, as punishment, have to throw herself onto the floor in front of the others at chapter and do such penance as would fill the others with fear. After all, she said, she had acted for the good of the community. This was the end of the matter for the time being, but a year later, in 1488, after the return of the two sisters, the controversy flared up again.

When the two nuns returned from Derneburg, the abbess convened the elders and counsellors to consult them on how to proceed with the twelve girls who were now old enough to start in the convent school. The unanimous advice of the experienced nuns was that these girls should be divided into two school classes so that they could be better looked after and more intensively taught. As the diarist notes in her displeasure, Abbess Elisabeth Pawel did not act on their advice but placed all the girls in the care of Dorte Damman, who had enjoyed the more intensive instruction at Derneburg and who had suggested to the abbess that, in order to pass on her experience, she would teach all the girls together. Setting a new course was not as easy as she anticipated. Even though the abbess gave Dorte Damman full authority over the girls' education, the convent *scholastica, the previous teacher, reacted by withdrawing from everything because she could not bear the harshness of the new school regime. As the outcome of the affair demonstrated – or so notes the diarist – it would probably have been better if the girls had been divided into two classes because, presumably in the certain knowledge they were doing things better and right, Dorte Damman and her fellow sister who had accompanied her to Derneburg turned the convent against them through their unusual strictness. The situation deteriorated so badly that in the daily chapter the abbess had yet again to forbid the nuns to reproach the two sisters for their stay in Derneburg. According to the diarist, because of the severe penalties she threatened 'no one now dared to say anything, either good or bad'.[1] The abbess's attempt to use the education of the next generation as, so to speak, an informal means of somewhat narrowing the gap between the reform monasteries and life in the Heilig Kreuz Kloster had failed.

What, then, was it about the teaching reform in the monasteries? It was very important to the reformers, the bishops and abbots of the *Bursfelde Reform Congregation, that nuns should have sufficient knowledge of Latin for a good understanding of the liturgy and the ability to read the theological reform literature independently. In fact, this was so important to them that they encouraged the women to employ a (male) Latin teacher to take over this task with the convent pupils should the competence available in their own convent be insufficient and they not be able to supply suitable teaching staff from their own ranks – as had been the case at the Heilig Kreuz Kloster.

---

1   *Ideo nemo audebat loqui vel dicere aliquid neque bonum neque malum*, fol. 43r.

The results of these educational efforts were impressive. Johannes Busch writes approvingly that in the reformed Augustinian convent of Marienberg near Helmstedt the girls and nuns had, under their teacher Tecla, made such good progress in singing and the scholarly branches of learning that they knew how to interpret Holy Scripture and write letters or reports in a masterly manner. He testifies to his assessment 'as I have seen and examined it for myself and is evident from the enclosed letters'. Marienberg was also dependent on outside support. Magistra Tecla had come to Marienberg for some time specifically to teach the pupils but was obviously better able to deal with the situation there than Dorte Damman at the Heilig Kreuz Kloster, because the letters demonstrate the enthusiasm of her then-pupils, who obviously missed her badly after she left.

School Lessons in Ebstorf

The Marienberg nuns shared their enthusiasm for their teacher with the convent schoolgirls at Ebstorf. The Ebstorf girls wrote countless essays and texts for school lessons which provide a lively and striking impression of their daily school life. Here the charisma which distinguished the then-*magistra* in Kloster Ebstorf becomes apparent. It was not only her teaching talent but also her careful, comprehensible explanation of Latin grammar that impressed and enthused the schoolgirls, because suddenly they really understood the contents and meaning of the liturgical chants and Latin prayers:

> She construed the whole text of the Rule of Benedict with us word by word, explaining each verse first literally and then according to the sense. Oh, what a pleasure it is to hear and read the sacred readings in the divine worship, the words of the holy gospel from the mouth of the Lord, the words of the holy fathers of both the Old and the New Testaments! For Bernard of Clairvaux rightly claims: 'If there is paradise on earth, it is either in books or in enclosure.' By contrast, how tedious and tiresome it is to stand in the choir and read and sing and to understand nothing![2]

---

2   *Totum textum regule nobis construxit de verbo ad verbum, quemlibet versum primo secundum literam, deinde secundum sensum. O quales delicie sunt audire vel legere in divino cultu sacras lectiones, verba sancti ewangelii ex ore domini, verba sanctorum doctorum tam veteris testamenti quam novi. Vere enim dicit Bernardus: 'Paradisus si est super terram, aut in libris aut in claustro est.' E converso magnum tedium est stare in choro,*

The records of the convent schoolgirls at Ebstorf tell of (poor) food, baking, dyeing, bathing, the cold, contemplation, mass – and, perhaps most extensively, of school. Alongside the many enthusiastic descriptions, they also reveal the reality of school, which could often be hard, especially in winter. One of the pupils begins her account quite prosaically by mentioning the barely tolerable winter cold. The tremendous frost, she writes, condemned her to idleness, for her hands were frozen stiff and so was the ink, which hardly wanted to turn liquid on the stove. She thought she could still sew gloves from the rest of the woollen fabric her parents had bought for a cloak for her at the market. Although the *magistra* had taken precautions against snow and rain with wooden shutters in the school, the warming house (calefactory) was now either dark or the rain was coming in. The previous year, she writes, it had been particularly unpleasant in the school because the windows had been broken everywhere. The *magistra* had then procured new stained-glass windows with beautiful images for the school, which her relatives had donated to the convent at her request.

The ambitious educational goals of the reform movement also had their downsides. The diary-like notes on the last pages of the notebook kept jointly by the schoolgirls convey an idea of everyday school life – and perhaps of the other side of the teenagers' frenetic desire for knowledge. They read as if this particular convent schoolgirl had given vent to her anger as well as her contempt – or it might be a literary *topos* used for a composition exercise:

> Why do you envy me for learning well? Dogged repetition of reading bears fruit in my knowledge. I just put my abundant natural talent to good use. One who is gifted easily absorbs instruction. You have a poor memory; your shallowness does not allow you truly to devote yourself to literature. You are so slow in declining when you are taught grammar; you are beaten all through school by the cruel blows of the rods. You become a joke to everyone if you do not speak perfectly![3]

---

    legere, cantare et non intelligere. From a miscellany with hymns, vocabulary, grammar, reform reports and observations by young nuns on convent life; late 15th century, Klosterarchiv Ebstorf, Hs. V 2, fol. 207v.

3 *Cur invides mihi, quod bene disco? Assidua repetitio legendi fructificat in me sciencia. Affluens ingenium meum utiliter expendo. Qui est capacis ingenii, faciliter capit doctrinam. Tu labilis es memorie, vanitas tua non sinit insistere litterature. Tam morose declinas si informemeris in alphabeto, diris virgarum plagis ad omne incitaris studium. Cunctis ridiculum effeceris, si non perfecte dicis.* Klosterarchiv Ebstorf, Hs V 4, fol. 99r.

For all the effort that was put into educating the girls to live a communal convent life characterized by mutual *caritas* and *devotio*, it was probably not possible anywhere for things to proceed entirely without tension within the community.

2. The Convent as Cultural and Educational Space

Convent Entry and Convent School

'Whenever the instruction in learned knowledge decreases in the monastic houses, the impact of religious life will most certainly perish'[4] – or so a young nun from Kloster Ebstorf recorded in her notebook at the end of the fifteenth century, presumably picking up on one of the Latin proverbs taught in the convent school. While earlier scholars considered the religious life of women to be intellectually undemanding, we now know that coping with the communal life of women in strict enclosure was very demanding and required the mastery of scholarly Latin for the choir services, the ability to infuse one's tasks with profound theological meaning and a knowledge of economics for the administration of the convent estates. The understanding of the Latin liturgy, the related insight into one's own tasks and the inner ordering of convent life were of an importance which was not to be underestimated. The women needed a thorough, intense education, something they could only acquire in the convent or through private lessons within the family, because Latin schools and universities remained closed to them until well into the modern era. Scholarly knowledge thus had to be passed down from generation to generation within the convent. Education in the convent school was, therefore, very attractive to girls and women; and families repeatedly tried to have daughters who were destined for the 'world' and marriage educated in the convent school. The nuns, on the other hand, rejected communal lessons with girls who were later to marry because this disturbed the withdrawal from the world by these convent residents and simply made it more difficult to observe strict enclosure.

Schlotheuber, Ebstorf, p. 221.

4 *Quandocumque in monasteriis deficit sciencia doctrine, tunc certe eciam destruitur effectus religiose vite*, Klosterarchiv Ebstorf, Hs V 2, fol. 207v.

The problem became clear when the founder of the Cistercian convent of Wienhausen, Duchess Mechthild of Braunschweig-Lüneburg (d. 1261), had it recorded in a document that, in accordance with custom, only girls who later took their vows should find a home in Wienhausen. A temporary admission of pupils into the convent for education or training alone was not to be permitted. Mechthild of Braunschweig-Lüneburg wanted an exception to be made for the daughters of the ducal family as a special privilege of the founding family. It suited both the convents and the families to admit the girls early so that they could attend the convent school at the age of six or seven, as soon as they were of an age to learn. While the convent communities wanted the girls to decide in favour of a religious life as independently as possible, their families, on the other hand, had an interest in an early, binding decision on the future status of their daughters – be it spiritual or secular.

But when and how did one enter the convent? Tilburg Remstede, nine years old, was already one of older girls when she was solemnly admitted to the Benedictine convent of Lüne on 10 January 1482. Katharina Semmelbecker had just turned four when she arrived at Lüne on 1 May 1487, the feast day of the Apostles Philip and James. Here Katharina met her biological sister Elisabeth, who had been living in the convent for a year. The girls' age and the day of their admission were carefully noted down by the officeholders, as were all further steps and rites associated with each girl's entry into the convent. The steps leading to admission often took up to ten years and were very important for both the girls and the community as well as for the families. The first was the solemn admission, followed by investiture and, at the earliest a year later, profession. As a rule, this was preceded by graduation from the convent school. Finally, the 'consecration of virgins', celebrated as the *crowning of the nuns, formed both the conclusion and in some respects the climax of the initiation rites.

Religious life as an alternative to marriage was highly attractive to women and their families. The nuns enjoyed great prestige in late-medieval society as 'brides of Christ, the king of kings'; and their spiritual marriage to the heavenly bridegroom was celebrated in the ceremony of the nuns' coronation. Admission to a convent gave the girls access to a learned education and a career in responsible leadership positions, for they not infrequently presided over communities of sixty to eighty nuns, numerous lay sisters and a large number of domestic servants. The women were responsible for managing both the extensive landholdings belonging to the convent and revenues such as from the salt works. According to wills from Cologne, until the middle of the fourteenth century, when the population declined due to the plague, half of all children were destined for religious life. Even at the turn of the sixteenth century, from the prestigious Nuremberg patrician family of Pirckheimer, six of Willibald Pirckheimer's sisters and three of his five daughters entered a convent (see Chapter IV). Only Willibald's sister Juliane entered into marriage. In the late Middle Ages, women's communities could certainly pick and choose their future convent members. The reform statutes for the Benedictine convent of Lüne from the end of the fifteenth century stipulated that if parents asked that a child be admitted to a convent, their repeated request should be granted, provided the status and reputation of the girl and her family had been carefully scrutinized. If the provost and convent agreed to her admission, at least six months were to elapse before her solemn induction (*introductio*). On the first presentation, the provost was to ask the child herself whether she wished to enter and remain in the convent of her own free will. She was then given a black tunic, a long veil and, as further head-covering, most especially a 'nun's crown', which consisted of two strips of white cloth, each a finger wide, crossed over the top of the head (see Figure 12). The new clothes were but symbolic references to the girl's destination for a religious life, because she had not yet entered the spiritual estate.

Since the dowry for a wedding befitting a girl's status was very expensive, parents tried to limit girls' permission to marry unless the marriage contributed to the success of their family politics. The relevant arrangements for the next generation were usually made by noble and patrician circles at the end of *pueritia*, when their children were six or seven years old – namely, before they were handed over to relatives or friends in neighbouring towns, or to other courts, or to monasteries or convents for education. At twelve, girls came of age and could enter into marriage without the consent of their parents. Even the staunch monastic reformers of the fifteenth century took the needs of lay society into consideration: the reform statutes of the Benedictine convent of Lüne set the minimum age for admission to the convent at five and the maximum age at twelve. The nuns were generally true to the rules of their statutes. In some cases, however, they also accepted younger girls. In the following case, a family relationship to Provost Johannes Lorber (1506–1529) may be assumed: on 25 July 1518 'Sister Cecilia Lorber came to this convent in her fourth year, on the day of the blessed virgin Gertrude. We fetched her in a little cart, and she remained here with us'.[5] The panel painting of lay brother Johannes transporting four nuns from Kloster Wolmirstedt to the newly founded convent in Old Medingen in a kind of hand-drawn wagon might reflect such practice.[6]

Fig. 10 History of Kloster Medingen, Panel 4. Lyßmann (1772) after paintings from 1499. Repro: Christine Greif.

The girls themselves could only take a valid vow of profession when they reached the age of majority. Then, however – as an alternative, one which many fathers and mothers may well not have had in mind – they could also enter into marriage against the will of their parents. If their

---

5   *Item eodem anno, in die sancti Jacobi apostoli, venit in istud monasterium soror Cecilia Lorber, anno etatis sue IIII⁰ de in die sancte Gertrudis virginis. In rotulam traximus eam, et mansit hic nobiscum,* Chronicle of Lüne Convent, Kloster Lüne, Hs. 13, fol. 78v, cf. *Die Chronik,* ed. Stenzig (2019), p. 154

6   Johann Ludolph Lyßmann, *Historische Nachricht von dem Ursprunge, Anwachs und Schicksalen des im Lüneburgischen Herzogthum belegenen Klosters Meding,* 1772, Plate 4.

family wished to bind the girls to a religious life prior to this, church law provided two possibilities for entering a convent while still a minor: *oblation and 'tacit profession'. In the case of oblation, the parents made a legally binding vow on behalf of their underage child by offering him or her to the altar of the spiritual community in question – in other words, by 'sacrificing' him or her. Through the parents' vow of oblation the child had entered the clerical state, whereby this decision did not, in principle, require any further confirmation by the adolescent. The 'tacit profession' usually took the form of the handing over of the *habit and is therefore called an 'investiture' in the sources (from the Latin *vestis*: robe; clothes). Investiture also corresponded to entry into the clerical state – albeit with the reservation that this had to be confirmed later, at the age of majority. Phrases such as 'virgins consecrated to God' (*virgines deo sacratae*) are not, therefore, mere vague descriptions but clear legal terms which denote the completed passage of the girl concerned into the spiritual state of a choir nun.

While oblation was quite common in the Cistercian convent of Wienhausen, after the monastic reform of the fifteenth century the Benedictine nuns in Lüne rejected this path to entry and preferred investiture. In preparation for the investiture ceremony, the provost gave an address to the girls in the chapter about the strictness of the rule, the 'perpetual enclosure', the renunciation of private property, the contempt for everything worldly, the complete separation from – the 'forgetting' of – parents, and the girls' relinquishment of their own will. The investiture itself was integrated into the celebration of a mass, during which the girls' parents and relatives were permitted to enter the nuns' choir. While the families and the girls sat in the middle of the nuns' choir, the convent followed the ceremony from the choir stalls. The nuns' crowns which the girls had worn since their admission were now taken from them and laid in front of the figure of the convent patron, St Bartholomew, where they were kept until the coronation of the nuns.

Mechthild von Eltzen, who had come to Lüne in 1506 at the age of six, celebrated her investiture just two years later. The prioress of Lüne, Mechthild Wilde, led the girl to the steps of the altar, where the provost received her. He took off her nun's crown (*vitta*) and the upper garment (*toga*) while he spoke of stripping off the former existence; and then he consecrated the novice's habit. With the verse 'the Lord robes you' (*induat te dominus*), based on Ephesians 4:24, the provost dressed her again in the habit and cincture. Finally, he took up a cloth, covered the novice's head with it and cut off her hair. It was hair like this, braided into plaits, that was discovered by the scholars of the Heilig Kreuz Kloster near Braunschweig when they searched the empty convent for usable objects during the nuns' exile (Chapter I.1). Afterwards everyone enjoyed a celebratory meal together, and Mechthild and the other girls received smaller or larger gifts. To mark the occasion, the mother of Adelheid Stüver gave her daughter a silver statue of St Aldegunde, on whose feast day she had been born; another mother gave her daughter a silver figure of St Clare; others gave silver spoons, a wine jug or money. In Lüne, the ceremonial investiture within the framework of mass marked, as a 'spiritual wedding', the transition to the religious estate and thus the final farewell to parents and to the life of the world in general.

Leaving the Convent School and Profession

The lessons at the convent school were entirely geared to the liturgical tasks and demands of life in strict enclosure. At age five to seven, the time spent in school was quite long and demanding by the standards of the time. Magdalena Schneverding came to Lüne in 1515 at the age of seven and was admitted to the convent school a year later, invested in 1520 at the age of twelve and left the school in 1523. At this point she had, therefore, already been living in Lüne for eight years. The ceremonial leaving of the convent school then took place at chapter in the presence of the convent and the provost. He officially released the girls 'from the scholastic yoke' (*a iugo scolasticali*). The education of the girls in the convent school was of the utmost importance to the convent. Here the course was set for the attitude and skills of the rising generation. In a typical mixture of Low German and Latin, a Cistercian nun from Wöltingerode noted down a programmatic poem below the text on the first page of a book on martyrs; the third stanza runs: 'The study of the arts should be a prelude to salvation: indeed, let us understand scripture! Without it, monastic – alas! – devotion remains in idleness: not to read is evilly done.'

Salutis ad preludium / sit artis nobis studium: / wolan, die scryft vorstan!
quo sine stat in ocio / claustralis – heu! – devocio: / nicht lesen is ovel dan![7]

The punchline of the stanza is provided by the Low German phrases that follow each Latin rhyming couplet: *scryft* (scripture) can be understood as literature in general but applies especially to the Holy Scriptures. Just as at university, the study of philosophy in the form of the seven liberal arts (*artes*) has the purpose of preparing students for the higher faculties, including that of theology; a deeper understanding of the basic sciences is also necessary for nuns to live convent life appropriately. Otherwise, the greatest sin of monastic life threatens: idleness.

The Nun's Coronation

The nun's coronation, known as the 'consecration of a virgin' (*consecratio virginis*), formed the climax and conclusion of the nuns' admission ceremonies. Nuns' crowns were widespread in late medieval northern German convents, but in southern Germany they can only be found in isolated cases. The essential elements in the ritual crowning of a nun were obviously derived from the secular marriage ceremony of late Antiquity. Traditionally, only the bishop enjoyed the right to crown nuns because their coronation signified the official recognition of their virginity by the church. The consecrated nun's crown anticipated their coronation in heaven, to which the virgins were entitled after the last judgement as a reward for their virginity, this being understood as a bloodless martyrdom. The nuns' crowns consisted of white strips of material laid over the head in a cross shape. Crosses of red silk were sewn onto the front and, more frequently, onto all four sides, as well as on the top of the crown. This is clearly visible in the depiction of music lessons from Kloster Ebstorf (Figure 27), in which the organ player, the two seated women in the garden and (seen here in the detail) the nun teaching the others to read music wear the ribbons with the red crosses over their veils.

---

7   Late 15th century addition to a 13th-century *Martyrologium* from Wöltingerode, Herzog August Bibliothek Wolfenbüttel, Cod. Guelf. Helmst. 498, fol. 1r.

Fig. 11 Benedictine nun with nun's crown (detail from Figure 27).
Photograph: Wolfgang Brandis.

The transmission of the nun's crown shown in the next illustration is a stroke of good fortune. It was only purchased from private ownership in 2000 by the Abegg Foundation on the Riggisberg near Bern. Until then medieval nuns' crowns had only been known from written sources or from illustrations. It consists of precious white silk ribbons with gold borders laid over the head in the shape of a cross, with five medallions where the ribbons cross: on the crown a red square with five golden dots; on the forehead a lamb of God (*agnus dei*); on the sides a cherub and an angel with a lily sceptre; and at the back of the head the Old Testament king David in an attitude of worship. At the end of the fourteenth century, the light silk bands were sewn for stabilisation onto a blue silk cap, to which the red trimming also belongs. The embroidery and especially the medallions on the nun's crown correspond to the descriptions of the famous nuns' crowns from the Rupertsberg, which Hildegard of Bingen describes in the letter to Tengswich of Andernach (d. 1152/1153) and in her visionary work *Scivias* ('Know the Ways') and which the nuns there wore over their loose hair.

II. Education 51

Fig. 12 Nun's crown from the twelfth century. ©Abegg Foundation, inv. no. 5257.

In her vision, Hildegard sees some of the nuns adorned with a golden circlet, displaying on the forehead a lamb, on the right a cherubim, on the left the figure of an angel, on the crown of the head the image (*similitudo*) of the Holy Trinity and a human being. This nun's crown comes very close to that description. In Hildegard's vision, it is no longer the tangible object, but already the heavenly crown which Christ placed on the head of his brides, the virgins, in their eternal life, in parallel to the crowning of Mary as the first of the virgins.

In Lüne, as in Ebstorf, the girls wore somewhat simpler nuns' crowns, which instead of medallions were decorated with red crosses as symbols of the stigmata of Christ. The unconsecrated nuns' crowns were initially given to the girls without the red silk crosses. Later, the abbess presented them with the crosses as gifts on special occasions. They were sewn onto the white fabric strips retrospectively. During the coronation of the nuns, the bishop consecrated the white strips of cloth, which had been deposited with the convent patron St Bartholomew at the time of their investiture as a sign of their promise of chastity; and then he placed them on the girls' heads in a solemn ceremony. The liturgical configuration of the celebration was based on the story of the wise and foolish virgins (Matthew 25:1–10). This biblical parable is about the return of Christ, the hour of which is unknown. Ten virgins – all personifications of the bride – go to meet the bridegroom by taking their lamps and setting out. The five foolish ones only have their lamps with them; the five wise ones also have oil. In the night, only the wise ones find their way to the bridegroom. Future nuns were to emulate these five. In the ceremony, this was staged as follows: with lighted candles in their hands and their heads uncovered, the candidates approached the bishop through the nuns' choir. There they received the crowns, which signified their final arrival and privileged position in the spiritual world.

3. The Heiningen Philosophy Tapestry

The nuns, especially in northern Germany, were well acquainted with Latin and with the learning of their time. As a rule, therefore, they were able to explore theological, philosophical and many other topics independently. This meant they belonged to a group of literate people which even in the late Middle Ages was still small. How, then, did the nuns themselves perceive the universe of education and where did they locate themselves within it?

A Demonstration of Education

The Philosophy Tapestry from the Augustinian convent of Heiningen is a very special means of demonstrating education: in 1516, the nuns in Heiningen produced a monumental tapestry, the visual rendition of a universe of knowledge into which the community – all the nuns, the lay sisters and the convent pupils – inscribed themselves.

Fig. 13 Heiningen Philosophy Tapestry. ©Victoria & Albert Museum, London, Accession No. 289–1876.

The tapestry measures almost five by five meters, everything revolving around one personification: Lady Philosophy. It must have taken many years to create such a monumental tapestry, from its design to its realization and the detailed embroidery of the figures with their speech scrolls.

Even though the tapestry reveals a great love of detail and the numerous speech scrolls require detailed studying, the overall structure is clearly recognizable. *Philosophia*, crowned, as imagined in Boethius' *The Consolation of Philosophy*, is enthroned in the centre; in her all knowledge is gathered. Two circles enclose the celestial sphere of knowledge, the source of which is Philosophy in the centre. While the sciences, which explain the immaterial forces at work in the cosmos and on earth, are framed by trefoil arches resting on pillars, this heavenly sphere of divine order is separated from human knowledge by a square frame. Earth-bound education rests on four authorities as the foundation of knowledge: Ovid, Boethius, Horace, and Aristotle. These highly respected classical authors were regarded as the origin of the academic disciplines. The first large display of Humanism north of the Alps happened about 100 years earlier, when a large group of Italian humanists participated at the Council of Constance (1414–1418), schooled as they were in the texts of Antiquity. Their education and culture deeply impressed the Holy Roman Empire gathered at Lake Constance. Renaissance culture had also gained acceptance in the convents of northern Germany. Eloquent and well-read, the nuns quoted Ovid: 'One should cultivate the arts in these times when faith stands or falls with fate'[8] – a far-sighted quotation in view of Luther's *Ninety-Five Theses* published only a few years later in 1517. Despite their enclosure, the nuns in Heiningen were apparently well acquainted with the fact that social change was on the horizon. From Aristotle, they selected a very pertinent admonition for a community tackling such a major undertaking as this tapestry together: 'Bad is the companion who hinders the common task'.[9]

The Tapestry Speaks

The Philosophy Tapestry is not a purely abstract or prefabricated view of the universe of medieval knowledge: rather, the women (and men) of Heiningen have integrated themselves into it. On the edges, in the outermost square frame, an inscription which surrounds the entire tapestry names Prioress Elisabeth Terwins as the driving force. The tapestry itself 'speaks': 'In 1506, our honourable Domina Elizabeth Terwins had me made by the professed nuns consecrated to God', and

---

8 *Cura sit ingenuas pectus coluisse per artes / Nunc cum fortuna statque cadique fides*, a combination of *Ars Amatoria* Book II.121 and *Ex Ponto* II.3.10.

9 *Pravus quoque socius est qui impedit commune opus*, a quotation of the *Topics*, one of the six books of the *Organon*, by Aristotle in the translation of Boethius, similar also in John of Salisbury's *Metalogicon* III.10.54.

then lists in order of seniority the sub-prioress Margaret Hornborch, the bursar Anna Lunemans, the other officeholders and the total of thirty-six choir nuns, six lay sisters and four novices in the convent.[10] The provost and the priests are also listed. Reference is made to the founding of Heiningen and its reform, which, as a second act of foundation, had made possible the blossoming of the convent at the turn of the fifteenth century. At the same time, this a snapshot of the convent of Heiningen with all its members. After a period of decline, they had all worked together to breathe new life into the convent through the reforms in the fifteenth century. To achieve this, the nuns and the entire community of Heiningen inscribed themselves into the universe of education and the long traditions of learned knowledge.

The Academic Disciplines and Christian Ethics

The intellectual roots of the academic disciplines and the educational universe lie in philosophy as the undisputed 'art of the arts' (*ars artium*). The speech scroll above Lady Philosophy declares that she encompasses everything a human being can know and that through her it is possible arrive at theology, the highest academic discipline – if knowledge is augmented by the grace of cognition. Following the systematics of Plato and Aristotle, the knowledge encompassed by philosophy is divided between five medallions, which are identified by female personifications displaying characteristic objects and epithets: 'Physics' (natural sciences) with a cylindrical medicine tin; 'Mechanics' (applied sciences) with a protractor; and 'Logic' (explained as 'knowledge for disputations') with a book. In addition, we find 'Practice' (moral philosophy and politics); and 'Theory' (speculative philosophy and searching for truth), the latter identified by a mirror.

---

10   *Anno domini MDXVI venerabilis domina Elisabet Tekwins priorissa me fieri fecit per has deo consecratas ac professas virgines: Margretam Hornborch suppriorissa, Annam Lunemans procuratricem...*

Fig. 14 Philosophy enthroned and surrounded by personifications (detail from Figure 13).

In the second large ring, we then find the Seven Liberal Arts, the *artes liberales*, personified by male and female figures and starting with the basics of Grammar, Rhetoric and Dialectic – or the Trivium, a term related to 'trivial', i.e. basic meaning. Building on this foundation, the Quadrivium was taught: Music, Geometry, Astronomy and Arithmetic. The Liberal Arts do not stand here alone and separate but are accompanied by and paired with the gifts of the Holy Spirit. Here the individual Arts are framed by rhymed mnemonic verses, such as were presumably taught in school. The seven gifts display quotations from the Old Testament on their speech scrolls, the contents of which always refer to the particular discipline of the Liberal Arts next to which they stand. Hence the academic disciplines, which, as the nuns knew only too well, can be used for both good and ill, are each restrained by a principle of Christian ethics in this blueprint for an ordered universe of education. Thus, Grammar is said to teach the art of writing and the manner of speaking;[11] and Wisdom is placed next to her in the form of Solomon,

---

11   *artem scribendi docet ista modumque loquendi.*

who warns us to be modest, emphasizing that all wisdom comes from God and is eternal in him. Grammar was the key qualification for all those educated in the convent, who were expected to converse with one another in Latin and also to compose their works in this language.

From 1516, the tapestry was kept in Kloster Heiningen and survived all reforms, the Reformation and the Counter-Reformation until the convent's dissolution in 1851. Whoever wanted to decipher the message had to circumnavigate the tapestry, because the figures and texts are arranged as on the axes of a wheel. Like the Wienhausen Tristan Tapestry (Figure 17), the textile was probably laid out in the convent for special visitors on feast days. Due to its monumental size, only the convent church or the nuns' choir could conceivably have been used for this purpose. The Philosophy Tapestry must have meant a great deal to the community because it was kept at Heiningen for many centuries. In 1876, it was purchased for the Victoria & Albert Museum in London, where the intention was to gather exemplary arts and crafts from all over Europe to act as models for budding craftsmen. Pieces like this one influenced the Arts and Crafts Movement with the medieval revivalism of William Morris and other artists; the *memoria* of the Heiningen nuns, of their craftsmanship and their names has thus continued under different auspices into the present.

III. Nuns, Family, and Community

Convent and world were interconnected in many different ways. When they entered the convent, the girls and women also made the legal transition from their own family group to their new family, the community of choir nuns. Whereas their father or a male relative had previously been their guardian, this duty was now assumed by the convent provost, who as the 'bride's best man' represented the nuns' bridegroom, namely Christ. The families remained connected to the community of nuns in many different ways, often celebrating high feast days in the convent and maintaining their family tombs there. As a highly respected alternative to marriage, the convent also represented a special space in which to reflect on spiritual and secular models for the conduct of one's life. Likewise, role models such as Elisabeth of Thuringia could be preserved, negotiated and imbued with meaning: Elisabeth had not entered a convent but had, in active service to others, dedicated herself to nursing the sick. In the Middle Ages, families were understood as a community of their members living in both world and convent and as a cross-generational network of the living and the dead, equally commemorated by the nuns in their prayers.

1. Life History and Family Influence

Family ties between the Heilig Kreuz Kloster and Braunschweig were close. This can be seen, for example, in the family van dem Kerkhove. Through the generations, many women from this family of tailors, an old patrician family whose members had long served on the town council, lived in the Heilig Kreuz Kloster. The men of the family officiated as *procurators, secular advocates for the community of women, on Braunschweig town council; and the van dem Kerkhove had a right to a place for their daughters in the convent.

The Limping Girl

In 1483, the Braunschweig citizen Margarete van dem Kerkhove, a friend of the convent, came to the convent and asked the community to take in her daughter, who limped. Yet she did not wish the daughter to be accepted into the convent as a future nun, but initially only that she could live there as a guest with the other girls. The daughter was seven years old when she came to the Cistercian nuns of the Heilig Kreuz Kloster on the Rennelberg. She lived with the nuns without being bound by vows of any kind, as the diarist points out. She wore a white habit and participated in the Liturgy of the Hours as well as interceding for the deceased, an obligation to which the convent was bound. Sometimes she studied in the school with the future choir nuns; on other days she worked alongside the lay sisters. She did not wear a *scapular, the dark upper garment of the habit, over her shoulders, nor did she follow the rule of the order – she remained a guest. Her uncertain status stemmed mainly from the fact that her family did not wish to see their daughter admitted as a lay sister, and the convent would not agree to her admittance as a nun because of her physical ailment. Being a nun was a question of status.

Almost seven years passed before unfortunate circumstances meant the daughter was almost the only one left in her family. Both parents had died in the meantime, as had all her brothers and sisters. In this situation, the girl's relatives advised her to ask the abbess to grant her permission to return to the world. Mechthild von Vechelde, abbess of the Heilig Kreuz Kloster, gave consent on one condition: namely, that the girl, who had lived with the nuns for so long and had been educated for this life, would continue to remain chaste and would not marry. With that, the abbess released the familiar guest, having first removed the robe she had worn in the convent. Of course, the abbess's authority ended at the convent walls. Back in the world, the girl did not feel bound by any promise. She married in the very same year and gave birth to a son, thereby ensuring the continuity of the family. The diarist does not comment on this breaking of her promise but concludes the narrative with the terse words: 'Let us not talk about that in detail now, but return to our own affairs'.[1]

---

1   *de qua non est dicendum per sigula, sed nunc revertamur ad propria*, fol. 55r.

The Reception Party for the Weferlingen Daughters

The convent performed an important function for the families in several respects. For the wives and daughters in particular, it served as a special space and shelter which provided an alternative to marriage and, not least, access to scholarly knowledge. Through this mutual dependence, convent and lay world were bound together by close relationships, which became critical when questions arose about the admission of future members of the convent. On one St Anthony's Day, 17 January 1496, the wife of the knight Ulrich von Weferlingen came to the convent, bringing with her two girls named Katharina and Elisabeth. The noble family of Weferlingen had probably been connected to the convent since its foundation and maintained their family tomb there. The convent accepted the two girls into its community in accordance with an earlier agreement and their father's will, on condition that they would agree to enter the convent of their own free will after a probationary period.

For the convent, it was a balancing act. For the nobility and the patriciate in particular, their daughters' entry into the convent was an important instrument in their family strategy. Especially if the families had the right to a *prebend, the financial outlay was much lower than a marriage in keeping with their status, amounting to barely a tenth of the dowry. Because the family estate became the property of the husband's family on a daughter's marriage and served as widow's dower to provide for her after the husband's death, families could prevent the fragmentation of their property by having one or more daughters enter a convent. For the convent community, on the other hand, it was crucial that future nuns had made their decision in favour of a spiritual life as independently as possible and viewed the religious way of life positively so that community life was not damaged by their inner reluctance.

When the probationary year of Katharina and Elisabeth von Weferlingen had passed, the elder of the two sisters refused to receive the clerical garments. 'We let her go free', the diarist notes, after the abbess had stripped her of the white robe, the promise to enter a religious life.[2] The younger girl, on the other hand, was keen to stay in the Heilig Kreuz

---

2   *dimisimus eandem libere discedere, exuta candita tunica a domina nostra,* fol. 122r.

Kloster and decided to become a nun. In the meantime, her mother, the wife of Ulrich von Weferlingen, had become a widow. In addition to the two older girls who had already spent a year in the convent, she had three other younger daughters, the youngest of whom, Fia, had taken it upon herself to take up the place left vacant by the departure of her sister Katharina. She wished to pray for their father and, as far as she was able, to come to the aid of his soul, which was presumed to be in purgatory. According to the diarist, Fia convinced her mother through 'fervent pleading',[3] with the result that the latter brought the four-year-old to the convent. The convent accepted Fia. In the same year the oblation of both daughters was celebrated as a spiritual wedding, at which the mother took perpetual vows on behalf of the children, who were still minors. These vows signified their passage into the status of *religious. The major celebration was set for 16 June 1499, St Vitus's Day, and the widow of Ulrich von Weferlingen invited friends and relatives of the family to the convent to celebrate her daughters' wedding day together.

Unfortunately, many of the invited guests obviously made their excuses because the diarist mentions with regret that this meant they had gone to great length to put out a 'great spread' of everything 'because of the nobles who were expected, but it was all in vain since only very few came'.[4] The convent had wanted to prove to the family that it was accommodation worthy of their status. The family of the Weferlingen daughters as the brides, on the other hand, had to pay for the festivities and the widow spared no effort or expense. Four courses of meat alone were served; there was venison, chicken, and beef for guests to fill their bellies. The convent 'accepted it gratefully on the day, but afterwards I heard several times that almost everyone was displeased by the overabundance', the diarist notes critically as a warning for future similar events.[5]

---

3   *sero et mane singulis diebus instanter peciit*, fol. 122v.
4   *lectisternia et cetera preparamenta, que propter curiales venturos exquisita erant, incassum extenta videbantur, quia perpauci erant, qui aderant*, fol. 131r.
5   *gratissime accipiebant, sed ut postea multociens ab aliquibus audivi et intellexi, omnibus ferme displicuerat. Hoc ideo exaravi, ut si in futuro simile mihi aliquid procurare convivium vel prandium occurrerit, caucius mihi habere valeam*, fol. 131r, see discussion in the 'Prologue: Voices from the Past'.

The Convent Throws Out the Provost

The most important office, the link between the convent and lay society, was that of the provost. As the highest-ranking clergyman in the convent, he was responsible for the supreme supervision of its religious life alongside the abbess. His main task was to ensure the nuns were provided for through the estates and to regulate all secular affairs for the nuns, including maintenance of the convent buildings.

In 1488 Heinrich Karstens, who admittedly still owned his own farm near St Cyriacus Abbey in Braunschweig, was provost and at the same time *canon in the Heilig Kreuz Kloster. The abbess of the Heilig Kreuz Kloster, Elisabeth Pawel, was not very satisfied with him. Heinrich Karstens was hardly ever present, but constantly spent his time on the Cyriakusberg, where he was having a new house built for himself. The absence of the provost had a severe impact on convent life. Sometimes the women did not have enough bread for the convent; sometimes there was a lack of wood, or of coal and in general of all the necessities of life: 'Whatever the provost was required to provide for us from our own estates could not be obtained without anger and harsh words from the abbess'.[6] Quite obviously, the nuns suspected that the provost was appropriating their property for his own building project. Worse still, he had turned almost the entire *familia*, all the secular servants who lived and worked on the neighbouring farm, against the nuns. The abbess found herself in a difficult position. Normally she would have discussed this abuse of office with the procurators, an office usually held by high-ranking Braunschweig citizens, who were responsible for representing the affairs of the nuns of the Heilig Kreuz Kloster on the town council. During these years this office was held by the two councillors Albrecht von Vechelde and Bodo Glümer. Yet Heinrich Karstens seemed to have been a respected, influential person in Braunschweig: the procurators declined to intervene because they did not want to annoy him. They were probably afraid of endangering their own affairs, or so the nuns heard from third parties. Nothing could be done, and the women had to put up with the damage caused.

Eventually, however, it all became too much for the abbess, and she

---

6 *quodcumque debebat nobis dari de nostra bona, non potuit nobis fieri sine ira et indignacione domine nostre*, fol. 29r.

resorted to a very effective expedient, one which illustrates the close lines of communication between the convent and the world. During the daily chapter meeting, the abbess gave permission to the whole congregation to complain to their relatives and friends about the provost and to ask them for advice on what could be done. She herself enquired from the good friends of the convent how the community could obtain different governance, that is, a new provost. They advised her to summon to the convent some of the twenty-four *guild masters, the political representatives of the guilds, and explain the situation. The abbess followed their advice, and the guild masters promised to support the community's request.

The effect was immense, but its consequences were not without problems for the convent. The twenty-four guild masters decided not only to dismiss the provost Heinrich Karstens, but also to remove the two procurators, Albrecht von Vechelde and Bodo Glümer, from office. They appointed two new councillors in their stead, namely Jakob Rose and Konrad Scheppenstede. Of course, Albrecht von Vechelde and Bodo Glümer were profoundly angered by this turn of events. The abbess tried to reconcile them with the convent by all means possible, sending them gifts and asking them to remain loyal friends of the Heilig Kreuz Kloster, but all in vain: they remained angry. Moreover, the deposed provost took revenge in his own way and took whatever he could with him from the provostry.

2. The Family and the Convent Community

As the example of the dispute with the provost and the lobbying of the Braunschweig families demonstrate, the convents were integrated into a tight network of families bound together by ties of friendship. Many of these families remained connected to a particular convent for generations, and their closeness can be traced back to its founding days. Both sides, the families and the nuns, benefited from this. The convents offered both men and women special access to salvation, but also to careers as religious – women as abbesses or office holders; men as provosts or parish priests in the parish churches under the supervision of the convent, for example. Through these networks the communities of nuns often exerted their influence very effectively.

The Families of Origin: Nobility and Patriciate

In principle, anyone and everyone could choose a religious life and enter monastic houses, but in practice the options for women in particular were predetermined by the status of the family from which they were descended. The civic or episcopal Latin schools were open to sons, who could, therefore, often make the decision about their way of life, whether spiritual or secular, much later, namely in adulthood. Then they could also enter a religious community against their parents' will and choose between a whole spectrum of religious ways of life that were more or less open to the world. In order to enter a community of Benedictines or Cistercians, the old monastic orders, daughters needed the support of their families, who contributed to their keep by means of a dowry. As the example of the Heilig Kreuz Kloster shows, the girls came from families who were in a position to make this financial outlay and who had long had ties to the convent. These were usually noble families from the surrounding area or members of the urban patriciate. Their coats of arms can be found in the objects handed down in the convents to this day. For example, the coat of arms of the von Bodendike family – a leaping brown stag with red antlers and a jagged white chevron on its coat – is set on a keystone in the cloisters in Kloster Lüne and is also immortalized on several tapestries, each of which was produced around 1500 during the period in office of Prioress Sophia von Bodendike, including the *Bartholomäuslaken*, a wall hanging showing the legend of St Bartholomew, the convent's patron saint. Around the first eight of the nine scenes there are short captions explaining the action. In the last roundel, the nuns are depicted adoring the saint who wears over his arm his flayed skin but is smiling with a heavenly crown on his head. The caption gives a short prayer instead 'O kind patron, help us',[7] with a further prayer line written as speech bubbles coming from the two nuns kneeling at the top: 'O glorious patron, blessed Bartholomew!'[8] Around the whole tapestry runs a longer rhymed prayer in the voice of the whole convent, imploring Bartholemew as 'God's friend' to assist the nuns in joining him in the 'hall of heaven':

---

7 *O pie patrone, adiuua nos.*
8 *O gloriose patrone / Beate Bartolomee.*

Saint Bartholomew, apostle of Christ, outstanding teacher of the Indians, incline your ear to our cries, that lifted up towards the Lord by your help, we may merit to become heaven's citizens like you. Intercede for us to the Lord, glorious friend of God, that by his grace granting, for the memory of our patron, we may behold you, God, face-to-face in glory, and live eternally. Holy Bartholomew, patron, teacher, good apostle of God, be our aid in the hour of death, place us in the hall of heaven, so that we may merit to enjoy the face of God without end, amen. In the year of our Lord 1492.[9]

Fig. 15 Bartholomew tapestry of 1492. Photograph: Ulrich Loeper ©Kloster Lüne.

---

9   *Sancte bartholomee, Christi apostole, Indorum doctor egregie / nostris aurem clamoribus appone, / ut tuo ad dominum sustentati iuuamine / tui conciues mereamur adesse. / Intercede pro nobis ad dominum, gloriose / dei amice, vt ipsius gracia largiente / Patroni pro memoria te, deum, facialiter / uideamus in gloria, viuamus immortaliter. / Sacer bartholomee, patrone, / doctor, apostole dei bone, assis nobis mortis in agone, / nos in aula celorum repone, / vt facie dei sine fine perfrui mereamur, amen. / Anno domini M^o $cccc^o$ $xcij^o$.*

While family members were allowed to enter the convent on special feast days, the nuns' enclosure meant they were not permitted to leave the convent to attend family celebrations or to care for sick relatives. For that reason, they had to rely on letters for communication. Among the letters of the Benedictine nuns in Kloster Lüne are quite a number congratulating their siblings on their weddings; in them the nuns regret that they cannot attend the celebration themselves because of their secluded way of life but promise to send holy guests with the gift of good wishes instead. Anna von Bülow thus congratulates her brother Vicke von Bülow on his second marriage and explains the spiritual significance of the celebration: Christ, her bridegroom, and Mary, her mother-in-law, would be present at the wedding just as they were in Cana when Jesus was instructed by his mother to turn water into wine.

The cultivation of good relations also included sending small gifts, although the nuns themselves owned no property and were therefore dependent on the work of their own hands in this respect. For example, the three sisters Elisabeth, Mette (Mechthild), and Tibbeke (Tiburg) Elebeke, living as nuns in Kloster Medingen, wrote a Low German prayer book for their sister Anna, who had married the mayor of Lüneburg, Heinrich von Töbing. For the volume they translated texts from their own Latin prayer books and adapted them to the life of their secular sister. Another nun from Kloster Lüne was apparently worried about her brother, to whom she wrote an admonition to study hard as well as good wishes for his recovery, because she had heard from their mother that he was ill. She said that he should commit himself to his talent for study, because now it was up to him what he made of it: after good beginnings, Judas had ended up a traitor; Saul, on the other hand, had turned into Paul. Although the brother had obviously studied and had certainly learnt Latin, the siblings wrote to each other in Low German – perhaps because of family ties.

The Monastic Community: Abbess, Prioress, Nuns, Lay Sisters, Provost, and Scholars

Medieval convents were large and often very influential spiritual institutions. As we have already seen, it was by no means only nuns who lived in them: the often extensive buildings housed very different social groups, both men and women.

A monastic community was always structured hierarchically. The abbess led the convent and represented it externally, while a number of further office-holding nuns assumed functions in its internal organization, such as prioress, precentrix (*cantrix*), cellar mistress (*celleraria*) or schoolmistress (*magistra, scholastica*) and formed a kind of 'inner council'. This council assisted the abbess in major decisions, they signed important documents together and led the way in ceremonies such as processions. The elders (*seniores*) in a convent also performed an advisory role, whereby their 'age' was measured according to the date when they entered the convent or took their vows. The communities could vary greatly in size, from a mere dozen to ten times that number of women: *houses of secular canonesses usually comprised twelve to fifteen women, convents an average of sixty to eighty women, as well as the novices and girls who had not yet professed but were already living in the convent.

Since the women lived in strict enclosure, they were assisted by lay sisters who undertook the necessary work outside the enclosure and ran errands for them. While the choir nuns, through their spiritual marriage to Christ, occupied a high rank in medieval society and were a 'good match' for Christ as 'son of the highest king', the lay sisters represented a different social order and usually came from less affluent families, such as the urban middle class. This is also the reason why, in the case of the girl with a limp, her patrician family resisted giving her to the convent as a lay sister rather than a choir sister.

Lay sisters typically entered the convent at an age when they were fit for work, took only simple vows and were cared for in the convent throughout their lives. They did not go through the convent school, so they did not learn Latin and had reduced prayer obligations so that their work did not suffer. Yet they learnt to some extent to read and write in the vernacular, as is evident from the letters and devotional manuscripts they wrote for themselves. They were not bound by any fixed rules of enclosure, and enjoyed greater freedom of movement, albeit under some control.

A rule from the 1470s for the lay brothers and sisters in Kloster Medingen stipulates that they were not to use their right to come and go more freely to smuggle strangers into the convent or, conversely, to go into town to visit relatives without express permission. They were to dress plainly and not, for example, wear two-tone red and green, tight-fitting garments with silver buttons – a prohibition that, like so many others, provides us with an insight into what was fashionable at the time. Above all, however, they were forbidden, under threat of excommunication, to write their wills without the knowledge of the provost – too great was the fear that property would be lost for the convent.

Maids and servants such as day labourers came from the same social group as those doing similar jobs in the town or for the nobility. They looked after the mills, brewery, fishponds, farms, vineyards, and the rest of the convent property. Sometimes they came to the convent together with members of a family whom they had also served in a secular capacity, even though the convent rule forbade *religious to be assisted by personal servants. The prebendaries found in many convents also represented an important group – men and women who decided, mostly towards the end of their lives, to live with a religious community that would then take care of them – a provision for their retirement. It was not uncommon for them to possess special skills, have detailed knowledge of sewing, be learned lawyers or trained craftsmen which was very useful to the convent. They transferred their inheritance to the convent when they entered, took on many smaller and larger tasks for the community, such as running errands, and were provided with all the necessities of life in return.

On the whole, a monastic community thus followed the model of a family, starting with the 'head of house' as the mother of the entire community. This is clear from the very title of the office. The term 'abbess' has a long journey through many languages behind it, beginning in the bible itself. Its basis is the intimate Aramaic address for 'Father', *abba*, which Jesus uses in the Lord's Prayer. The abbess represented and took responsibility for the community to the outside world and for this reason was also allowed to leave the enclosure. The reputation and prosperity of the convent often depended on her family connections: for example, when in case of conflict it became necessary to assert the interests of the convent in lay society. She also had the power to punish the nuns and the duty of supervising discipline in the convent. The office of abbess was extremely demanding. In the Lüne letters, obituaries praise the head of house (which in convents sometimes was the prioress) as 'sweet mother and loyal shepherdess' whose loss is mourned by the nuns like 'lost sheep'.[10] The

---

10 *pium sit relictis oviculis deflere tam dulcem matrem ac fidelem pastricem*, Letter 131,

inscription on the last panel from the cycle in the house of the abbess in Kloster Medingen praises the work of Margarete Puffen, who had been the first prioress during the monastic reforms and who had successfully managed to be promoted to the higher-status form of abbess in 1494. It does so in Latin verse and from the point of view of the convent:

> She taught us, the handmaiden of Christ, with all gentleness and piety in the holy reform and observance and abolished fully the vice of personal property. She scattered the flowers of true religion and reform and rejected all error. All the deeds of her predecessors she gilded with her own deeds; and like an angel of the Lord she walked among us and never tired of working for us day and night.[11]

Men were also necessary in this community: canon law forbade women not only to speak publicly on issues of dogma, but also to preach and to administer the sacraments. As shown by the example of the nuns in their Braunschweig exile, they organized the Liturgy of the Hours and the chapter meetings themselves, but in several areas they came up against the limits imposed by canon law. For the celebration of mass and the sacraments, the women needed priests. These could be secular clergy, the provost or even monks who took over the spiritual ministry known as 'care of the souls' (*cura animarum*). The small group of clerics who assumed responsibility for pastoral care in the convent was usually headed by a provost (Latin *praepositus*, anybody 'appointed to position as superintendent, governor or administrator, reeve, provost, mayor'). Frequently he was not only the chief cleric but also assumed responsibility for all the administrative and legal matters of the community. The powers of the provost could vary greatly from convent to convent, depending on whether the foundation in question belonged to a religious order such as the Cistercians. If that was the case, the monks took over the task of spiritual ministry to the women;

---

written by Margarete Snitkers, prioress of Altkloster in Buxtehude, to the convent in Kloster Lüne after the death of their prioress, Sophia von Bodendike, on 19 February 1504.

11 *Hec cum omni mansuetudine & pietate nos Cristi ancillas / sanctam reformacionem & observanciam edocebat. / Et omne vicium proprietatis obstruebat./ Vere religionis et reformacionis sparsit flores / Et reprobavit omnes errores. / Omnia predecessarum suarum facta factis suis inauravit. / & quasi angelus domini inter nos ambulavit / atque die ac nocte pro nobis laborare nunqvam cessavit.* DI 76, No. 58†, urn:nbn:de:0238-di076g013k0005801.

III. Nuns, Family, and Community

and the abbot who governed the men's community was the competent clergyman. Then only the task of administering the nuns' secular affairs (*cura temporalium*) fell to the provost, who was assisted by cantors, deacons and scholars. As a rule, a whole group of clergymen thus lived at or near a convent; apart from the provost, the confessor was the most important point of reference amongst them. In addition, representatives of the church hierarchy preached at services; led the nuns through the liturgy of masses and high feast days; heard confession; led processions such as the exodus from the Heilig Kreuz Kloster; administered extreme unction; performed the last rites before death and the funeral rites.

Men were also needed for the concrete administration of goods and produce on the farms, as experts for the brewery, mills and agriculture. Some of them were *lay brothers who, like the lay sisters, became part of the clerical estate; others were laymen such as stewards or farmhands, who did the heavy physical work. For example, on illustrations of feast days in the convent the nuns playing the organ are assisted by boys who tread the bellows and also ring the bells (see Figure 30 in Chapter VI.3), an activity which can also be seen when welcoming the nuns in their new home in Medingen. The old nuns and novices leave the old site (*Oldemeding*), weeping, following Provost Ludolf; the younger nuns greet them in a welcome procession with banners, a cross and the statues of the patron saints Mary and St Maurice.

Fig. 16 Procession to the new convent in Medingen. Lyßmann (1772) after Medingen 1499. Repro: Christine Greif.

The extent of the male guardians' power to make decisions depended on many circumstances. The nuns could be very persistent when it came to their spiritual care, both for good and bad. In the mid-fifteenth century, for example, Kloster Lüne was drawn by Provost Dietrich Schaper into serious unrest in the town of Lüneburg during the so-called Prelates' War. Schaper vigorously defended the interests of the Lüneburg nuns against the financial claims of the town council, a stance which made him many enemies on said council. When, in 1451, this finally resulted in a trial at which the provost was accused of disloyalty, squandering convent property and leading a dissolute life, the convent appeared in court under the leadership of Prioress Susanne Munter and presented a witness testimony written in Low German defending the provost and declaring the charges levied against Schaper to be unfounded.

The fact that the close interaction of the sexes and these diverse social groups functioned for centuries in a relatively small space was due to their body of rules and the ingenious arrangement of this space. They spent most of their time in separate areas, but were nonetheless aware of one another and, as in the convent church, could still sing together, even though the nuns could not be seen by the other groups. This was due not least to their common goal, namely, to enable a spiritual life in enclosure dedicated to the praise of God.

3. Representation and Status

The Tristan Tapestry

What is a story of adultery doing in a convent? The nuns of Wienhausen embroidered no fewer than three large-format tapestries depicting the love story of Tristan and Isolde, complete with love potion and bed scenes. The largest of them (2.3 metres high and four metres wide) is particularly revealing for an understanding of the meaning of these tapestries.

III. Nuns, Family, and Community

Fig. 17 Wienhausen Tristan Tapestry. Photograph: Ulrich Loeper ©Kloster Wienhausen.

It depicts coats of arms and scenes from the story in alternating strips; a band of Low German inscriptions runs between them; and on the sides the pictorial narrative is surrounded by climbing roses and ivy. Just like the Ebstorf World Map, these coats of arms combine the local and the global: first comes the imperial eagle, then the Braunschweig lion – but in the top right-hand corner we also find the coat of arms of the legendary King Arthur, and the Kingdom of Jerusalem is prominently represented. In between these features, the nuns placed themselves: their family coats of arms, or at least elements which also appear in the symbolism of their families, such as the cross of St Andrew, the griffin or the lion. Whenever there were important visitors, for example from the House of Guelph, which, in the person of Duchess Agnes of Landsberg, had co-founded the convent, the tapestries with their courtly themes of hunting, battle, love and dragons could be brought out to decorate the rooms for festivities.

The nuns also memorialize themselves on the tapestries through their own interpretation of the Tristan story. At the centre of the Tristan Tapestry, both literally and figuratively, are the women and their astuteness. After Tristan sets off for Ireland to fight Morolt in the first strip and returns wounded (the direction of travel back and forth across the Irish Sea can be seen from the fact that the horse looks once to the left and then to the right as it watches Tristan row), the second strip has in the middle the two scenes with Queen Isolde and her daughter of the same name. They drag Tristan, who has disguised himself as a minstrel, into the fortress-like city of Dublin and heal him. While the two crowned women stand tall with their ointments, small, sick Tristan crouches between them. The bottom row of images repeats the depiction of the women's power to save from illness and threat. When Tristan faints from the poisonous fumes emitted by the dragon he has defeated, the three women find him (the servant Brangäne has joined them), literally pull him out of the swamp, bathe him and escort him to the royal court. In the bathtub he again sits small among the vigorous, active women; one of them, the young Isolde, has seized his sword. In the known versions of the Tristan story she raises her weapon in this scene to take revenge on Tristan for the death of her uncle Morolt, but the Low German inscription on the tapestry turns this around: 'There stood Lady Brangäne and healed him; Lady Isolde anointed him. Then she bathed him. Lady Isolde held the sword'.[12] Threat has turned into protection; and it is clear who holds the threads of the narrative as well as of the embroidery: the nuns, who turn forbidden love into a story about the fight against evil and salvation from sickness and death by women.

Fig. 18 Bathing scene from the Wienhausen Tristan Tapestry. Photograph: Ulrich Loeper ©Kloster Wienhausen.

The Black Knight Maurice Intervenes

A unique testimony has been preserved from Kloster Medingen which provides us with some insight into how the nuns themselves conceived of their history. There are fifteen pictorial panels from 1492 with detailed

---

12   *do stot vrv Braniele – vnde hel ene vrv Isalde salvede ene – do badde se ene vrv Isalde helt dat svert.* DI 76, No. 5, urn:nbn:de:0238-di076g013k0000500.

captions in Latin and German explaining how, since its foundation, the community had been divinely guided and how heaven had repeatedly intervened to further the convent's interests. The originals, which hung in the abbess's house, were destroyed by fire in the eighteenth century, but thanks to 18th century copperplate engraving where the Protestant chronicler of the convent history very accurately copied the preparatory drawings for the panels, even including the notes for the painter regarding the colour of the nuns' habit and cloaks, the iconographic programme can be reconstructed. Previous chapters already introduce depictions of nuns on the handcart (Figure 10) and of the feast marking the consecration of the new convent (Figure 16), but the nuns' view of their own history becomes even clearer in the pictures which show how they have repeatedly and energetically been helped by saints. On Panel 9, the Virgin Mary, patron saint of the Cistercians, orders the construction of a new convent; and on the next one, John the Baptist, one of the patron saints of the city of Lüneburg, personally clears the land for it.

Fig. 19 St Maurice threatens Provost Dietrich Brandt. Lyßmann (1772) after Medingen 1499. Repro: Christine Greif.

The saints' active solicitude for the nuns is particularly clear on Panel 13, which depicts a scene during a Christmas mass with Provost Dietrich

Brandt, who held office at the end of the fourteenth century (1380–96), as the inscription *Tidericus prepositus* reveals. He kneels with raised hands before the patron saint of the convent, St Maurice, depicted as an armed knight, who presents his sword and in a speech scroll exhorts the provost to provide the nuns with what is due to them: 'Give my daughters what you owe them'.[13] The nuns, dressed in their white festive robes, kneel in two groups in the background.

Accompanying texts explain in Latin and Low German what is meant by the scene. The Low German text reads: 'When the previous provost had died, they elected Master Dietrich Brandt, who once during Advent withheld the provisions due to the nuns and gave them nothing to eat. During Christmas mass, when the provost was sitting on his chair by the altar, it came to pass that he saw St Maurice in front of him with his sword unsheathed, and the saint said to him: "Give to my dear children what you owe them". Then the provost rose and fell to his knees and the whole convent joined him, though they did not see him, only the provost did'.[14]

Thus the patron saint intervenes in his own person and with some force. It is as if the figure visible in miniature on the altar suddenly springs into action larger than life. The scene allows us an insight into the way space is organized in Medingen. The rendering of the space is of necessity highly simplified, but it is obvious that the nuns are depicted as observers, albeit distant ones. From their seats they follow the events at the high altar. As the caption describes, the nuns have fallen to their knees on seeing their intimidated provost falling to his. In the centre of the image stands the high altar of the convent church with *paten, chalice, and book; across it at the back is an altar-like rectangular panel bearing the statues of Mary and Maurice to the right and left of a crucifix. The climax of the celebration of the mass, the transformation of bread and wine into

---

13 *Da filiabus meis ad quod teneris.*
14 *Alse de vorige Provest vorstorben was, koren se wedder hern Dyderick Brant dede tho ener tyd den junckvrouwen in den adventen ere provene vor enthelt un jum nen eten gaff. So is id geschen tho Wynachten under des hilgen Kerstes miße, alse de provest upp synen stole sath by dem altare. Sach he vor sick stande Sanctum Mauricium mit enen openbaren swerde, un sede tho em alsus. Giff mynen Kynderen wes du jum plichtig bist. Do stunt de provest upp un vell upp syne Knye und al de ghanße sammelinge mit em. men se seghen en nicht averst de provest allene.*

the body and blood of Christ, is imminent: the chalice is already on the *corporal, the rectangular base for the communion vessels; the paten, the plate for the bread, is half covered by it. To the right lies an open book, the missal, from which the priest was meant to read the words of consecration. If the depiction were liturgically correct, the volume would, seen from Christ's position, be on the right-hand side of the altar, where the Gospel was read out. The provost would be standing in front of it with another, assisting priest. Yet this is not a snapshot of a historical situation. The panel was only created one hundred years after this incident is said to have taken place. The event is concentrated symbolically, preserved for the memory of the community and recognizable to fifteenth-century viewers as history which is of ultimately timeless validity. This is why the figures on the altar – Maurice, the armoured knight with the fluttering standard, and the Madonna – correspond to the statues that could be seen on the main altar in the convent church.

The large altar statue is lost; the small statue of St Maurice that has been preserved in Kloster Medingen shows the same type of armoured knight with curly hair and fluttering standard. It was commissioned by Abbess Margaret Puffen in 1506 and made by the renowned sculptor Hermann Worm whose dragon stamp (as canting arms symbolising his name 'worm' = dragon) and hallmark to show the purity of the gilded silver is visible at the front. At the feet of the saint clad in duckbill-style sabatons (iron shoes as part of plate armour), above an intricately worked octagonal base, an engraved scroll has the statue speak to the viewer: 'In the year of our Lord 1506, the venerable Lady Margaret, the first abbess in Medingen, had me made in praise of the Lord and St Maurice'.[15] The statue completed the furnishings of the new abbess's office. While the portrayal of Maurice in the Medingen manuscripts follows the general template for saints, namely a youth with red cheeks and armour only sketched in schematically on the blank parchment, in the commissioned works which were executed in Lüneburg by professional craftsmen he is depicted as a black knight in fashionable ceremonial plate armour, with feathers and precious stones adorning the crown on his head.

---

15 *Anno domini m°dvi venerabilis domina margareta abbatissa, prima in meding, me fecit fieri ad laudem domini sanctus mauricij.* DI 76, No. 90, urn:nbn:de:0238-di076g013k0009002.

III. Nuns, Family, and Community

Fig. 20 St Maurice. Lüneburg: Hermann Worm 1506. Photograph: Ulrich Loeper ©Kloster Medingen.

For the nuns, the chivalric St Maurice was of considerable importance: he made the convent attractive to the surrounding nobility. Today, one might speak of a 'company logo' or 'mascot', even if this only partially reflects his significance for the identity of the nuns. His accompaniment of them runs like a golden thread through the history of the convent: a statue of Maurice travelled with the first nuns from Magdeburg, where he was the patron saint of the diocese, and was carried ahead of their procession from Old to New Medingen (Figure 16). The importance of the saint in the furnishings of the convent is also evident from the fact that the statue was one of the few items saved during the fire in the late eighteenth century, along with the abbess's ceremonial crosier, also displays Maurice as a black knight.

The community of saints surrounded, protected and adorned the nuns' devotions. In the inventory of the furnishings of Kloster Medingen compiled in the mid-eighteenth century, the following are listed for the nuns' choir alone: a triptych with apostles in two rows; another shrine to the apostles from the fourteenth century; a large wooden crucifix; a painting from 1504 with the head of Christ; a painting on which the scene on the Mount of Olives is expanded to include the figures of the Virgin Mary and St Bernard of Clairvaux; a life-size Man of Sorrows; and a wooden annunciation group in a niche. All this set the scene for and framed both the abbess's throne with its carved canopy and the space-filling choir stalls, which held almost one hundred seats (see Figure 5 for the comparable space in Kloster Wienhausen). The statues of saints were not simply room ornaments: the heavenly patrons were the nuns' networks for eternity. They were the promise that the women's prayers would be answered – right down to the very tangible form of the Christmas meal, which Maurice won for them as their very own knight.

IV. Love and Friendship

In the convent, love and friendship have a long tradition. Love linked the nuns with their bridegroom Christ. His love created a community in which the women not only felt connected to one another but were also able to include others, creating a fellowship which opened the door to a close relationship with God. Their function as mediators between God and mankind meant the nuns played an important part in this process. Thus bonds of love and friendship assumed a major role in the nuns' everyday lives both inside and outside the convent. For women who spent their lives in enclosure and hence could not personally make their concerns heard in a medieval society, one which relied heavily on actual physical presence, these relationship networks were of crucial importance: relationships to the bishop and the ducal family, to the urban patriciate, to theologians and abbesses and neighbouring convents, to the families and friends of individual nuns – to some extent, such communication defined their sphere of action. From the cloister they utilized every opportunity to maintain and cultivate these bonds: through letters, gifts, intercession, advice and mutual aid. All shades of love and friendship can be found in the lives of the nuns. In writing, this is reflected in the friendly correspondence with other nuns or the impressive intellectual exchange between siblings, as well as mystical texts containing declarations of love for their bridegroom Christ which were inspired by the passionate language of the Song of Songs.

1. Friendship Beyond Convent Walls

Friends in Need Are Friends Indeed

The diary of our nun from the Heilig Kreuz Kloster begins with the death of the abbess Gisela von Damme on 8 October 1484. In that year the plague raged in Braunschweig, the disease from which she may have died unexpectedly after only two years in office. The death of the head of the convent constitutes a crisis for any community, one in which the Heilig Kreuz Kloster received help from the neighbouring Cistercian monastery of Riddagshausen: 'Our close friend',[1] a monk from Riddagshausen, visited the nuns and comforted them with a sermon on the 'death of Deborah, Rebecca's nurse'. The diarist notes that comparison with the biblical loss of Rebecca's 'nurturer', the great-niece of Abraham, was a 'sweet consolation'.[2] 'Friends in need are friends indeed'[3]: the nuns in Lüne also knew this and emphasized the great importance of friendship in times of emotional distress. For example, 'good friends'[4] looked after the possessions of the nuns of Heilig Kreuz Kloster when they had to leave their convent in 1485. Good friends also helped when the convent wanted to set up its own dairy farm but was in danger of failing due to the resistance of its own provost. First they laboriously persuaded the provost, then they made it possible to establish a herd by means of donations: 'At this time (1486), a certain Heinrich Wilken fell ill in the head and offered up a cow in honour of Heilig Kreuz Kloster for his recovery; this cow was the first. Soon other good friends gave us other cows and then we began to have them on our farm'.[5] Friendship can thus be expressed in very concrete terms: in cows, in small gestures or even in the fact that nuns visiting Wienhausen were 'most honourably' sent home by the abbess in her own carriage 'for the sake of old friendship'.[6]

Love of God that inspired the ties of mutual friendship and connected the earthly to the heavenly realm, with religious women bearing particular responsibility for the latter: they were, so to speak, 'experts' in divine assistance. Friends pray for one another: during a riot in Braunschweig, on both sides also involving relatives of the nuns,

---

1 *intimus amicus noster*, fol. 1v.
2 *dulciter est nos consolatus*, fol. 1v.
3 Literally: 'Necessity proves who your friends are' (*in necessitatibus amici sunt probandi*, Letter 13).
4 *boni amici*, fol. 7r.
5 *Ipso tempore valebat male in capite quidam vir Hinricus Wilken, et offerebant I vaccam in honore sancte crucis pro sua sanitate, et illa erat prima; mox alii boni amici nostri dederunt nobis alias, et tunc incepimus eas habere in nostra curia*, fol. 10r.
6 *remisit nobis honorifice nostras sorores cum suo proprio curru et servo et aliqua dona misit nobis propter amiciciam*, fol. 22r.

'our *domina* secretly asked some sisters to pray for the liberation of their friends'.⁷ In this case, it took longer than desired for the turmoil to pass but the nuns were practised intercessors. A large number of the surviving letters invoke a specific act of friendship: mutual intercession for the living as well as the dead. The fact that these relationships defined the nuns' sphere of action is shown by the following story: a friend of the convent, probably a canon of the collegiate church of St Blasius in Braunschweig, had demonstrated his affection by showing the nuns – who were, of course, not permitted to leave the cloister – the tunic of St Anne from the treasury of relics in Braunschweig. The women won him for an important diplomatic mission, namely the wooing of a possible candidate for the all-important office of provost in Heilig Kreuz Kloster.⁸

Sibling Love in the Klara Kloster

Friendship networks that did not stop at the convent walls also connected the Nuremberg humanist Willibald Pirckheimer (1470–1530) with sisters and daughters who lived as nuns in the neighbouring convents. One thing immediately becomes clear when reading the countless letters exchanged between them – the ladies possessed wit and humour. These letters provide us with special testimony to the role played by friendship in correspondence across convent walls. The humanist Erasmus of Rotterdam (1466–1536), who enjoyed widespread fame, wrote admiringly that if England had its Mores – the learned family of Sir Thomas More – then Germany had its Pirckheimers. In January 1520, Willibald's sisters Sabina and Eufemia thanked their brother, a weighty man in any sense, for a lavish new chasuble, the measurements for which had obviously been based on his own physique: 'When we looked at the chasuble, we realized that you had had it made according to your own stately figure. It is handsome and large. When you become a priest and our confessor, it will be just right for you'.⁹ Letters and gifts played an important role in friendly

---

7   *rogavit domina nostra aliquas sorores secrete, ut facerent aliquam oracionem pro liberacione suorum amicorum*, fol. 27r
8   *peciit, quod nostrum optimum vellet facere contra ipsum sacerdotem*, fol. 32r.
9   *Wir sehen das meßgewant dafür an, du habst es nach dir lassen machen. Ist ye ratlich und*

relations between the siblings. On 7 July 1524, St Willibald's Day, his daughter Katharina and his sisters Klara and Caritas (1467–1532), the latter the abbess of the Nuremberg convent of the Poor Clares, sent him homemade confectionery made with rose oil; and in turn Willibald sent them glasses and mead for St John's Day.[10] To a certain extent, gifts could replace personal presence and could, therefore, also be carriers of meaning as part of symbolic communication. In June 1520, Willibald offered to send Eufemia and Sabina chain mail for their practice of asceticism. The sisters gratefully declined: 'You wrote to us in your previous letter with regard to one or two rusty old coats of mail. We thank you for being so well-meaning. However, because we are not used to riding, we would know of no other use for them than the scouring of pans'.[11] Then, with a twinkle in their eye, they remark that even their dressing gowns are often too coarse for them, such tender martyrs are they. Further, because Caritas had already sent them hair shirts from Nuremberg, they write: 'So keep your chain-mail shirts yourself'.[12]

Willibald who agreed with Erasmus of Rotterdam in his criticism of Catholic monastic life and his scepticism of Protestants and most particular his dislike of 'runaway' monks who had fled the monasteries, had obviously poked fun at the nuns for what he saw as their pointless ascetic practices. In summer 1520, all three were still able to take this ironic use of iron with humour. Yet Willibald does not conceal his ambivalence towards convent life from the Protestant reformer Philip Melanchthon and adds that – like everyone else – he previously had been under the wrong impression that he was well advised in allowing his daughters to lead a religious life: 'For, to confess it openly, like others I was mistaken at the time and thought it best if they "became religious", as they call it'.[13]

Before the Reformation, religious life as an alternative to marriage

---

groß. Wenn du ein pfaff wirst und unser peichtvater, wird es dir gerecht sein, Letter 665.
10 Letter 885.
11 *Du hast unß verganger zeit geschriben eines oder zweyer rostiger panczer halb. Dancken wir dir dennoch, das du so gutwillig pist [...]. Dieweil wir aber der reyterey gancz ungewont sein, westen wir sy nit anderst, denn die pfannen zu fegen, ze nuczen.*
12 *Darumb so behalt deine panczer selber*, Letter 696.
13 *Nam, ut ingenue fatear, errabam tum cum caeteris putabamque natis optime consultum, si religionem, ut vocant, ingrederentur*, p. 388.

had been an established choice for the female members of the respected Pirckheimer family and also attractive for Willibald's own family, since six sisters and three daughters had entered convents. His sisters Sabina and Eufemia lived in the Benedictine convent of Bergen near Neuburg (Bavaria). From 1521 onwards Sabina was abbess of the Bergen community, followed after her death by her sister Eufemia. Willibald's youngest daughter Caritas also entered Kloster Bergen in 1517. His sister Katharina lived with the Benedictine nuns in Geisenfeld, while Walburg lived in the convent of the Poor Clares St. Jakobus am Anger in Munich. Willibald's sisters Caritas and Clara lived in the community of the Poor Clares in Nuremberg, which his daughters Katharina and thirteen-year-old Crescentia also entered in 1513. Admittedly, Crescentia remained 'a child' all her life and was dependent on care. When she died in 1529, Willibald expressed criticism to his elder daughter Katharina regarding the role of convents in the provision of care and repeated the apparently widespread view that monastic life made people peculiar. Katharina attributed this criticism to the 'enemies of convents' and replied to her father: 'But, dearest father, do not let your heart be weighed down and do not let the enemies of convents persuade you that we create so many fools. I hope we have fewer of them in our convent than in the city itself'. According to Katharina, only one nun was really mad; two others were a little strange, but perfectly useful. She continues, 'We have no more such people', and asserts that this particular cap did not fit: 'We would not like, even unwittingly, to be the cause of this'.[14]

As with all deeper relationships, the bond between the siblings was also subject to stresses and strain over the years. Willibald Pirckheimer could react quite touchily at times. When his daughter Barbara married in February 1518, he told Caritas that, incidentally, he preferred to deal with ordinary people rather than the highly regarded. His comment presumably referred to his lifelong friendship with Albrecht Dürer, who was not a member of the Nuremberg patriciate. When, therefore, Caritas advised him to be more careful about making such remarks in

---

14 *Aber, hercz lieber vater, [...] wolst dir dein hercz nit beschwern laßen und dir die closter feynt nit eintragen laßen, das wir so vil narren machen. Ich hoff, wir haben ir in unßerm closter nit als vil, als in der stat sein. [...] Nit mer hab wir solcher leut. [...] Wollten auch mit unbescheydenheyt nit gern ursach sein*, Letter 1253.

public, he became furious and refused to speak to or visit his sisters for over a year. He did not come at Easter either, with the result that the whole city took notice of their dispute. This put the Poor Clares in a difficult situation because they urgently needed their influential brother to mediate their concerns in the city. Since Willibald refused to accept an apology from Caritas, Klara now took the initiative – and Klara knew how to handle her brother. She wrote to him at the end of July 1519, saying bluntly that anyone who liked to dish out criticism must also be able to take it: 'I have often been present when you have startled and reviled the worthy Mother, in private as well as in front of other people, and certainly often slung numerous nasty words at her. Balance, then, one thing against the other. We are all human'. She blames her own directness on the heat of the summer and the fireflies which appear around St Margaret's Day (20 July), concluding her long letter with the words that this is 'because I have written it just as it came into my head. And forgive me if I have been too harsh. We are now in the dog days, when St Margaret's little worms have perhaps been going round in my head'.[15] In a second letter, from September the same year, Klara invokes – even more clearly and obviously with humour – the image of nuns as simple-minded and fearful as shared by the nuns themselves and by many others: it was no wonder that they, such 'poor little nuns', feared the great man Willibald, 'since we are often frightened even by a mouse so that we do not know where to put ourselves'.[16] Klara possessed good powers of observation and her brother was aware of her frank, straightforward manner: 'But, sweetest brother, I want to write to you straightaway about how my heart feels. You know full well that I don't go in for fuss or flattery'.[17] This combination of candour and a need for protection proved successful, and at Christmas 1519 Willibald showed he had come round and dedicated his edition of Fulgentius to Caritas.

---

15 *Ich pin oft mit und pey gewest, daz du dy wirdig muter allein und auch vor den leuten also entseczt host und also geschmecht und sicher oft vil poßer wort poten [...] Darumb rechen ains gegen dem andern ab. Wir sind alle menschen. [...], denn ich in allein auß meinem kopf hab geschriben. Und verzeich mir, wo ich zu grob pin geweßen. Es sind yzunt die hunczlag geweßen, mochten mir vileicht sant Margen wurmlein im kopf umb sein gangen*, Letter 613.
16 *Es ist kain wunder, dass wir armen nundlein einen solchen großen man furchten, so wir doch oft vor einer meuß erschrecken, das wir nit wißen, wo wir beleiben sollen*, Letter 617.
17 *Aber hercz lieber pruder, ich will dir geleich schreiben, wie es mir umb das hercz ist. Du waist wol, ich kann nit vil verworens noch federklaubens*, Letter 613.

Just how cleverly the women were able to play on the image of simple-minded nuns can be seen even more clearly when, in April 1525, Willibald composed a letter of petition on behalf of the Poor Clares to Christoph Scheurl (1481–1542), advisor to the council and mediator in the dispute over demands by Nuremberg council, which had adopted the Reformation. Klara thanks her brother for all the effort he has put into writing to 'Doctor Troll', using the nickname for Christoph Scheurl which the nuns had bestowed on the friend who had previously admired them so much but who, since becoming one of the Protestant reformers, had been so critical of them. She claims that Willibald had chased away Caritas's tears with the letter, that she had laughed even though she was so sad. She goes on to report that Caritas had been very pleased with the petition and had immediately passed his text on to Scheurl's aunt Apollonia Tucher so that she could write the letter in her name to her nephew. According to Klara, Caritas had not revealed to Apollonia that he, Willibald, was the author so that she would not let it slip to her nephew in a moment of weakness. Instead, Klara wrote that Caritas had added a bit of nuns' gossip to the letter so that no suspicion would arise as to its authorship: 'The Reverend Mother has included some silly nuns' gossip because your letter is so well and sensibly written that suspicion might arise it had not sprung from her own head'.[18] These remarks advise us to be cautious with regard to the attribution of authorship in convents; collective authorship must always be considered a possibility for letters and other monastic writings. Pirckheimer's letters were read out in front of the entire convent and the replies, even if written in the name of individuals to specific addressees, were presumably agreed with the community in the same way.

Klara's entertaining letters to her brother are written in German. The literary relationship between Willibald and his sister Caritas took place on a different plane. It could be said that the latter's letters are characterized by a difference in tone; not only because the siblings communicated with each other in Latin but also because Caritas occupied a firm place in humanist circles, primarily through Willibald's mediation. Willibald and the German 'arch-humanist' and

---

18 *Dy wirdig muter hat etlich ainfeltig nunnen teding dar ein geseczt, wann dein prief so wol und vernunftiglich geseczt ist, das man einen arckwon mocht gewynen, er gieng nit auß irem kopf*, Letter 917.

poeta coronatus Konrad Celtis (1459–1508), had bestowed on the gifted sister the honorary title of *virgo docta Germana* and placed her in the tradition of learned women, influenced not least by Celtis's recent discovery of the works of the canoness Roswitha von Gandersheim (c. 935–973). Moreover, the correspondence between Willibald and Caritas is characterized above all by notable affinity and profound intellectual debate. This intellectual plane later enabled them to come to terms with the literary expression of Lutheran criticism, a process that obviously also clarified their own positions.

In his early letters Willibald refers to Caritas as his 'most beloved sister' and, citing Horace to describe their spiritual kinship, as the 'second half of my soul'.[19] Like the Nuremberg patrician and humanist Sixtus Tucher, whose correspondence with Caritas probably contributed to the raising of her spiritual and intellectual profile, Willibald also took a serious interest in religious matters. For him the Poor Clare obviously stood for the spiritual side of Humanism, for a high esteem for the transcendent as opposed to the earthly, for truths of timeless validity. As late as 1529, Willibald wrote: 'Human affairs should never be given preference over divine matters'.[20] For her part, Caritas chose the image of the 'hidden pearl',[21] to describe Willibald's astuteness and wisdom, revealed in his understanding and interpretation of the Greek and Latin texts. Emphasizing her words with a quotation from Psalm 33:9, in 1502 she wrote to him about how beneficial and important it was for the virgins, busy with divine worship both day and night, to have a teacher such as him, one who taught them a deeper understanding of the sacred scripture enabling them to 'suck honey from the rock and oil from the hardest stone. For you can imagine for yourself how tiring it otherwise is constantly to sing psalms, yet be unable to pluck the fruit of liturgical chant'.[22]

According to Caritas, the ability to interpret the liturgy in a

---

19 *soror charissima ac meae dimidium dimimae*, 20 December 1503; referencing Horace's Carmen 1.3, where he says this about Virgil.
20 *divinis nequaquam humana praeferenda censeam*, Letter 44.
21 *margarita abscondita*, quoting Matthew 13:46.
22 *Revera res esset magnae utilitatis, si ingeniosae virgines, divino cultu die noctuque mancipatae, talem haberent praeceptorem, qui doceret eas, mel sugere de petra oleumque de saxo durissimo; alioquin frequenter psallare et fructum psalmodiae non posse carpere, quam taediosum sit, ipse cogitare poteris*, Letter 33.

meaningful way – ultimately the ability to transcend everyday life – was crucial for cloistered nuns. Caritas herself enjoyed a particular mastery of this. In the letters addressed to her by Willibald, Christoph Scheurl and Konrad Celtis, the quality of her words is a recurring theme. In 1514, her brother wrote to Caritas about how much her letter had comforted him after his rescue from considerable danger: 'For apart from the fact that I love you in a singular way, I do not know why all your letters do me so much good and have impressed themselves so devoutly into my deepest soul'.[23] The young Christoph Scheurl informs her that he carefully preserves her letters so that he has them on hand to refresh his exhausted spirit;[24] and that he reads them time and again in order to enjoy them. The tributes paid in these letters were certainly part of epistolary rhetoric, the *captatio benevolentiae*, but they were only effective if they captured the true essence of the matter.

An impressive example of Caritas's ability to use words to be a friend to friends in need and her gift of – also humorously – deriving meaning from everyday situations can be found in the letter she wrote in 1502 to the unfortunate Konrad Celtis, who had recently been assaulted. She assures Celtis that he had all her sympathy because he had recently fallen among bloodthirsty robbers, been savagely beaten and robbed of all his possessions. She had no doubt, she continues, that he belonged to that select band of true philosophers who have the capacity for enduring all adversity with equanimity, even when every earthly thing had been taken from them – indeed, to those very philosophers who preferred the treasure of true knowledge and wisdom over all earthly goods. Such men would, therefore, be comforted by adversity rather than oppressed by the injustice they had suffered, which is why it was more beneficial than harmful for the wise to suffer such blows.[25]

Friendship entails, then, not only an obligation to support, but also to speak out. Hence Caritas does not stop at this general reinterpretation

---

23 *Nam praeterquam quod te unice diligam, nescio quemadmodum tua me cuncta delectant scripta penitusque sancte animae meae inhaerent*, Letter 37.
24 *quocum animum defatigatum recreare queam*, Letter 68.
25 *et si non diffidam excellentiam vestram esse de numero perfectorum philosophorum, qui cuncta adversa aequanimiter norunt tollerare, etiam si omnia caduca et transeuntia eis auferantur, modo carum thesaurum verae scientiae et sapientiae, cunctis opibus preciosiorem reservent, quapropter in adversis magis consolantur quam de illatis iniuriis contristentur, profecto non ignari talia pati sapientibus magis prodesse quam obesse*, Letter 45.

of painful events as an experience vital to the formation of genuine philosophical equanimity: 'What did the robbers do other than free you from the worry of worldly goods? What did they do when they beat you other than give you an opportunity to school yourself in practical virtue?' According to Caritas, Celtis actually had cause to be grateful to the robbers because the incident had, above all, allowed him salutary exercise in the highest virtue, namely holy suffering (*sancta patientia*), because according to the Apostle James he who suffers temptation possesses the perfect work (*opus perfectum*). Thus the outstanding philosopher Celtis (*eximius philosophus*) unexpectedly becomes a great theologian (*optimus theologus*) who accepts adversity (*adversa*) not only with equanimity but rather with joy – and does so all the more in view of the sufferings of Christ, which the Son of God had taken upon himself not involuntarily but of his own free will, in the form of vilification, beatings, robbery and the harshest death. Celtis could, therefore, regard himself as an honourable emulator of Christ. Reflection on this, writes Caritas – quoting Bernard of Clairvaux – is 'the highest philosophy'. In addition, she goes on to say she does not believe the attack was a coincidence. Rather, it was due to divine providence that this affliction had befallen him, Celtis, precisely at a time when the Passion of Christ was being celebrated, namely during the holy season of Easter: Christ had wished to offer him the opportunity, as it were, not simply to comprehend his holy Passion in his, Celtis's, mind, but actually to experience it on his whole body.

Caritas succeeds in providing Celtis with a new perspective on the experience which had so oppressed him. The abbess interprets the threatening situation in which Celtis had found himself in religious terms and elevates it in a way which the humanist would have considered appropriate for a religious woman (*religiosa*). Indeed, Celtis then thanks her warmly for her sympathetic letter on the occasion of his attack by robbers. He sends Caritas a copy of *Norimberga*, his learned description of Nuremberg, enclosing with it a verse dedication to her, which reads: 'Full of consolation, bringing means of healing, which quickly erased from me the intense pain and grief of my soul'.[26] Her words to him

---

26 'Ad Charitatem [...] carmen': *Dulce solamen mihi epistola mox / virgo reddebas variis medelis / quae mihi tristes pepulere et acres / mente dolores*, April 1502.

quickly made him forget the pain of his body and the distress over the loss of his possessions.

Friendship and love were of great importance in the conditions enforced by enclosure. They represented the 'cement' or 'glue' which bound together the members of the convent, the lay sisters and the clergy, the different communities and all the participants in their internal and external networks. The nuns reflected on the various forms of friendship and love which these respective relationships brought to the fore and employed them pragmatically in their communications. The foundation on which the community was built was their relationship to one another as 'brides of Christ', which, as a 'bond of love', predetermined their interaction. In 1484, a nun from Lüne gave articulate expression to this idea in a letter to a friend in another convent: 'For we have all been chosen by Christ and been gathered together to honour his name. Although admittedly unworthy, we are all glued together by the bond of love for Christ'.[27]

Fig. 21 Two nuns wearing crowns, the initials GLM und GF on a capital in the cloisters of Kloster Ebstorf. Photograph: Wolfgang Brandis ©Kloster Ebstorf.

---

27   *Nam a Christo omnes electe ac in unum congregate ad glorificandum nomen ipsius et, licet indigne, tamen conglutinate in vinculo amoris Jesu Christi*, Letter 235.

Above all, in creating a sense of community this bond of love created the potential for the women to develop and grow in their shared striving towards God. At the end of the fifteenth century, the dean of St Jakobi in Rostock wrote to the provost of the nuns in Lüne, Nikolaus Schomaker, that 'it is not knowledge of God but love for God that makes us blessed'.[28] The nuns, in turn, emphasize to their provost their own knowledge that he cherishes them as his dearest friends above all others, locating their close relationship in body and spirit within a finely differentiated framework: as a convent, they, the nuns, are, as it were, the limbs of his body and their spirit is 'glued together' with his spirit.[29] This elevated tone of friendship is not entirely disinterested: faced with Nikolaus Schomaker's imminent death, the women wanted to ensure the provost did not favour others over them in his will – a concern that was by no means unfounded.

It is striking that the image of being inseparably 'glued together' is one repeatedly used for spiritual friendship. For example, at the end of the fifteenth century, a nun from Kloster Lüne writes how delighted she had been to receive a letter of consolation and gifts from a friend in another convent as a 'sign of love'. For, she continues, my soul is 'glued to yours as Jonathan's soul was to David's and, if I could, I would strip myself of my robe for you as Jonathan did for David'.[30] Unfortunately that is not possible, she continues, so instead she sends a veil and sweet, spiced fish and a little basket of sweets and titbits. What, then, is the meaning of the 'glued-together' souls and David's friendship with Jonathan? Why is this image not only invoked as a role model by this nun, but frequently echoed in other convent letters, too?

---

28 *quare non cognitio Dei, sed amor in Deum nos beatos efficient*, Letter 18.
29 *conglutinatus*, Letter 24.
30 *Attamen pro inditio caritatis immense, qua anima mea conglutinata est anime vestre, veluti anima Jonathe conglutinata est anime Davidis et dilexit eum Jonathas quam animam suam* (1 Samuel 18:4), *ita ego diligo vestram reverentiam in visceribus Jesu Christi* [...]. *Et si foret michi possibile, quod ego tantilla possem me expoliare tunica nostra et reverentie vestre eam prestare, quemadmodum Jonathas fecit Davidis, hoc ex fundo cordis libenter facerem*, Letter 189.

2. The Idea of Friendship

In the Old Testament the 'classic' pair of friends were Jonathan, the son of King Saul, and David, the youngest son of Jesse, whom Yahweh summoned from the flocks and elected to be king. As the son of the ruler, it was actually Jonathan who ought to have assumed the kingship, but he remained steadfastly loyal to his friend David, in opposition to his own father. When Saul persecuted his friend, Jonathan saved David's life because he recognized that God had called David and considered God's authority higher than that of his father. Jonathan renounced his own right to kingship in favour of his friend. The power of his renunciation brings about a deepening of his friendship with David which is constantly aligned to the will of Yahweh; in turn, their friendship achieves a hitherto-unknown intimacy in the passage quoted by the Lüne nun: 'And it came to pass, when he had finished his conversation with Saul, that the soul of Jonathan was joined to the soul of David, and Jonathan loved him as he loved his own soul'. Jonathan and David entered into a covenant of friendship (*foedus*); and Jonathan removed the outer garment (*tunica*) that he wore and gave it to David, as well as the rest of his clothes, even his sword, his bow and his belt: 'Then Jonathan, the son of Saul, arose and went to David in the forest, and strengthened his hand through God, and said to him, "Fear not, for the hand of my father Saul will not find you, and you will be king over Israel, and I will be second to you; but my father Saul also knows this". So they both made a covenant before the Lord'[31]. David's later lamentation for his slain friend and the latter's royal father was adopted as an Old Testament reading in the church's Liturgy of the Hours.[32] In the Old Testament friendship is a gift from God, a 'holy consolation'[33], a treasure and means of healing in life that offers protection against all kinds of adversity. Friendship is the higher quality of life, rooted in faith in God and opening new horizons for friends. God is always the third party in this relationship.

The lofty ideal of unbreakable friendship and love which was strong enough to overcome even death was already known in Antiquity.

---

31 *Percussit ergo uterque foedus coram Domino*, I Samuel 23:15–18.
32 2 Samuel 1:17–27.
33 Jesus Sirach 6:14.

Horace's line about Virgil as 'other half of his soul' became proverbial, as the letter by Willibald referenced above shows; while Virgil, for his part, coined the unforgettable phrase 'Love conquers all'[34] and described friendship as a force of perpetual growth. Cicero's definition of friendship in his *Laelius de Amicitia* (44 BC) became particularly influential: for him, friendship is nothing other than an 'agreement in all matters divine and human infused by benevolence and love'.[35] Cicero believes that, apart from wisdom, no better gift than friendship was given to mankind by the immortal gods, but that all the characteristics of this friendship exist in the many possible forms of mutual accord.

Based on Cicero and inspired by the Christian transformation of the concept of friendship, which is witnessed before God, the twelfth century English Cistercian abbot Aelred of Rievaulx (1110–1167) developed a powerful idea of spiritual friendship in *De amicitia spirituali*. In the prologue, Aelred, elected abbot by the monks in 1147, recounts how Cicero's book on friendship had fallen into his hands, a work he had considered unsurpassable until, after entering the monastery, he had discovered something incomparably more sublime, namely the essence of spiritual friendship. His book *On Spiritual Friendship* is conceived as a dialogue. He begins the first book by welcoming the friend entering the room with the words: 'Behold I and you, and I hope the third among us is Christ'.[36] The presence of Christ turns their friendship into a 'holy covenant'. In lucid language Aelred explains to his readers precisely what he feels Cicero lacks: namely, the shared, connective love for Christ, which elevates and enriches every bond of friendship. In a striking scene, he also describes the relationship between love and friendship. When he looks around the monastery, so the abbot writes, he loves all his brothers, the perfect and the less perfect, dearly and deeply – but only a select few are suited to a genuine, lifelong bond of friendship which creates the potential for spiritual development by opening a way to share worlds of inner experience and spiritual ascent. Aelred develops a powerful ideal of spiritual friendship which, in harmony with a person's love for God, opens new horizons of knowledge for friends through their joint ascent

---

34 *omnia vincit amor*, 10th Eclogue, 69.
35 *omnium divinarum humanarumque rerum cum benevolentia et caritate consensio*, Lael. IV.
36 *Ecce ego et tu, et spero, quod tertius inter nos Christus sit*, II,1.

of the path to the inner soul. According to Aelred, 'holy love' which embraces a friend leads upwards to that blessed love which allows us to embrace Christ. In the end, we savour to the full this most spiritual of all the fruits of holy friendship, awaiting perfect bliss. Then all the fear which now fills us is banished; all the suffering we must now bear for one another is overcome.[37] The formative aspects of the consolation and help gained from friendship, benefits invoked by so many letters written in monasteries in the late Middle Ages, are also laid out here, as are the sharing of joy and sorrow. What also becomes apparent is the importance of a frank word like that of Klara Pirckheimer at the right time and the commitment to sometimes difficult truth among friends and the part played by friendship in forging a community. Aelred also provides a biblical model for the various roles and different forms of friendship within the spiritual community: Jesus entrusted Peter with the keys to the kingdom of heaven and therewith his church; while he revealed the secrets of his heart to John. Peter is destined for action; John is reserved for love: 'I wish him to remain so until I come, says the Lord'.[38] This special bond is strikingly expressed in the devotional image of Christ embracing John (see Figure 22). Aelred's ideal of friendship bears fruit, and allows his monastery of Rievaux to blossom. Upon Aelred's death in 1167, the chronicle reports that he had doubled everything there: monks and brothers, land and goods and all the equipment, but that he had tripled discipline and love within the order.

The bonds of friendship between the nuns, which they invoked in their letters and demonstrated in their gifts, recall all the aspects and levels of meaning which had been known, and repeatedly re-interpreted, from Antiquity onwards. Indeed, as was already understood in classical antiquity, ideal and reality could be poles apart, especially when it came to friendship. Often the practical nature of friendship appears to dominate in everyday monastic life, but the formative, connective Christian ideal of friendship always resonates. The women were skilled in deploying, for their own purposes, the immense potential inherent in establishing relationships and spiritual closeness; they were also versed in cultivating and preserving it as a

---

37 *De amicitia spirituali*, III, 132.
38 Book III, 117; referencing John 21:22.

crucial network of friendships. In the process, personal and collective friendship, intimacy and polite distance merge seamlessly. For example, in one letter, a nun from Neukloster Buxtehude addresses the prioress in Lüne as 'my special and dearest friend', whom she then informs, now using the polite plural form of address, 'that we' – namely the entire convent – 'have put a new roof on the church and the nuns' choir'.[39] The singular voice of the writer is interwoven with the plural voices of the collective.

The conditions which prevailed in enclosure shaped the specific ways in which the nuns cultivated and expanded their many and varied friendship networks, which were crucial to the functioning of their institution within society. They cultivated old and traditional relationships and created new ones through formal requests for friendship with nuns in other convents – as 'pen friends'. What others cultivated as relationship networks in a society dependent on personal presence, the nuns knew how to achieve from enclosure using words and gifts. Friendship is based on a shared love for Christ; it offers comfort and support in times of need; it sometimes requires frank words; opens new spiritual horizons; enables collective growth; and delights through small gifts and small tokens of affection. The words chosen by the nuns in their letters and the references they summoned up were shaped by the high ideal of spiritual friendship. Love for Christ – in which they were experts – was the common bond which permeated and glued their networks together.

3. Christ Embracing John the Evangelist as Spiritual Bridehood

Particularly impressive in its representation of an intimate relationship is the sculpture of Christ embracing John the Evangelist, a type found mainly in southern German convents in the upper Rhineland and across the German south-west. It illustrated for the nuns the special relationship of love, trust and friendship between St John and Christ, offering them a figure with whom to identify in the form of

---

39 *mea specialis ac precordialissima amica, [...] dat wy, Dei cooperante gratia, unse karken et chorum wedder under dack ghekreghen hebben*, Letter 289.

the youthful, virginal Evangelist. On the cross, Christ had entrusted his mother Mary to John and thus – as successors to Mary – also the nuns. Due to his virginity, John was as physically close to Christ as the nuns; they were also united by their imitation of Christ, the *imitatio Christi*. This representation developed out of the account of the Last Supper, at which John, 'the disciple whom Jesus loved', rested his head against Christ's chest in anguish at the announcement of the latter's suffering. This gesture took on a life of its own as the embodiment of the close bond between the faithful soul and Christ, also known as 'St John's Love' (*Johannesminne*). The earliest examples derive from the twelfth century and are found in manuscript illuminations for the feasts of St John, as in the *gradual from the Swiss Dominican convent of St Katharinental (1312). This convent also possessed a similar sculpture since their chronicle reports that 'Master Henry from Constance made a sculpture of St John from walnut wood, one so beautiful that everybody was amazed, even the master himself'. This points to one or more workshops in the region of Lake Constance and the upper Rhineland which produced these and other high-quality figural groups, such as scenes of the Visitation. They were carved mainly for convents: the Augustinian canonesses in Inzigkofen (near Sigmaringen); the Dominican convent of Mariaberg (between Reutlingen and Sigmaringen); the Cistercian convent of Wald (near Meßkirch); and, around 1320, the Benedictine convent of St Martin in Hermetschwil (Switzerland).

Only a few of these groups have remained *in situ*. One such is the group from the Cistercian convent of Heiligkreuztal which represents the seated figures of Christ and John and at 101 centimetres high is almost two-thirds life size.

Fig. 22 Heiligkreuztal: Christ embracing John. Photograph: Markus Schwerer ©Staatliche Schlösser und Gärten Baden-Württemberg.

The back is hollowed out, since the group was not free-standing but originally kept in an altar shrine which was opened on special occasions. The medieval colour scheme was certainly more restrained – the remains of colour on other groups, such as that from Inzigkofen (now in the Bode Museum, Berlin), display similar decoration of the face with slightly reddened cheeks and mouths, but much less brightly coloured robes. The painting on the group from Heiligkreuztal was refreshed in the Baroque and, in keeping with period taste, given a lustre finish with a metallic sheen intended to imitate precious materials – a sign of the esteem in which the medieval devotional image was held by the community right up until the modern era. It is now housed in a niche where it can be seen at eye level, as was probably the case for the nuns. There Christ, bearded and with long, dark hair, sits on a bench with the beardless youth St John, whose hair is blond and curly. John's head has sunk onto Christ's breast and he rests with his eyes closed, while Christ, whose head and body lean towards him, rests his left hand on John's shoulder; their right hands interlock. It is the gesture of betrothal, established in Antiquity as the *dextrarum iunctio* and resembling the 'hand-fasting' (*hand-truwen*) mentioned in poems about Christ as bridegroom from the Lüneburg convents. The intimate gesture of the hands simultaneously evokes the Song of Songs, in which the lovesick bride says: 'His left hand under my head, and his right hand shall embrace me'.[40] The two figures, who both wear a long-sleeved undergarment with a gold hem and whose voluminous cloaks, draped over their knees, swing down in parallel folds to their bare feet, demonstrate perfect unity, literally hewn from a single block and inseparable. Christ's gaze is directed not at St John but straight at the viewer. Medieval literature attributes to the gaze an almost physical ability to emit rays; the eyes were regarded as the 'gateway for love'. The gaze thus constitutes the starting point for the growth of love, all the way through to physical union. A hexameter on the *gradus amoris*, the stages of love, puts this in a nutshell: the gaze leads to confiding conversation, which leads to touch and from there to a kiss – and finally to the act of union (*visio, colloquium, tactus, osculum, actus*). The exchange of gazes between Christ and the observing nun includes her in the bond of love between John and Christ; conversely, it also means that the virginal youth, John, assumes the place of the nun as the bride of Christ.

Physical closeness to Christ was a given for the nuns on several levels. In the Eucharist they received in the one form of bread both the body and blood of Christ, whereby he was meant to be present before their spiritual eyes in all his corporality. This is particularly vividly illustrated by the numerous sculptures of Christ in Wienhausen Kloster. The wound in the side of their statue of Christ as he is rising from the tomb has a hole behind which the relic of the holy blood owned by the convent may have been kept, so that the blood from Christ's actual body turned the wooden image into the real presence.

---

40 *Læva ejus sub capite meo, et dextera illius amplexabitur me*, Song of Songs 2:6.

Fig. 23 The Resurrected Christ. Photograph: Wolfgang Brandis ©Kloster Wienhausen.

The figure changed with the various church festivals. At Easter, two angels could be placed next to the central figure as a proclamation of the Resurrection, and a victory flag was placed in Christ's hand. Just as the priests had different vestments in the different colours of the church year, Christ and the angels also had 'holy robes', the colours of which signalled the times of fasting or joy for the nuns. The nuns had made these garments in their parament workshops out of the same sort of precious fabrics as the clerics' robes; some of the fabric used for the statues had come into the convent as their own trousseaux, so their own festive garments were tailored to fit Christ. Robes were also made for the figures of the Christ child, for whom not only clothes but also cradles have been preserved. Wienhausen's larger-than-life figure of Christ in the Holy Sepulchre could be dramatically revealed by the lowering of the lid – or the empty tomb demonstrated by opening the doors below.

Fig. 24 Holy Sepulchre. Photograph: Wolfgang Brandis ©Kloster Wienhausen.

The relics in the head of Christ transformed the sculpture into far more than a wooden figure: it was the Real Presence at the heart of the convent. Some representations of Christ also double as tabernacles and had inbuilt repositories for the bread which was transformed into the body of Christ.

Many texts from the mystical tradition in the convents unfurl dialogues with Christ which take up and continue the passionate language of love found in the Song of Songs. In the thirteenth century, three women associated with Kloster Helfta stand out. Their texts not only filled convent libraries but equally shaped lay devotion. They were Mechthild of Magdeburg (*c.* 1207–*c.* 1282), Mechthild of Hackeborn (*c.* 1240–1298) and Gertrude the Great (1256–1302). In her 'Herald of Divine Love' (*Legatus Divinae Pietatis*), the latter created a comprehensive liturgical exegesis. One of the visions recorded in the text for the benefit of her fellow nuns reads like the direct transformation into literary form of the sculpture of Christ embracing St John: when Gertrude assists in the nuns' choir at matins on St John's Day, John himself takes Gertrud's soul by the hand, transports her into spiritual rapture and leads her to Christ to rest together with her on Christ's breast (Book IV.4). He places her on his left, while he himself takes a seat on Christ's right, like the recursive reflection of the sculpture. Gertrude reports that she lays her head next to the wound in Christ's side and hears his heart beating. Thereupon she asks John why, if he had also sensed this while resting on Christ's breast, he had not written it down – to which John replies that his harkening to Christ's heartbeat was intended as a revelation for a time yet to come when the world, its love for God grown cold, would have to revive it. Gertrud does not cease her reenactment of the scene from the Last Supper there, but vividly develops it further. In a striking twist, John grants Gertrude's wish to see him in his heavenly form. Suddenly she sees him hovering on an 'infinite ocean within the heart of Jesus', as he had become so drunk with the desire to taste God that his Gospel burst forth from a vein in his heart and poured out over the entire world. When, time and again, the nuns revived the biblical story through the liturgy on St John's Day, the external eyes of the body that saw the sculpture of Christ embracing John helped the inner eyes of the spirit to access the entire cosmos which encompassed this story of an exceptional relationship. As John confirmed, this was uniquely possible for them in the convent: Christ's love had been given to him as a reward for his virginity, and thus it was promised to them, too.

The works of the women from Helfta and the devotional texts based on them, such as those by the Medingen nuns and many others, develop models of bridal mysticism which can be adapted across the sexes and boast a powerful impact. Far beyond the Reformation, the language and images of love developed by the nuns in the convent both gave wings to the imagination and shaped the bridal mysticism in religious literature, music and works of art.

V. Music and Reform

Convent communities always developed through an interplay with the religious and social conditions and needs of their time. Conversely, their vision of a religious life influenced society, since their particular way of life meant these spiritual women acted as role models in medieval society. From the very beginning, convent life was exposed to constant changes and processes of adaptation; almost every generation sought to bring its way of life closer to the original ideals of Christianity, to 're-form' it. The monastic reform of the fifteenth century was influenced by the *devotio moderna*, the 'new devotion', which, as a powerfully influential religious movement, was meant to bridge the gap between the individual and God through personal relationship. While earlier scholarship long regarded the late Middle Ages as a time of decline, we now know that it was precisely the great ecclesiastic and monastic reform of the fifteenth century that led to a blossoming of society and spiritual institutions and to a profounder religiosity. Enclosure, an expanded education that inspired the devotional practice and a remoulded liturgy prove this. Something else was obvious: the renewal of religious life became manifest in its music. One could hear the reform.

1. Secular Songs while Breaking Flax

It was in the summer of 1491 that Abbess Mechthild von Vechelde announced to the convent her intention to give permission for a *flax-breaking festival 'so that', as the chronicler says, 'we could look forward to it since we would have great entertainment in the breaking of flax and, if we wanted, could sing songs during it. This news pleased us very much, both the old and the young and those of middle age'.[1] A flurry of preparations began immediately. Because it was a long time since there had been a festival like this to mark the breaking of flax, the women tried to recall the old songs that were usually sung during this work and to adapt them for the coming festival. The middle-aged sisters and the younger nuns wrote down these songs; the girls – both the young and the slightly older ones – practised them with great zeal. So important was this pleasure to them, notes the diarist, that they did not consider what the end result of such foolishness would be, for they believed that such entertainment would be freely granted every year from then on.[2]

From the Songbooks

It can be assumed that numerous songbooks containing secular and spiritual song texts were written for such occasions and later passed down to us from the convents. When a suitable day arrived, 'our abbess had the linen brought and taken into our courtyard; and she ensured there was a wheel in the barn so that we could spend a cheerful day there breaking the linen. To help us, she allowed our *familia* to enter, both the men and the women, the confessor and the provost, the scholars and whichever of the others wanted to be there'[3] – in other words, also the servant-girls and the prebendaries. For this one day, enclosure, usually strictly observed in the Heilig Kreuz Kloster, was lifted. The nuns, especially the younger ones, and the novices, the maids and the lay sisters sang spiritual songs together – or even secular ones whose content was also acceptable to convent residents,[4] as the Cistercian diarist adds. When they no longer knew any further respectable songs to sing, they let the maids and the prebendaries sing secular songs and whomever wanted to join in on the singing.[5]

---

1   *hoc predixerat nobis, ut gauderemus, quia deduxionem magnam habiture essemus in roteracione lini nostri, et si placeret, aliquas cantilenas cantare apud linum. Hoc licenciaret nobis, quod verbum optime placuit aliquibus, tam de senioribus quam iuvenibus et mediocribus*, fol. 64v.
2   *non advertantes, quis finis huiusmodi vanitatis secuturus, putantes, quod singulis annis possit talis deduxio licenter offerri*, fol. 65r.
3   *Et cum dies oportunus accidisset, fecit domina nostra linum trahi et invehi in curiam nostram et procuravit rotam in testorio, ut ibi roterando letum diem duceremus super linnum, et permisit quasi pro adiutorio intrare familiam nostram, quam viros quam mulieres, confessorem et prepositum, scolares et ceteros, quicumque volebant*, fol. 65r.
4   *cantabant cantilenas spirituales seu minus seculares et, quando nil plus habebant cantare, de cantilenis honestis*, fol. 65v.
5   *cantare seculares cantilenas et, quibus placuit, cantabant simul cum eis*, fol. 65v.

A Godly Feast?

At that, time Salome, the daughter of Konrad von Schwicheldt, a member of the lower nobility, was living as a guest in the Heilig Kreuz Kloster along with a lay sister. They had come from neighbouring Wöltingerode to the Heilig Kreuz Kloster in Braunschweig so that the Braunschweig doctors could more easily treat Salome's serious illness, since the Cistercian convent of Wöltingerode was quite remote. There the monastic reform had already been introduced in the middle of the fifteenth century with a life lived in strict accordance with the rules; and it had since enjoyed the reputation of a model convent for faithfulness to reform. The lay sister from Wöltingerode was obviously shocked by the flax-breaking festival and such exuberance. The diarist notes, 'that some of the external visitors were scandalized by it, or so it seemed to me, and above all the lay sister from Wöltingerode, about whom I have already reported, was immensely indignant: she said she had never seen or heard anything like it before, but nevertheless she disliked such entertainment'.[6] The Braunschweig nuns, lay sisters, maids, priests and servants had fun: 'For our abbess, out of respect, they sang something appropriate to her. They did something similar for the provost, singing "O best prelate" and other songs they had composed impromptu'.[7] The day ended with small gifts for the singers and a communal meal for all the helpers. The provost was also taken with it, 'or at least he pretended to be'. The singers, male and female, received prizes and the confessor and some of the priests sent gifts, 'as if they were well-disposed towards us. Our abbess and individual sisters in office also gave a prize, even if it was not particularly valuable. In the evening our abbess gave food and drink to all who had helped'.[8]

---

6   *de quo eciam aliqui de extraneis scandalizabant, ut mihi videbatur, et conversa de Woltincrode, de qua supra scripsi, valde scandalizabat; dicebat se numquam vidisse aut audisse, tamen dispicuit sibi talis deduxio*, fol. 66r.

7   *Eciam domine nostre cantabant ob reverenciam aliqua sibi conveniencia, similiter fecerunt domino preposito cantantes 'O prelatorum optime' cum aliis pluribus cantibus, quos ad hoc composuerant*, fol. 66r.

8   *ipse prepositus simulabat omnia sibi grata, omnia sibi fore placita, et dabat precium, prout optabamus. Similiter fecit confessor et aliqui de sacerdotibus, et quamvis non fuerunt ibi, tamen miserunt quasi faventes nobis. Eciam domina nostra et singule officiate dederunt precium, licet tamen parvi ponderis. Hora cene domina nostra hiis, qui iuvaverant, dedit manducare et bibere*, fol. 66r.

Such large, exuberant festivities were probably common in many convents before the reform. Their importance for the harmonious co-existence of the various groups in the convent should certainly not be underestimated. The potential side effects were perhaps one of the reasons why the strict observance of enclosure emerged as one of the first demands of the reform movement. The tradition of convent festivals had evidently been curtailed in Braunschweig's Heilig Kreuz Kloster as well, but not completely discontinued. However, even this small festivity on the occasion of flax-breaking, one in which the whole monastic *familia* had taken part, now no longer seemed in tune with the mood music of the times. Some from the convent's social sphere, whose names and positions the diarist did not know, took offence at the festivities and induced the confessor and the provost to reprimand the nuns for this enterprise. Thus the diarist's merry account ends on a sombre note: 'And I have described all this in such detail because we had not been allowed such entertainment for a long time, nor were we able obtain it again for a long time, because it provoked great ill-feeling, since some were very displeased with everything that had happened on that day and condemned it severely. They also persuaded our father confessor to condemn us, to rebuke us, mainly, it seemed to us, to ensure that similar things do not happen more often'.[9] The provost Georg Knochenhauer reacted strategically when he avoided a similar situation in future simply by prohibiting the cultivation of flax in the convent garden – without revealing the reason, of course, so as not to offend the women of the convent.

2. Convent Reform

Music was indisputably at the centre of the nuns' lives, especially in the context of the liturgy, but by no means only there. The women singing in the nun's choir could not be seen; they were shielded from the gaze of laity and clergy, but their voices could be heard.

---

9 *Et hac omnia ideo per singula denucliacius prescripsi, que talis deduxio non fuerat permissa ex longo tempore, nec eciam per longum tempus potuimus simile aliquid optinere, quia maxima displicencia inde orta est, quia aliquibus valde displicuerant omnia, que illo die contingerant, et graviter diiudicaverant; confessorem eciam commoverant ad iudicandum et erguendum ac prohibendum, ut nobis videbatur, maxime tamen, quod huiusmodi non pluries contigit*, fol. 66v.

Where They Sing, There Set Yourself Down

The question of which song is pleasing to God occupies all religions. The Bible also offers a repertoire of love songs in the form of the Song of Songs, which was only included amongst the canonical books because it could be understood as an allegory of God's love for his people. Nonetheless, the erotic potential behind and alongside this book continued to inspire and to retain its explosive power. In a letter to a widow who had asked for advice on education, the church father Jerome stated categorically that young people, especially girls, should not read the Song of Solomon under any circumstances. It was above all the great Cistercian abbot Bernard of Clairvaux who, in the twelfth century, enabled the potential of this 'Song of Songs' to bear fruit, interpreting it as the basis for the highly personal love (conceived as transcendental) of an individual soul for her bridegroom Christ and developing it as a theological and spiritual approach of considerable appeal. The nuns' devotional texts are, therefore, full of quotations and images from the Song of Songs praising the heavenly bridegroom Christ as the heavenly bridegroom and Mary as a role model for the bride of Christ and first amongst virgins. Just as the songs of the Old Testament were repeatedly understood in new ways and blossomed in new contexts, so was everyday life in the Middle Ages shaped by fluent transitions between spiritual and secular songs.

On the one hand, the songs and chants of everyday life and church festivals followed fixed norms; on the other, every religious order, such as the Cistercians, had their own tradition. Moreover, each monastery or convent celebrated their own patron saints and special feasts. The well-informed could recognize monks and nuns by their singing. The soundscape of the convent was varied – and by no means only spiritual, an aspect which admittedly sparked controversy time and again. In addition to the sung liturgy which accompanied the nuns' lives and in which changes became an audible feature of reform, this also affected oral traditions brought into the convent from the outside world.

Writing a sermon for her fellow sisters in a North German convent, a nun begins with a 'pretty little song', which she says secular people 'usually sing with pleasure'.[10] It tells of a blossoming apple tree under which lovers desire to meet, wishing that summer would never end, as it says in the refrain: 'And she shall be my love all summer long, and that shall last very long; long, long shall last, even longer shall that last'.[11] Similar songs with refrains such as the 'long, long' repeated here are also entered by the nuns into their devotional books. These include, for example, a song which the nun Winheid wrote in her devotional book in 1478. It relates how King David himself plays the harp for the nuns to dance and Mary is called upon in the refrain to lead the heavenly dance:

> King David plays the harp for the dance, he plays the harp well and eagerly, we may well long for it, what joy is in the kingdom of heaven! Mary, honey-sweet Mary, Empress Mary, help us, noble, fine virgin, so that we may perform this dance.[12]

Secular and Sacred Music in Dialogue

We can assume that on occasions such as the flax-breaking, songs of this kind were reworked to suit the occasion and then actually sung. In this way secular and spiritual song texts cross-fertilized one another – a creative and quite characteristic mixture with which we are already familiar from the convents. The song texts found, for example, in the Wienhausen Songbook, a collection from the fifteenth century, are not actually offensive, but certainly include texts which gently mock the clergy and which one can imagine being received with a frown by the provost. The song 'Little Donkey in the Mill' (*asellus in de mola*) is one such song. It tells of a donkey who signs off work at the miller's in order, with his 'i-a' (hee-haw), to succeed as a Latin singer in the choir and forge a career as a cleric: 'I sing in the choir in order to obtain a big *benefice; when I open my mouth,

---

10 *myt welker lust io pleghen to singende de seculares eyn suverlick ledeken*, SUB Dresden, Msrc. Dresd.A 323, fol. 60v.

11 *Unde de schal aver sommer myn lef syn, dat schal overlangh syn, langh, langh scal dat syn, noch lenger schal dat syn*, fol. 60v.

12 *Koningh David, de herpet den danz, / he harpet den wol na vlite, / dar uns wol na verlanghen mach: / wat vroude is an hemmelrike! / Maria, Maria honnichsem, Maria keyserinne, / help us, eddele juncvrouwe fin, / dat we den danz vulbringhen*. (Dombibliothek Hildesheim Ms J 29, fol. 71v).

"i-a" comes out; I don't want to carry sacks any longer'.[13] Similar mockery of the clergy's ability to read and sing the liturgy is also visible on a keystone in the cloister of Kloster Ebstorf. It shows the donkey standing on its hind legs, its mouth open, in front of a large lectern, while the open book in front of it reveals the letters 'I' and 'A', which it sings. Opposite the donkey is a wolf dressed as a deacon with a thurible and a candle; judging by the wolf's open snout, it howls along with the donkey's braying.

Fig. 25 Keystone, 2nd half of the 14th century. Photograph: Wolfgang Brandis ©Kloster Ebstorf.

---

13 *pro magna prebenda ik to kore singhe. dum clamo, vox est ia; de sack schal myk nicht wringhen*, Wienhausen, Klosterarchiv, Hs. 9, fol. 15v.

The secular songs on the occasion of the flax-breaking festivities also created similar offence to the guests from the reformed convent of Wöltingerode – the sick nun and her aide (a lay sister) – because their reform liturgy had been kept simpler and stricter and these people were thus critical of polyphony or accompaniment by musical instruments. This was another decisive feature of monastic reform.

The Reform – A Second Foundation with New Rules

This alone shows that introducing monastic reform into a convent was by no means an easy undertaking. Religious communities enjoyed a way of life which had often been established for many generations and which they sometimes defended with all their might. For this reason a bishop, a senior member of the order or sometimes even the territorial ruler attended the introduction of reform in order to make the gravity of the situation clear to the nuns. The first thing they did was to take stock of the situation in the convent, known as a visitation, which was then coupled with binding recommendations for the women. After that, the men's task was over. They could not undertake the task of familiarizing the nuns with their new daily routine, with the conditions of strict enclosure, with managing the convent economy so as to put food on the common table, or with the reform liturgy. As a rule reformed nuns from neighbouring convents were summoned to instruct and guide their sisters. Being called upon to aid reform in another convent was a very honourable, but sometimes difficult, task. Accepting the monastic reform meant a new beginning in the eyes of all involved; it became a second act of foundation, one that the Heiningen nuns decided to record for posterity on their Philosophy Tapestry. Some of the women took on leadership functions in the new convent; others later returned to their own convent, with the result that close relationships developed between the reform convents – the nuns' networks.

From the visitation records[14] in Kloster Medingen, we know precisely what the reform theologians considered to be the decisive characteristics of a convent life which obeyed the rules because they recorded this in sixteen points. The first, and for them the most important, was to follow the Liturgy of the Hours, at night just as scrupulously as during the day.

---

14   *Carta visitationis*, Stadtarchiv Lüneburg, a 1479 March 31.

In the second paragraph, they stipulated the unconditional community of property. All personal property was to be donated to the convent. In addition, it was important to them to prevent the nuns from having direct contact with the secular world around them. For this purpose, a window for communications, probably covered by fabric or a grille and equipped with a turntable (*rotula*), was to be installed; it was only to be used with the special permission of a 'window sister' (*fenestraria*), yet to be appointed, and the prioress. In the confessional, an iron grille also served as a screen so that confession could be heard without direct contact. Through the introduction of strict enclosure, upon which all convent doors had to be fitted with double locks, they intended to prevent nuns from leaving the convent without permission (active seclusion) and, except in dangerous situations, to deny entry to all outsiders (passive seclusion). Only the provost and the abbess were each to have a key for faithful safekeeping. The next paragraph demanded the strict implementation of the prohibition on speaking, which was to be observed without exception in the dormitory, refectory, choir, and cloister. No conversations were to be allowed anywhere after compline and before the end of prime. In addition, they imposed 'chapters of fault', at which the nuns in the chapter had to confess in front of the community any rule transgressions such as breaking the ban on speech and atone for them. This strict examination of their own behaviour in the penitential chapters furthered the ability of the nuns and monks to reflect on their own actions, which is why the reformed way of life led not least to a high degree of self-discipline.

Since the reform required change in all areas of life, it had to be 'learnt'. For this reason, the next paragraphs stipulated the following for Medingen: two Cistercian nuns from a neighbouring reformed convent were to be summoned to instruct the Medingen nuns. This requirement was to be adopted 'without grumbling or resistance' (*sine omni contradictione et rebellione*) until everyone had been familiarized with the demands of living in accordance with the rules (*in regulari vita*). Some nuns ate well because they were better placed thanks to their families, while others in the convent went hungry: in other words, the differences in status characteristic of the society around them filtered through into the community. To prevent this, a decisive component of the reform was the provision of meals for all nuns. This communal meal was to be introduced into the refectory, accompanied by table readings from religious texts taken from the prioress's canon of readings. Of course, the new rules had to be enforced in part against the will of some individuals, which is why the installation of a penitential cell was prescribed in Medingen in accordance with the Cistercian statutes so that punitive measures could be taken. Strengthening community life also dictated that sick nuns no longer had to go home to their families to be looked after: a room was to be converted into a sick chamber and two sisters were to be delegated to bring meat, fish and whatever else was needed to the sick. Supplying about sixty to eighty nuns and the lay sisters with all the necessities of life throughout the year constituted a great logistical achievement. It required the provost's full attention and capacity for work, which is why his residency and presence were mandatory unless there was a compelling reason keeping him away. After all, it was his responsibility to ensure that all the nuns were provided with food and clothing.

As can be seen clearly here, convent reform also had an economic side, because the convent properties and revenues had to be sufficient to provide for the entire convent, the lay sisters, and the servants for twelve months of the year. Adoption of reform therefore entailed reorganization of the estates, whereby the professionalisation of their economic management becomes apparent in the creation of account books, for which the nuns frequently assumed responsibility themselves after the reform. Strict care was taken to ensure that no greater number of girls were allowed entry to a convent than its economy could later provide for as nuns. Since the convent depended on good relations with the girls' families, the problem of rejecting candidates was referred upwards to the next level in the hierarchy, namely the bishop. The *Carta* decreed that new sisters could only be accepted with the express permission of the bishop until a final quota had been established. All in all, the entire convent had to become firm in their grasp of the rules, which is why it was stipulated that the Cistercian regulations and statutes should be acquired in writing, if possible, in order for the nuns to see clearly what was permitted and what was not. As a final point, the Medingen reformers addressed a very central concern: women's convents in particular had often taken in girls from the secular world for training and education only. This option was very popular with families because there were no other institutions providing education for women in the

Middle Ages. Families were willing to pay well for it, and the religious communities often depended on this money. This practice was now to be stopped because tension was caused by the close association between girls who would become future nuns and those who would later return to the world and marry. Secular pupils were, therefore, no longer to be admitted so that the sisters could devote themselves to divine worship without being distracted. Only those who wished to be robed as a religious person in the future were to be admitted.

The Monastic Reform as a Narrative of Progress

'After performing these tasks, the bishop departed and left them *cartam visitasionis* and a new seal', reports the Medingen Chronicle in the eighteenth-century copy of Abbess Clara Anna von Lüneburg. Some of the points listed were probably implemented immediately, as demonstrated by the report on the commissioning of the required Cistercian Rule from the *scholastica* and of the mandated table readings from the *vicarius*. The implementation of the reform is impressively rendered in visual history of Medingen mentioned before, as penultimate panel of the series commissioned by the abbess to show the convent going from glory into glory.

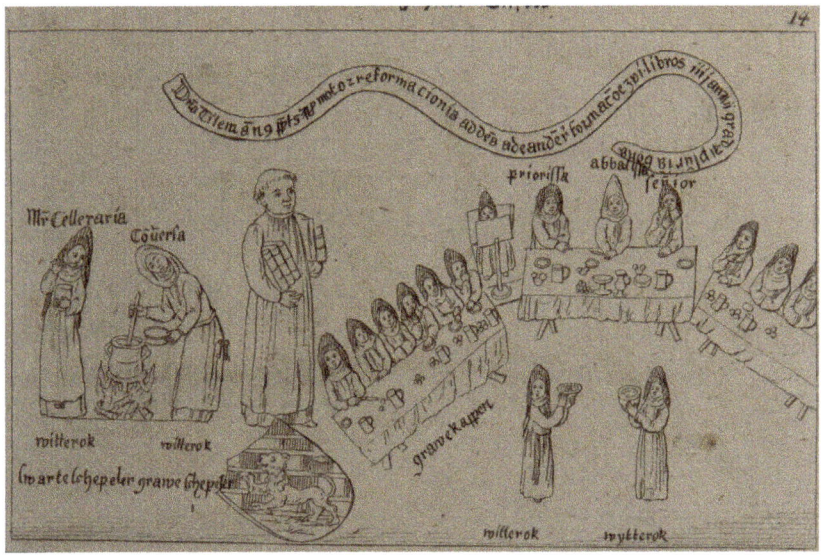

Fig. 26 Communal meal after the reform. Lyßmann (1772) after Medingen 1499.
Repro: Christine Greif.

As is typical of medieval images, representation and interpretation are inextricably linked. The results of the reform are arranged together in a bird's-eye view as visible signs of renewal. On the left stands the nun in charge of the food, tasting the stew prepared by the lay sister in charge of cooking. This marks the fact that the nuns no longer individually cooked their own soup (or 'did their own thing'), but that the food was prepared and eaten together. The engraving also copies the annotations added to the sketches for the painter, probably an artist based in the city. These annotations not only record the functions of the women, such as Mater celleraria – the sister acting as steward of kitchen and cellar and here tasting the soup – but also the colours of the garments. The habit worn by the order was also a visible sign of the reform because the black veil (*swarte schepeler*) for the *celleraria*, meant to be worn with the white dress (*witte rok*), had only become pointed in the reform. A black habit marked a nun as a Cistercian; before the reform, they wore a white round veil like the ones used by other orders.

The officeholders are enthroned at a separate table with the abbess in the middle and the prioress on her right; to the left and right the convent community sit at long tables – the same arrangement as in the choirstalls (see Figure 5). In the background a sister is visible on a high chair with a lectern, reading aloud during the meal so as to combine physical with spiritual nourishment, as required by the Visitation Act – actually a practice which had existed since the start of monasticism, but one which could only be put into action if there was a common table around which the whole community gathered. The aforementioned canon of readings of the Medingen prioress has not been preserved, but we know from medieval libraries such as that in Kloster Ebstorf or the library of the Dominican Sisters of St Katherine in Nuremberg that saints' legends, providing *exempla* for the nuns' own lives, sermons together with interpretations of the liturgy were read out at table, knowledge indispensable for the nuns' understanding of their own way of life. In a nice circular way of events, the German version of this book, 'Unerhörte Frauen', has been used as table reading in the Benedictine Abbeys of Münsterschwarzach and Maria Laach – a fact which certainly would have pleased the nuns of Medingen and the other convents discussed here.

In the picture the provost appears in the refectory with folio-sized books under both arms. The accompanying text explains that these are six liturgical manuscripts which he had commissioned in Braunschweig, his hometown.[15] The provost is depicted as much larger than the nuns, but this portrayal of him does not mean that those who designed the cycle had failed to master rules of perspective. Rather, it derives from medieval conventions for measuring importance: the special significance of the provost for the convent and for the new beginning represented by the reform is illustrated here by the representation of him as bigger. With his coat of arms, the Guelph lion awarded to him by the duke, the provost carries with him not merely the liturgical books with their music but, as it were, the reform itself.

The Nuns' Networks

For the practical instruction of the Medingen nuns in the new way of life, reform nuns from neighbouring convents were called in, as suggested in the visitation report. The abbesses from Kloster Derneburg and Kloster Wienhausen, as well as three nuns and two lay sisters from Wienhausen, arrived in Kloster Medingen for three weeks in order to introduce and implement the work of reform. While introduction of the reform in the Cistercian convent of Wienhausen had led to fierce arguments and even violence and in Kloster Mariensee the nuns had even cursed the convent reformers with Latin chants, this mediation ensured that the reform process in Kloster Medingen evidently went smoothly. After only a few weeks, communal meals had been introduced and private possessions handed over: 'The nuns brought everything they had kept in their private household, including precious things such as rings or money, all they had saved also for comfort in their old age, books etc., to a collection point'.[16] On Laetare Sunday (4th Sunday in Lent, named 'Rejoice'), they 'left their keys with the prelates and prioress, as well as everything they privately owned in terms of gold, silver and money. Each person had previously provided themselves with all the necessary goods, meat, fish, beans, peas, groats, honey, oil, butter, cheese, etc. All

---

15 *he gaff ock VI sangboke de leth he scriven tho hyldensem dar he bordich uth was.*
16 *Daselbst haben die jungfrauen alles, was ihnen heußlich gewest, auch zieraht als etwa ein ringlein, gulden oder pfenig, alles was sie ersparet auch zum zieraht des alters köstlich gehabt, bücher und anders mehr an einen sonderen ohrt des closters gebracht*, chronicle compiled on the basis of the convent archive *c.* 1700 by Abbess Clara Anna von Lüneburg, p. 98.

this they left cheerfully, gladly and willingly'. The chronicler adds: 'But they also noted that the flesh was still weak'[17] – the biblical reference to Matthew 26:41 ('the spirit indeed is willing, but the flesh is weak') probably a veiled hint in the otherwise consistently positive picture of the nuns' willingness to reform the convent, suggesting that some found it more difficult than others to relinquish their possessions.

Moreover, the rules governing fasting could naturally be enforced more strictly with communal meals than if individual nuns kept their own households. On the other hand, communal meals gave everyone the chance to enjoy any delicacies equally. The Wienhausen Chronicle notes that Susanne Potstock, the first abbess after the monastic reform, gave out 'not only half a jug of beer every day, but on fast days a whole jug' for each nun and also 'a certain quantity of ginger, figs and raisins during Advent and during the fasts, and a cake made of wheat during the fasts'.[18] The provost had to provide bread and beer; also, in the case of Wienhausen, 12 fat pigs, 10 three-year-old cattle, 30 mutton or sheep, 4 tons of fresh butter, 6 tons of herring, dried cod, 3 tons of cheese, 120 chickens, eggs, almonds, rice, vegetables, milk and much more on an annual basis.

Susanne Potstock had brought personnel from Wienhausen as support. Amongst them was Margarete Puffen, a nun in the convent. In 1479 she was elected prioress in Medingen in the presence of the abbot of Scharnebeck, the provost of Ebstorf and town councillors from Lüneburg because the old prioress, Mechthild von Remstede, who was already bedridden during the reform, could no longer fulfil this office. Puffen was officially released by Kloster Wienhausen for this task. A year later, Kloster Derneburg offered spiritual friendship to the newly reformed convent, thereby officially admitting Kloster Medingen to the network of reform institutions in Lower Saxony. The convents which had helped each other with the reform continued to provide mutual assistance beyond the actual reform period. From Kloster Derneburg, whose abbess had first helped to reform Kloster Wienhausen and then

---

17 haben sie überlaßen den henden ihrer prelaten und domina ihre schlüßel, auch alles, was vordeme eigenthümlich gehabt an golt, silber und gelt. Es hat sich eine jede persohn versorget gehabt mit notdürftigen vitualien, fleisch, fisch, bohnen, erbsen, grütze, honig, öle, butter, kese etc. Solches alles haben sie frölich, gerne und willich verlaßen [...] aber steht dabey, das fleisch ist doch auch schwach gewesen.

18 it. Alle Tage einen halben Krug Bier, aber an denen Fast Tagen einen gantzen [...] eine gewiße qvantität an Engeber, Feigen und Rosienen zur Adventszeit und in der Fasten. it. einen Weitzen Kuchen in der Fasten, in: Chronic des Klosters Wienhausen, ursprünglich bis 1692, nachträglich bis 1793 geschrieben, p. 27.

Kloster Medingen, via Kloster Wienhausen, a family of successive spiritual generations was created in which mother and daughter convents were in regular contact, not least through their lively correspondence.

In Seclusion

The convent reform had far-reaching effects on the daily life of its inhabitants, male and female, of the nuns, lay brothers and sisters and the group of clerics and pupils around the provost. The reorganization of the estates made it possible to run the economy more effectively, from which the necessary alterations to the buildings had to be financed: a common dining hall; a common dormitory; the walls, locks and doors which were necessary to maintain enclosure. The nuns' choir was furnished with further sacred pieces. After that, the provost was only allowed to enter the area for the washing of the feet on Maundy Thursday; and from then on secular guests were only permitted on high feast days, such as the investiture of their daughters. In the church, they were now even more strictly separated from the nuns. To this end, the area under the nuns' choir, which belonged to the parish church and was intended for its congregation, was vaulted over. In a directive four years after the visitation, the Bishop of Hildesheim and Verden reminded the provost of the obligations arising from the visitation and instructed him to build the promised guest house so that the enclosure of the nuns could be all the more bindingly observed. On pain of excommunication, the nuns were no longer allowed to receive secular guests or to supervise pupils from outside the convent.

Antiphonal Singing

The community of nuns was organized into two groups, which sat opposite each other in the nuns' choir, as can still clearly be seen in Kloster Wienhausen to this day (Figure 5). The liturgy was a dialogue – with God, but also with one another. The singing was led by a precentor, the *cantrix*, and her deputy, the *succentrix*, who, alternating, sang the antiphons, psalms and chants of the Liturgy of the Hours and, in addition, the more complex *sequences and chants on feast days, for example for the Easter celebrations. The texts and the manner of their performance were noted down in large parchment choir books, which were expensive and very time-consuming to produce. When the chants for the church year were changed, these choir books also had to be rewritten. It is in this context that the image of the Guidonian Hand (Figure 27) used in music lessons has come down to us from Kloster Ebstorf; and from the manuscripts there we also know that the first thing to happen after the reform was that the nuns, working night shifts, wrote down the new liturgical chants on slips of paper. These chants were quickly learned by a few nuns in order then to perform them as antiphons in two choirs of six nuns each until the entire community had mastered the new repertoire.

3. Music Instruction in Kloster Ebstorf

Books are complex sign systems. This is all the more the case when they contain not only script and illustration but also musical notation. These signs must literally be deciphered, their meaning recognized and then transposed into practice in performance, rendered audible in divine worship or devotion, all of which demands a system of several stages. These are 'narrative images', which do not depict reality but seek to explain to the viewer multi-layered facts within their semantic context. How this process worked at the time is seen particularly graphically in the double page from a manuscript for music instruction in Ebstorf, which is densely decorated with symbols, pictures and texts.

Fig. 27 Guidonian Hand. Klosterarchiv V 3, 15th century, fols 200v–201r.
Photograph: Wolfgang Brandis ©Kloster Ebstorf.

A Mnemonic for the Singers

The depiction of the double page with the Guidonian Hand combines this visual aid for learning intervals with music theory definitions, mnemonic verses and little scenes as illustrations. The hand, which assigns notes within the hexachord system to the joints of the fingers to aid memorisation, is intended to facilitate the learning of liturgical chants through the conception of intervals. In conjunction with the towers on the right, illustrating the graduation of the scales, the concept is based on the pedagogy for religious music associated with the name of Guido of Arezzo (*c*. 992–after 1033); depictions of the hand are transmitted from the twelfth century onwards. The texts explain that thorough contemplation of the 'artful hand' (*manus artificialis*) opens the way to understanding its musical components, provided they are studied closely. This is underlined by an accompanying animal scene: a monkey, sitting casually with crossed legs next to an owl, provocatively holds a mirror in which the profiles of both animals can be seen, along with the monkey's spotty fur. A pictorial commentary, the scene holds up a mirror to students of music: which animal do they wish to follow, the wise owl or the silly monkey? The admonition to the nuns is quite clear: anyone who evades the step-by-step didactic introduction to music offered here will not gain a true understanding of its spiritual content. The two squirrels on the right demonstrate how the road to revelation is to be opened: by cracking nuts, a popular image for the value in working one's way through hard shells to the tasty kernel.

Fig. 28 Owl and monkey looking in the mirror (detail from Figure 27).
Photograph: Wolfgang Brandis.

On the left side, too, symbolic animal scenes are assigned to the two nuns: the one making music and the one teaching. The suggestion of a roof arches over the depiction of teaching; a nest with two storks can be seen on its battlements. One of them feeds the young in the nest; the other one, its beak open and its head thrown back, signals nature joining in with the jubilation of Creation. This also provides us with information about the musical lesson taking place underneath. It is part of the tenderly affectionate upbringing of the girls in enclosure by means of role models: with a stylus, her writing tool, the pupil sitting on the low chair traces the line marked out for her by the teacher's pointing hand. On the left, a nun playing the organ demonstrates that learning to read musical notation is worth the effort. Music lessons in general, as emphasized in the various tracts from Kloster Ebstorf, are not primarily about the acquisition of theory. On the contrary, the nuns should apply what they learnt so that the celebration of the liturgy could bring them joy.

At the same time the leaf of parchment with its detailed diagrams illustrating musical theory, the professional notation and, not least, its rich decoration with images documents what could be achieved in the field of manuscript production and illustration through training in the convent. Finally, the page layout and the adept use of colour are proof of great skills in graphic design. The materials for the long production process were largely produced in the convent itself. The parchment (from animal skins) and paper (from rags) were rarely produced in the convents themselves, but were usually bought in from outside as the basis for writing. The further preparation of the material, though, lay with the scribes. They smoothed and prepared the parchment further; cut the quires to size; and pricked out the lines on the writing material with the pricking wheel, a tool which allowed several pages to be set up at once by rolling a small wheel with sharp points over the pages. In addition, they boiled the ink, for which recipes have survived: for example, for the boiling down of oak galls. They also cut the feathers of different species of birds to produce nibs for strokes of different thicknesses. These quills then had to be regularly re-sharpened when they became blunt. Protective parchment covers were made for the household-management books by the nuns themselves. 'Hardcover' leather bindings over wooden boards were also occasionally made and repaired in the convents to protect the precious parchment or paper blocks and to make the manuscripts 'library-ready', sometimes also chained, as surviving staple marks show.

Moreover, a slim sample book from Kloster Medingen, written in Low German and containing the alphabet, the Lord's Prayer, the Hail Mary, and other daily prayers, shows that templates were also provided for the lay sisters which they could use as a guide when creating their own prayer books.

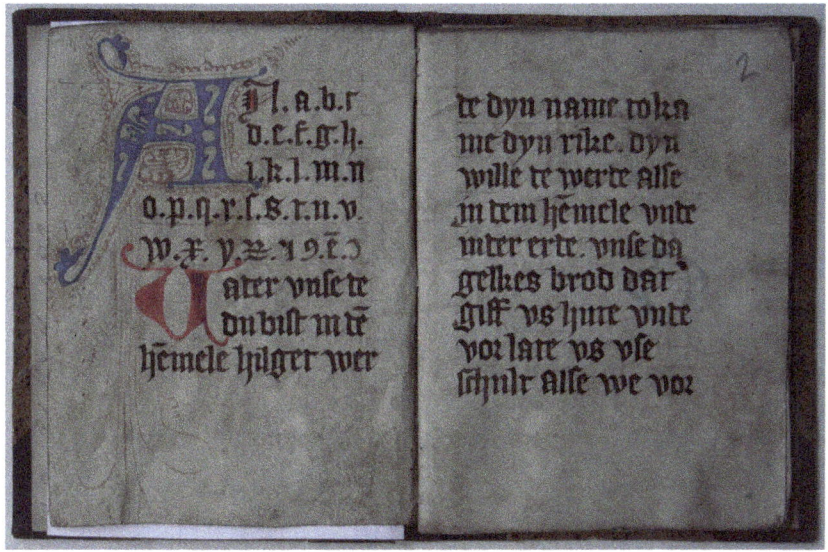

Fig. 29 SUB Göttingen 8° Cod. Ms. Theol. 243, fols. 1v–2r, *c.* 1500. Photograph: Hans-Walter Stork ©SUB Göttingen.

The Reform – An Intellectual Training

The reform of the liturgy in the fifteenth century thus demanded intensive intellectual and musical training, which was part of building a community. In 1495, an elderly nun in Kloster Ebstorf noted, with a withering look at the younger singers, that she had never heard such bad choir singing in all her sixty years in the convent. She admonished them:

Make an effort to sing and read correctly, observe the pauses for breath and the caesuras in half verses and help the precentors on both sides of the choir faithfully. Do not sit there in silence and let them sing alone as often happens! You should now make an effort. Things will become clearer to you with time so that you will then understand all the better what you are to do.[19]

There were clear monastic guidelines on 'how to sing and how we should recite the psalms', which were quoted and commented on in Kloster Ebstorf:

We are not to drag out the psalms too much, but sing them in a well-rounded way, with a lively voice, that is, resonantly, evenly and regularly, not trailing and all too slowly lingering, but also not too quickly so that it does not sound frivolous and skittishly skipping. We should strike up the verse together and end it together and observe the pause together in the middle and at the end of the verse.[20]

All in all, 'we are to sing manfully' (*Wy schollet synghen menliken*, respectively in the Latin text: *viriliter*). This means, first and foremost, the performance style of firm, straight singing, but it is also a remarkable demand. Especially after the reform, the nuns saw themselves as part of a culture of singing that could and should be cultivated in women's convents as well as men's monasteries.

So it is above all the singing that, from a musical point of view, stands at the centre of the reform. The organ is the only musical instrument for which there is firm evidence in convents, although its use was not uncontroversial. Indeed, the renunciation of organ-playing is mentioned

---

19 *Dot flit, dat dar rechte sungen vnd lesen wart, pauses et predominantes halden warden vnd dot cantrici, succentrici truweliken helpen, vnd saet nicht vnd swiget vnd latet se so nicht allen singen, wo vaken schut. Gy moten nu dar flitich in syn, idt wyl nu myt der tyd an juw langen, vp dat gyt deste beth wanen, wen gyt don schollen.* (Archiv der Emder Gesellschaft für Kunst und Altertümer, flyleaf).

20 *Wy en schollet de psalmos nicht langhe natheen, ßunder de scholle wy rotunde hen synghen myd leuendigher stempne. Dat iß: ßatighen vnde euene vnde like, nicht to hanghende vnde alto langhsem to slepende, vnd ock nit alte drade to singhende, dat id nicht lichtfertighen vnd huppafftighen en lude! Wy schollet dat varschk lyke tho ßamde anheuen vnd tho lyke enden vnd in dem myddele vnd em ende des verschkes to lyke pausam holden.* (Kloster Ebstorf, Hs. VI 11, fol. 79v). This is based on a Latin treatise attributed to Bernard of Clairvaux: *psalmodia semper pari voce, aequa lance non nimis protrahatur, sed mediocri voce, non nimis velociter sed rotunde, virili, viva et succincta voce psallatur; syllabas, verba, metrum in medio et in finem versus, id est initium, medium et finem simul incipiamus et pariter dimittamus. Punctum aequaliter teneant omnes.*

as a feature of the reform in Kloster Ebstorf, along with the renewal of the liturgical books. As always, regulations and implementation are not necessarily synonymous. In Medingen, even after the reform, it is certain that an organ was used at least during Easter, since the abbess's official manual states that during the girls' communion the *hymn 'This is the bride of the highest king' (*Hec est sponsa summi regis*) should be sung to organ accompaniment. Moreover, as we have seen (Chapter III.2, Figure 16), on the panels depicting the history of the convent organ-playing is portrayed as an ancient tradition. Throughout the sources, music-making – whether on real instruments or 'the harp-playing of the soul', as inner participation is called in the texts – is depicted as part of the angelic choir, of the jubilation of the spirit which moves people and even animals. As instruments of jubilation, the organs and bells were silent only during Holy Week and during an *interdict, when they were replaced by 'wooden bells', the tongues of a standing rattle which instead gave out the necessary acoustic signal to call the nuns to prayer. In the Medingen prayer book written and illuminated by the nun Winheid (of Winsen) in 1478, a nun plays the organ while a boy treads the bellows and rings the bell. The text for this comes from the Easter hymn *Laudes Salvatori*.

Fig. 30 Nun playing the organ. Dombibliothek Hildesheim Ms J 29, fol. 119r. ©Dombibliothek Hildesheim.

The soundscape of the convent, with bells, organ and the nuns' singing, which could be heard but not seen, must have been impressive and was certainly one of the reasons why participating in services in convent churches was also attractive to lay people. After the convent reform, when the Medingen nun adapted the manual for the provost and added more chants, she also included responsories in the vernacular for the congregation and for the first time codified some of the chorales which are still sung in worship today, such as 'Gelobet seist du, Jesu Christ'.[21] At Easter, the nuns in the gallery intoned the Latin sequence 'Praise to the Saviour', and after each verse, the laity responded from the nave with the vernacular 'Christ is risen'.[22] This is explicitly justified in theological terms when it says of Easter: 'The laity join in the praise because on this day all nature rejoices'.[23] In the common liturgy, the barrier of enclosure is overcome, and the church space expands for heavenly song. The Medingen Easter prayer books depict how heavenly choirs and the local congregation sing together on Easter morning:

The angels sing the Easter hymn 'Let us rejoice today' (*Exultemus et letemur hodie*); the nuns join in with 'The day is dawning' (*Illuxit dies*, a line from the *Laudes Salvatori*); and the laity respond, as they did during the Easter service in Medingen, with the German stanza 'This day is so holy' (*So heylich is desse dach*).

The liturgical performance, repeated every year in the rhythm of the church feasts, made comprehensible and tangible the wide spiritual horizons beyond the material world and opened a space for reflection on the deeper meaning of life. Music could thus become the place where lay people and members of the convent came together in shared closeness to God.

---

21 *Evangelisches Gesangbuch* (Protestant hymnbook) no. 23; *Gotteslob* (Catholic hymnbook) no. 252. Translated into English as 'O Jesus Christ, all praise to Thee' by Arthur T. Russell.

22 *Deinde 'Victime paschali laudes', laycis laudem canentibus 'Crist is' quia indignum valde est, ut dicit Gregorius, quod eo die Laudes debitas taceat lingua carnis quo videlicet die caro resurrexit auctoris.* Bodleian Library, MS. Lat. liturg. e 18, fol. 48vb. 'Christ ist erstanden' was translated by the English reformer Miles Coverdale in his *Goostly Psalmes and Spiritual Songs* as 'Christe is now rysen agayne'.

23 *Et layci canant laudem quia omnis in hac die rerum natura iubilat*, fol. 49rb.

Fig. 31 Dombibliothek Hildesheim Ms J 29, fol. 52r. ©Dombibliothek Hildesheim.

VI. Reformation

When the Reformation was introduced into the imperial city of Nuremberg in 1525 and Catholic mass was banned, the Nuremberg patrician and learned humanist Willibald Pirckheimer, who had openly declared his allegiance to Protestantism in the previous years, wrote a desperate letter at Easter to his humanist friend and Luther's confidant Philipp Melanchthon. He begins his letter: 'With you, my Philipp, I see myself compelled to seek refuge; I implore your advice and help ...'. The reason for Willibald's despair was the situation in the Nuremberg convent of the Poor Clares, over which his sister Caritas Pirckheimer presided as abbess and where his daughters lived. During Advent 1524 the Franciscans had already been taken away from the nuns as pastoral carers and confessors, and now the monasteries and convents in Nuremberg were gradually being dissolved with gentle pressure or even force. Only the Poor Clares steadfastly refused to give in to the council's urging. In his letter of advice,[1] the Protestant preacher Andreas Osiander found unambiguous words, especially for Abbess Caritas Pirckheimer: there would be no peace in the convents unless they first rooted out the weeds and got the *Birckamerin* (Caritas Pirckheimer), out of there. In moving words Willibald describes to Melanchthon how the women had long been deprived of all spiritual support, including confession and the Eucharist; and how he himself considered the priests they were offered as replacements to be untrustworthy. On the contrary, they took such delight in abusing the poor women and behaved so arrogantly towards them that the nuns were likely to become more obdurate than to change for the better: 'This sex, as you know, wants to be persuaded, under no circumstances to be forced'.

---

1 *Ratschlag über die Klöster*, 31 May 1525.

Of course, it soon becomes clear that Willibald Pirckheimer could not approve of a breach of monastic vows. When, in 1525, Willibald allowed his daughter Katharina to remain faithful to her vows, her reply reveals she was well acquainted with Luther's criticism and her father's point of view: She 'does not think she will be blessed in the nun's habit, but still thinks she will please her heavenly bridegroom better in that than in a gown bedecked with pearls'. As a sign of gratitude, the daughter calls him not only her biological but also her spiritual father. Willibald's criticism of monastic life was ignited by the narrow-mindedness of the mendicant friars in theological and philosophical matters – these 'most impudent scroungers' who lived off the labour of others. In terms of systemics, his criticism referred first and foremost to the doctrine of justification through works: to what was, in his eyes, a misunderstood clinging onto liturgical rites which had been introduced at some point in the past – the ceremonies – or onto regulations governing asceticism and fasting, the origins of which were unclear. The Protestants, on the other hand, took as their starting point the grace of God alone, *sola gratia*, and had scant regard for the efficacy of pious works. The Protestants' criticism was, therefore, also directed primarily at the papal practice of indulgences, which positively flourished in the years immediately preceding the Reformation and especially in the Jubilee Year of 1500.

1. The Papal Legate Arrives in Town

In December 1502, there was only one topic of conversation in Braunschweig, namely the imminent arrival of the papal legate, Cardinal Raymond Peraudi, who, as a high-ranking diplomat for Pope Alexander VI, had been sent to northern Germany in 1500 to announce the Jubilee Indulgence. The legate was still in Erfurt and subsequently in Magdeburg, but from there he was already conducting negotiations about his reception with the city of Braunschweig and the old Duke William II the Younger of Braunschweig, who died in the summer of the following year.

The Announcement of the Legate

Initially, the arrival of the distinguished guest was a long time in coming, but on 18 February 1503, a Saturday, suddenly everything went very fast. The word in town was that Cardinal Raymond Peraudi would be arriving in Braunschweig in two days. The entire clergy was to march in procession to meet the papal legate outside the gates as a sign of respect – the Cistercians from Riddagshausen and the Benedictines of St Giles with their abbots, the Dominicans and the Franciscans – and all were to do so in full ecclesiastical regalia. The provost of the Heilig Kreuz Kloster with his chaplains and scholars was also invited. Indeed, not a single ecclesiastical order in Braunschweig was forgotten; only the nuns of the Heilig Kreuz Kloster were excluded, as the diarist notes with regret – for the protection of their virginity and their duty to observe enclosure. Yet they did not want to do without women altogether. To ensure the procession did not lack glamour, all the girls in the town who had reached the age of majority were called upon to take part, dressed in black robes, their hair adorned with caps and green ribbons, although some respected widows were entrusted with the supervision of the girls. The richer families were meant to help the poorer ones to ensure everyone presented a dignified appearance. A high-class reception naturally included music; and everyone who owned an instrument was therefore called upon to play and sing. A magnificent reception ceremony for the cardinal, one befitting the status of the rich and powerful Hanseatic city of Braunschweig, was a matter of honour. Usually on such occasions, cities presented themselves as well-ordered, peaceful communities in imitation of 'heavenly Jerusalem', the biblical ideal of a civic community in which everyone, rich and poor, lived together happily and safely.

On that cold Saturday in February 1503 Henry the Elder of Braunschweig-Lüneburg, the old duke's son, had received the cardinal in his ducal seat, the neighbouring town of Wolfenbüttel. The timing was convenient, because the next day the cardinal was to accompany the duke to the Augustinian convent of Steterburg to celebrate the spiritual wedding of the latter's daughter, Elisabeth, during mass: she was to receive the habit and the nun's crown in Steterburg, as was the custom there. The Braunschweig town councillors were also invited to the ceremony and the banquet there, but when they arrived, the church was already so full that they could find neither a place to stand in the church nor anywhere to stable their horses. After a few hours, therefore, they returned to Braunschweig, tired and still hungry. This was also particularly annoying because the cardinal had granted full remission of all their sins to everyone who had taken part in the celebration. Moreover, so that the event would not be forgotten, Raymond Peraudi also granted a major indulgence to all those who visited the convent on the anniversary of the investiture ceremony of the duke's daughter. A few years later, in 1515, Elisabeth was appointed prioress to lead the community in Steterburg and to guide it through the difficult years of the Reformation.

Since the papal legate was already in nearby Wolfenbüttel, the councillors in Braunschweig assumed the cardinal would enter the city the following day. Preparations for the arrival were made in great haste. At the sixth hour on Monday morning everyone, including the priests of the Heilig Kreuz Kloster, marched in their finery and an orderly procession to meet the cardinal outside the city walls. When the priests from the Heilig Kreuz Kloster had left, nothing held the servants, maids and prebendaries there any longer and they ran after them. 'Unfortunately we were not invited', noted the diarist, 'but we still fervently hoped that the cardinal would visit us and give us the pope's blessing and absolution. In the meantime, we made intensive preparations for his arrival and rehearsed the Easter chant with which we wished to receive him'.[2]

For the time being, it did not come to that. At the eleventh hour, Provost Georg Knochenhauer and the clerics returned to the convent with their reliquaries and censers, just as they had left, but having accomplished nothing because the cardinal had not appeared. Henry's wife, Duchess Catherine of Pomerania, had not let the distinguished guest leave because she wanted him to sing mass for her the following morning. Thus the councillors ordered everyone to assemble again at the seventh hour on the following Tuesday to meet Cardinal Raymond

---

2 *Nos quoque, licet non eramus invitate, tamen sperante in proximo nos visitandas a prefato cardinali, [...] et quod personaliter deberet nos invisere seu visitare ac papali benedictione et absolucione letificare [...]. Inde ergo accepta fiducia preparavimus nos ad eius adventum affirmando omni studio cantum, cum quo ipsum suscipere gestiebamus, videlicet 'Advenisti' paschale et responsorium 'Audi Israel'*, fol. 174v.

Peraudi a second time. This time, as was now known, Duke Henry himself would, in company with other high-ranking nobles, counts, bishops and abbots, solemnly escort the legate to the town. This, in turn, aroused conflicting feelings in the council, for the previous years had witnessed serious disputes and a feud with Henry the Elder, who, when seizing sovereignty over the town of Braunschweig, had made harsh demands with which they did not want to comply (cf. Chapters I.1 and I.2). The matter was, therefore, delicate.

A Splendid Arrival – Without the Heilig Kreuz Kloster

Although 'not adorned with gleaming gold like the streets of Jerusalem', the streets and squares of the town through which the cardinal would be led were 'nevertheless swept clean and cleared of dirt', as the Cistercian nun stresses with some pride; the fronts of the houses were decorated with tapestries and flags; and in the windows stood musicians playing their instruments.[3] On Tuesday, the prelates, monks, clergy and girls now marched through the Stone Gate a second time to meet the cardinal and waited patiently for his arrival from the eighth hour in the morning until the first hour after noon, although already quite tired. When the company finally approached the town, those assembled intoned the verse 'Thou art come, O desired one'[4] and led the papal legate to the sound of kettledrums and trumpets through the streets of the town to the collegiate church of St Blasius inside the ducal castle complex and to a town palace that had been erected especially for him. The arrival of the cardinal left no one untouched; everyone who was able ran to meet him and ask for his blessing, which resulted in great pushing and shoving. Those who could not push their way through to him, remarks the Cistercian nun, were deeply annoyed.[5] Cardinal Peraudi's reception, it seemed, eclipsed all the receptions that had ever been held in Braunschweig.

While waiting for the return of the clerics to the Heilig Kreuz Kloster

---

3   *Strate eciam erant platee, per quas inducendus erat, et si non auro mundissimo ut platee civitatis Ierusalem, tamen scopis mundate et purgate; tapecia insuper et dorsalia ceteraque ornamenta erant dependencia pre foribus domorum, in fenestris autem stabant luzares reddentes diversos sonos musicales*, fol. 176v.

4   *Advenisti desiderabilis* from the Easter sequence *Cum rex gloriae*.

5   *et quicumque illic pervenire non poterat, grave ferebat*, fol. 177v.

on Tuesday, the maids in their impatience climbed up to the very top windows in the nuns' dormitory, hoping to see or hear something, but in vain. Finally, the scholars returned with the relics and recounted with what dignity and splendour everything had passed off and that only the white cloaks of the Riddagshausen Cistercians had been a little dirty. In imitation of Christ's arrival into Jerusalem, the cardinal had chosen a mule as his mount for entering the town and given everyone the papal blessing willingly and with a cheerful countenance until he had reached his palace, where he dismissed the people. The nuns of the Heilig Kreuz Kloster were sad and disappointed that they had not set eyes on the lofty guest from Rome, nor shared in the papal blessing. Provost Georg Knochenhauer showed some understanding and a few days later, together with the nuns' confessor Ulrich Pawes, set off for the residence of Cardinal Peraudi to persuade him to visit Heilig Kreuz Kloster in person and to console the nuns by giving them the papal blessing. He had previously informed the abbess of his intention so that she could in the meantime decorate the convent with tapestries and prepare it for the visit. To help in persuading him, the provost and confessor carried precious gifts with them, a gold-plated lamb of Christ and silk pontifical gloves, which the cardinal obviously liked and gladly accepted. He nevertheless sent his apologies, saying that due to other commitments he was unfortunately unable to comply with their request.[6]

On the men's return, the nuns took this news hard. The lay sisters had spent the whole day cleaning the convent from top to bottom; the *sacrista* had laid out the paraments in the choir and decorated the church with tapestries and wall hangings. The girls, in their choir robes and veils, had run from one corner to the other all day in their excitement; and quite a few of the choir nuns had emulated them – as the diarist notes critically – in order to see what needed to be done if he came, all the while singing in loud voices. 'It was especially hard for me', she admits in a rare personal remark, 'and for the others who have St Matthias as their personal Apostle, for it was St Matthias's Day'. What an honour that would have been! She comments: 'We had all worked so hard, preparing the convent and rehearsing the festive chants, that our

---

6   *offerentes ei agnum deauratum, cirothecas serico et auro more pontificalium cirothecarum ornatas cum aliis exeniis; visis autem cirothecis amanter eas suscipiens, benigne respondens excusabat se dicens illo die non valere desiderium nostrum implere certis ex causis*, fol. 183r.

old sisters had to laugh and opined that they had never experienced anything like it as long as they had lived'.[7]

The abbess made one last attempt and wrote to the cardinal asking him to honour the community with his visit. Together with the letter, she sent him two statues of the Virgin Mary, which she asked him to consecrate and endow with the privilege of indulgences. Her fervent pleas at least moved the cardinal to the promise of sending one of his doctors to the convent on Ash Wednesday to afford the nuns full remission of their sins and to place the consecrated ashes on their heads. He also consecrated the two Madonnas and conferred on each an indulgence of one hundred days for those who, in their devotion, prayed the rosary before them. If the appropriate number of prayers were said before the statues of the Madonnas, a total of 1,000 days of remission from purgatory could thus be acquired, a prospect which added to the appeal of the convent church and the community. This did not come cheap. The account book of the Cistercian nuns of the Heilig Kreuz Kloster lists the large sum of one mark, six shillings and one denarius for the cardinal's letters of indulgence and his remuneration. At least Peraudi kept his promise. On Ash Wednesday, one of his doctors of theology actually appeared at the convent. He imposed on the nuns the obligation to pray three paternosters: every hundred days they would pray one paternoster for Cardinal Peraudi, one for the pope and one for all Christendom. The abbess summoned the doctor come to her at the end of his visit so that she could talk to him about questions of progress in religion. Because his Latin was too foreign and she did not really understand him, she had to let him go without anything having been achieved.

The cardinal stayed in Braunschweig for four or five weeks, partly because he was suffering from gout. At the end of March, though, he

---

[7] *Et nos hec audientes indigne tulimus, quod in tanta sollempnitate talem destructionem incassum nobis excitaverant, nam die illo post refectionem converse purgabant in aliquibus locis, sacriste portabant preparamenta ad chorum, tapecia ad sanctuarium sternentes illud tapetibus et dorsalibus et scapualibus, puelle currebant cum cappis et peplis de loco ad locum, similiter et persone plurime conventus nostri discurrebant querentes et investigantes, quid agendum esset, si veniret, significabant, musicabant et alique aperta voce, que illis videbantur, edisserebant; quod quidem mihi et ceteris, quibus erat beatus Mathias apostolus, valde grave erat et moleste tulimus, quod non sufficiebat eis, quod multo iam studio in diebus precedentibus purgando et parietes fricando claustrum preparaveramus. Tantum namque in hiis laboravimus ob reverenciam adventus eius, quod seniores nostri ammirantes in gaudio dicebant: "Qualia talia numquam vidimus, quoad quidem viximus"*, fol. 183v.

wanted to set off for the northern provinces in the direction of Bremen. Because the attack of gout had not yet completely subsided, a light carriage was built for him to minimize the pain in his limbs throughout the journey. Then an incident occurred in which the nuns played a part. Some of the cardinal's companions wished to visit the Cistercian nuns before they left, also because they had not managed to persuade the cardinal to visit the Heilig Kreuz Kloster as the nuns had repeatedly requested. To this end and without further ado, the companions took the carriage which had been built for the papal legate and drove it to the convent cemetery – where the carriage promptly broke down. The nuns' confessor Ulrich Pawes noticed their misfortune and gave them some advice. Above all, he urgently exhorted them, as the diarist knew, 'not to join us in the convent, lest they disturb our devotions, because it was 21 March, the feast day of St Benedict'.[8] Even in the Heilig Kreuz Kloster in Braunschweig, which had not been reformed, enclosure was also carefully observed. Hence Ulrich Pawes kept the guests with him, gave them refreshments and gingerbread and whatever else he had in the house and they consumed every last morsel: 'There were 15 doctors of theology with their servants; and he thanked God when he got rid of them again in the evening with good fortune and without any major havoc'.[9]

Ten days after the accident with his travelling coach, on 30 or 31 March 1503, or so the Cistercian nuns notes, 'the aforementioned honourable and pious Cardinal Raymond Peraudi sent us his energetic penitentiary' (*devotissimus et reverentissimus sepefatus dominus cardinalis Raymundus ... misit ad nos suum penitencionarium, virum strennuum doctoremque eximium,* fol. 190v), that is, the member of his retinue who was responsible for the distribution of signs of grace such as indulgences. She continues:

> He gave us two gold florins and asked that we include the cardinal in our prayers so that he might return to the papal court in Rome in good health and in peace and might complete the mission he had been charged to

---

8 *dedit eis concilium, quid de curru facerent, et premonuit eos, ne ad nos intrarent, ne forte nobis impedimentum in nostra devocione facerent, erat enim eo die festum Sancti Benedicti,* fol. 190r.

9 *porrigens eis electuarium et tortas piperatas, quas nos mellificatas dicimus, videlicet honnickoken unde wat he sodens hadde, unde se eten dat ome al up. Erant enim doctores cum suis ministris viri, ut estimo quindecym, he danckede godde, dat he or vor dem avende mit heyle quid wart,* fol. 190r.

perform, for which God grant him mercy. Our abbess gladly agreed to
this request, but asked the learned man that, humbly begging, he might,
on his departure from the town, lead his master the cardinal along such
a route that he would pass our convent and at least visit our church and
gladden us with his fatherly blessing. The papal penitentiary promised
to carry out her request faithfully and to direct the cardinal's mind and
path in our direction. He was successful and the cardinal promised the
confessor Ulrich Pawes that when he left Braunschweig on Saturday, 1
April he would pass our cemetery on his way out of the town. If the
convent came to meet him with the priests in processional order, he, who
for his departure again rode the mule on which he had entered, could
pass us and give us the greeting of peace and the blessing with his own
hand.[10]

That was the plan. The Cistercian nun noted in her diary:

> It seemed like a major event to us and so we discussed whether the
> cardinal might not leave by another town gate and we might have left
> enclosure for nothing and made a laughing stock of ourselves. Hence
> the confessor set out once more to see the cardinal and learned from his
> own mouth that he had every intention of passing by us on his departure
> from the town and of bestowing the blessing of peace on us one by one
> by holding out to us with his own hand a pax board with the lamb of
> God and the cross for the kiss of peace. When the confessor heard this, he
> immediately sent for the abbess because time was running out, told her
> what he had heard and instructed her on how everything could proceed
> with dignity and honour. The abbess then gave instructions that the
> priests should precede us with crosses, relics and thuribles and intone
> the sequence 'Thou art come, beloved'; and then we should add 'Hear,
> O Israel' in antiphonal chant. When the cardinal approached, the abbess
> would step forward a little and prostrate herself before the papal legate

---

10   *misit nobis II florenos rogans intima devocione, ut personam eius cum omni frequencia
ipsius dignaremur suscipere in oracionibus nostris, ut cum salute et pace mereretur remeare
ad curiam Romanam et ut legacionem, qua fungebatur, posset ita perficere, ut deo gratum
esset et sibi meritorium aliisque proficuum in vitam eternam. Quibus peticionibus cum
domina nostra annuisset, peciit, ut reverendissimum dominum suum humili supplicatu ad
hoc adduceret, quatenus in discessu suo, si iter apud nostrum monasterium faceret, ne nos
inaniter transissiret, sed dignaretur ecclesie nostre ad modicum approximare et sic nobis
sua paterna benedictione letificare. Qui cum se facturum promittens valedicensque recessit
et negocium nostrum fideliter promovens animum reverendissimi cardinalis ad peticionem
nostram inclinavit innuitque confessori nostro propositum cardinalis, quando in sabbato
sequenti recessurus iter per nos faciens declinare vellet a turba ad cimiterium nostrum, et
qualiter illi obviam esset a conventu et clero nostro procedendum, quodque ipse personaliter
mulo incedens stantibus nobis per choros vellet per nos transsire et nobis manu propria
pacem esse porrecturus ac benedictionem daturus* (fol. 190v).

and then, rising again, kiss his hand and receive the blessing of peace. The nuns would then come forward two-by-two also to kiss his hand.[11]

When, on the day of his departure, the cardinal himself sent the nuns the news that he would personally visit and bless them, everyone reacted with great joy and prepared to meet the illustrious guest. The abbess permitted them to don their finest white Sunday robes. These robes, the Cistercian nun noted critically:

> I mention the robes here because it seems to me that in future we must take better care not to display such slovenliness again. One wore a very short robe; another had thrown a fur covering over her robe; one girl's coat shone white; another's was dirty and in tatters. Quite a few people were unpleasantly affected by this, which is why something similar should be prevented in future, if possible.[12]

While the convent, together with the provost, waited in their own rooms for the cardinal's arrival, lay people flocked from all directions and a tremendous crowd formed, filling all the streets and alleys from the cardinal's residence as far as the cemetery of the Heilig Kreuz Kloster. Because the nuns were not sure which gate he would be led out of, and the Heilig Kreuz Kloster was directly outside the gates of the town, the abbess had taken the precaution of sending out the

---

11 *Et quia videbatur nobis magnum negocium, tractabatur, et ne forte per aliam viam educendus esset et sic nos de clausuris non esset casse egresse fieremus illucio populo. Idcirco accescit confessor noster in presencia ipsius cardinalis et audivit ab eo, quod propositum habere declinandi ad nos in egressu suo de civitate et dandi singulis benedictionem pacem, porrigendi manu propria agnum dei vel signum crucis ad osculandum. Quibus auditis, quia iam instabat hora eduxionis, fecit vocari dominam nostram et proposuit ei, que audivit, et instruxit eam, quomodo se habere deberet et qualiter cetere omnes, ut omnia cum summa reverencia et honore fieri possent. Et hec omnia nostra domina ulterius dixit nobis, quando sacerdotes nostri cum crucibus et reliquiis et turibulis cantando, Advenisti desiderabilis'* (Cantus a02107) [...] *adiungeremus, Audi Israel'*(Cantus 006143). *Et qualiter illi appropinquanti domina nostra procedendo modicum deberet se prosternere ad terram, deinde surgens de terra accedere ad osculandum manum ipsius perceptura pacem, quam illi cardinalis porrigere vellet, et prima in accessu antequam oscularetur manum cardinalis osculare deberet manum propriam, sicque due et due accedentes veniam peterent; deinde in accessu ad ipsum manum propriam oscularentur et sic posce accedere ad manum ipsius osculandum* (fol. 192r).

12 *De cappis autem idcirco hic mencionem facio, quia videbatur mihi, quod in futuro esset precavendum, ne tanta difformitas in habitu nostro appareat sicut tunc: uni erat cappa nimis curta, altera pellicium extendebatur ultra cappam, unius cappa apparuit candida, alterius sordida et perfusa, unde eciam aliqua erant valde permote in animo – ideo, si potest, caveatur in futuro* (fol. 193v).

maids so they could let the convent know 'if the cardinal rode out of St Peter's Gate so that we could then set off in an orderly fashion'.[13] The maids passed the abbess's instructions on to street urchins, who were meant to inform the nuns. The boys, in turn, had no wish to squeeze through the throng either, so without hesitation they climbed up to the windows of a taller house and saw the town dignitaries, who were leading the cardinal out, coming through the old town and approaching St Peter's Gate. Because the street boys now believed that the cardinal would follow the town councillors directly, they ran to the convent at top speed to let the nuns know that the cardinal was approaching. The provost with his clergy and scholars led the procession with censers and saints' relics:

> and paused at the inner gate of our cemetery. The abbess with the oldest nuns, then the middle and youngest nuns together with the girls and the lay sisters, set off in processional order so that no one remained in the convent, and everyone left it, even the very old and the sick. Thus we waited for almost a quarter of an hour, with the huge mass of people all around us, until one of our servants shouted from the top of a tower that the cardinal had left by another gate and was already far away. When the provost became aware of this, he immediately urged the abbess that they should withdraw; and he himself moved into our church with his priests. As we followed them, we heard the people clamouring and shouting: 'Oh, what have we seen? Why have they allowed the virgins to go out and endure this shame for nothing?'[14]

A part of the crowd still ran after the cardinal at top speed via a short cut and managed to come close to him and receive his blessing together with those who followed. The diarist notes:

---

13 *ut considerarent diligecius, quando de valva Sancti Petri exiret, quia tunc adhuc competenter possemus exire*, fol. 194v.
14 *Prepositus cum sacerdotibus et scolaribus presedebant nos cum turibilis et sanctorum reliquiis et subsistebant iuxta portam interius cimiterium nostrum, et domina cum senioribus post eos, deinde medio cres et minores, deinde puelle et converse per choros; sicque stantes omnes singule in suo ordine, et nulla ex nostris mansit in claustro, sed omnes eramus extra tam seniores quam infirmi, exspectavimus ferme unam quadrans de hora inspectante nos undique populo, donec unus de familia nostra de cacumine turris clamaret, quia per aliam valvam divertisset, remocius fieret nobis. Quod prepositus intelligens premonuit dominam nostram, ut regrederetur, ipseque cum clero precessit ad ecclesiam nostram, nosque insequentes audivimus populum tumultantem et vociferantem: "O quid vidimus? O quare virgines fecerunt exire et afflictionem incassum ferre?"* (fol. 195r).

But we, when we had returned to the convent, lamented to one another our sorrow at having been enticed and embarrassed, asking ourselves in our hearts whether it might not, perhaps, be attributed to our negligence and carelessness that we now had to forgo the blessing of such a bishop. In the meantime, one of those who had accompanied the cardinal returned and told us that the venerable cardinal, when he had been escorted out of the town, had carefully inquired where the convent of the nuns called St Crucis stood, because he wished to pass by there; and that he had noted with great displeasure and a hard countenance the answer that the convent he sought was not at that town gate but another. Moreover, he had added: 'So that those nuns might not be deprived of the blessing they had hoped for, I shall grant them and all who wished to follow me and could not such indulgences and as great a blessing as those who followed me'.[15]

As a condition of this indulgence he stipulated the praying of a paternoster. Moreover, the Cistercian nuns adds, lest it seem doubtful to those who followed: 'We have heard not only from one person but from several that the cardinal looked very angry and then proclaimed the indulgence and the performance of the prayer that was linked to it'.[16]

As the Cistercian nuns heard later, the town's citizens accompanied the papal legate as far as the outer defences of Braunschweig. Then he sent them back to the town, although they had to be forced to turn back because they were reluctant to leave him. The cardinal then proceeded to Wienhausen, where he was received by Duke Henry of Celle and escorted by him to the nuns, who received him very worthily and honourably and on whom he bestowed a blessing and great benefits.

---

15 *Cum autem nos ad claustrum regresse conquereremus ad invicem, quod ita seducte et confuse fuissemus, dicentes in cordibus, ne forte propter neglienciam vel incuriam subtraxerit nobis benedictionem tanti pontificis. Interea rediit quidam ex hiis, qui post cardinalem abierant, et nunciavit nobis, qualiter reverendissimus dominus cardinalis, cum se extra civitatem pervenisse vidisset, diligencius inquisierit, ubi claustrum virginum, quod sancte crucis dicitur, conditum iaceret, quia ibi perduci cuperet, et cum quanta indignacione suscepisset responsum illius, qui ei intimabat, quod monasterium illud, de quo quereret, non apud illum vallvam, sed ab altera parte civitatis iuxta aliam valvam positum esset, quomodoque torvo vultu circumpiciens indigne hoc ferre ostenderit et quomodo post hoc subiunxerit: "Ne ergo ipse virgines moniales priventur sperata benedictione, dabo eis et aliis, qui me sequi cupiunt et non possunt, tantam indulgenciam et tam largam benedictionem sicut eis, qui me secuti sunt; et qui eis hoc ex parte mea intimaverit, singularem optinebit indulgenciam."* (fol. 196r).

16 *Et ne ambiguum videatur posteris, sciant, quod hoc non solum per unum, sed potsmodum per plures dictum, quod ita torve respexerit cardinalis et quod indulgenciam tantam dederit ac oracionem pro indulgencia consequenda pronunciaverit*, fol. 197v

2. Convents during the Reformation

As the example of the intensive efforts to obtain indulgences from the cardinal demonstrates, it was a matter of considerable importance to both the citizens of Braunschweig and the nuns to participate in the church's blessing of grace. Religiosity had by no means declined in pre-Reformation society, quite the contrary: the church reforms of the fifteenth century had intensified and deepened it.

The Indulgence as a Penitential Practice

What exactly are indulgences? Indulgences are part of the practice of penance, which consists of several steps: first, repentance of the heart (*contritio cordis*) for one's misdeeds; second, explicit confession of sins (*confessio oris*); and third, expiation of the temporal punishment for sin (*poenae satisfactionis*), which would otherwise have to be suffered in purgatory. Together, these three steps make up the sacrament of penance. With indulgences, it is not the sins themselves that are forgiven but the temporal punishments for sin, which remain even if the sin itself has been expunged – and which would otherwise have to be expiated in purgatory. Purgatory was understood as a time of purification of the soul before the last judgement, the time when God would finally sit in judgment on people's souls. In the medieval Catholic understanding, individuals could 'work off' these temporal punishments for sin themselves through prayers, almsgiving or pilgrimages; or they could simply buy themselves free with an indulgence. To this end, money or endowments were given to the church so that it would intercede for the sinner with its treasury of grace, the relics, and obtain for him remission of his punishment for sin, redeeming him from purgatory through the church's infinite treasury of grace. For this act the sinner gave his money to the church, giving rise to the sarcastic quip: 'As soon as money in the coffer rings, the soul from purgatory's fire springs!'

Enclosure disadvantaged the nuns; unlike their relatives in the secular world outside the convent, they could not approach the papal legate directly, but on the other hand it also gave them an exclusive, privileged position. As special mediators between God and the world, as brides of Christ who prayed for the salvation of mankind through their prayers, they enjoyed a high status in medieval society, one which no one could challenge – until the Protestant Reformation called the entire theological basis of monastic life into question. The central point of Lutheran theology was that no man could earn grace for himself, not even through a pious life and good works, a path which monastic life represented *par excellence*. While there had previously been consensus that that the intercession of the saints and also the prayers of nuns helped the soul in purgatory and saved it from torment, the Protestants were certain that not even the intercession of the saints was of any use, since they rejected it as not being anchored in the Bible and constituting a later invention by the church. Through the removal of its mediating function and the focus on the individual grace of Christ, the nuns' prayer was devalued and an important foundation removed from monastic life, which lived from the perpetual intercession for the community of patrons and their families. Martin Luther rejected monastic vows as invalid because, in his opinion, they constituted a bargain with God. Whoever wanted to live poor, obedient, chaste lives could continue to do so, but they no longer involved an obligatory, lifelong commitment to an institution.

Conversely, the features of the Reformation which made it attractive to many lay people – the opening-up of new forms of participation in theological discourse and active involvement in worship – were of only limited value to the women in the convents. They did not need German translations in order to read biblical texts, nor did they need vernacular chorales to join in the singing in church, or explanations of the mass in German. They had long been writing their own Bible-based manuscripts, singing hymns and sequences in their services of worship, and they had acquired sufficient theological competence.

Between Persistence and Renewal

While the monastic reform had intensified the religious life of monks and nuns, filling it with new horizons of meaning, the Protestant Reformation meant a break with the belief in the ability of monastic vows to secure salvation. This was new and by no means uncontroversial. Many communities of nuns therefore bitterly resisted the attempt to introduce Reformation teachings, which deprived them of their accustomed way of life and communities. An anecdote from Kloster Medingen illustrates this controversy. When, in 1524, Duke Ernst of Braunschweig-Lüneburg sent a New Testament in Low German to Kloster Medingen, Abbess Elisabeth Elvers was reputed to have burnt it in the brewery. The eighteenth-century history of the convent by the Protestant minister Johann Ludolf Lyßmann, who provides the only source for this, cites the incident as justification for the duke's order to confiscate the convent property 'when he received news of the blind zeal shown against the Holy Bible'. In the more detailed report, the event appears as an irrational act on the part of the abbess which, in the long run, did not prevent the conversion of the convent but did delay it:

> Thus, through the Reformation begun by *Luther*, the truth that is Protestantism finally began to be revealed in her time, even though the abbess, for her part, remained inimical to it until her last hour [26 May 1524]. The world-renowned Prince *Ernestus Pius* made every effort to introduce the Protestant Reformation in his whole country and hence especially in our convent as well. In 1524, in order to lay the initial foundation for it, he sent here the translation, in Low German, of the New Testament, completed the previous year by the blessed *Luther* and printed in Wittenberg. He did this so that the nuns could read it both for themselves and publicly when at table. However, the mere name *Luther* was enough to make her detest the entire book; therefore, without much hesitation, she took it to the brewery and threw it into the fire that had been built there.

What the Protestant pastor interpreted as an expression of irrational antipathy, the nuns saw as a rejection of the duke's unlawful interference in spiritual matters. The study of Latin texts in particular was an expression of the nuns' conception of themselves and their spiritual role, as had become clear in the measures implemented by the convent reform (Chapter V.2). From the nuns' point of view, the duke clearly exceeded his sphere of competence.

The further development of the conflict in Medingen is typical of the struggle to find a viable solution for convents in territories with Protestant territorial lords. It escalated under the abbess's successor, who took office shortly after the incident in the brewery. With Margaret Stöterogge, who like her predecessor came from the ruling patrician class in Lüneburg, a strong woman took office at the end of 1524 and held it for forty-three years. The fathers of both abbesses, Dietrich Elvers and Hartwig Stöterogge, were, as Lord Mayors, closely connected to the convent and also acted as executors for the provost of Medingen. They made sure that the convent was not disadvantaged vis-à-vis the provost's relatives and they were very familiar with its financial situation. Moreover, Margaret Stöterogge had direct experience of the monastic reforms: she had entered the convent in 1504 when it was still under Margarete Puffen, who, when she died in 1513, was praised in Latin hexameters on her gravestone as the 'renewer' or, literally, 'repairer' of that religious house.[17] Like her predecessor, Margarete Stöterogge had been raised in a convent which offered excellent theological and musical training; and for a while she certainly held the new role of table-reader, which had been created under the reform and always fell to the youngest nun. Accordingly, both abbesses reacted to the duke's continued provocation with a collective response from the convent and also the wider family networks. There was particularly close co-operation with the Benedictine convent of Lüne, situated just outside the town of Lüneburg. We are exceptionally well informed about their handling of the duke's reformatory advances thanks to the rich correspondence from that time. The Medingen abbesses are frequent correspondents, since both Elisabeth Elvers and Margarete Stöterogge wrote to relatives in Kloster Lüne and regularly exchanged views with Mechthild Wilde, who presided over the convent as prioress, on legal issues such as the ownership of benefices or how to proceed with regard to the duke.

The Conflict with the Duke

At the same time as he interfered in the sovereignty of the convent, the duke demanded that Provost Mahrenholz draw up an inventory of the goods belonging to the provostry. This was customary for ecclesiastical authorities in all Protestant states because the sovereign was, after all, also the supreme ecclesiastical ruler in his territory. The convent community naturally saw things differently. Mahrenholz made the list under protest the same year but assured himself of the backing of the entire convent, which in turn acted in consultation with the local bishop of Verden,

---

17 *reparatrix hujus ordinis domus.*

Christoph von Bremen, who was also bishop of Bremen. Above all, however, the nuns were supported by Lüneburg town council, which was largely composed of their closest relatives. Further interventions and encroachments by the duke followed one after the other: in 1529, the provost was removed from office and replaced by a captain who was subordinate only to the duke. This completely abolished the convent's election rights. All priests and scholars were dismissed along with the provost and the nuns were left with only one confessor. When this did not change the nuns' attitude, in 1536 parts of the convent were demolished, the most symbolic being the wall which protected enclosure. This had only been completed under Abbess Elisabeth Elvers in 1518 and concluded the reformation process, replacing an earlier wooden fence as the only demarcation.

The wall stood for the monastic seclusion demanded by the reform as well as for the exclusion of secular influence. Duke Ernst used this symbolic potential to demonstrate his own power. One third of the stones from the demolished walls he used to have the 'Fürstenhaus' built in Medingen as a dowager residence for the duchess; and, within sight of the convent, had his own likeness mounted on the façade as a portrait in the classical style. From the convent's perspective, the duke's actions constituted a counter-reform to their own, monastic reform: his 'deconstruction' of the convent razed to the ground the external sign of this monastic reform, namely, enclosure. With the destruction of the bell tower built by Provost Ulrich von Bülow and the severing of the clappers on the other bells, the outward sign of the praise of God fell silent, the sound which had marked the nuns' feast days and divine services for miles around. Monastic reform had achieved a new strictness in the observance of enclosure and of the rule, but this was now disrupted by the demolition of the nuns' choir. In 1542 the dispute reached a new peak: the duke forbade all contact between the women and Lüneburg with its surroundings and thus their family network. He summoned the abbess to Celle to confiscate the property of the provostry once and for all. This prompted Margaret Stöterogge to seek temporary shelter in Hildesheim as the nearest Catholic territory as a precaution. She took with her the convent's legal titles, the deeds and privileges in the convent archives. Some of the most valued manuscripts from the convent can therefore now be found in the library of Hildesheim Cathedral (see Figure 30).

A Lutheran Preacher as a Challenge

Most grievous was the appointment of a married Lutheran preacher who was a former monk. Accordingly, the nuns, like the Pirckheimer siblings in their correspondence (Chapter IV.1), referred to him as a 'runaway monk' (*ausgeloffen münnich*), someone who, in their eyes, had broken his oath of profession to God and therefore committed perjury. The interpretation of events from the nuns' point of view comes to light in the letters of complaint addressed by them to Bishop Christoph of Bremen. The bishop then obtained a letter of protection from Emperor Charles V, who, in a letter to Duke Ernst of Braunschweig-Lüneburg dated 29 February 1544, took up the nuns' arguments and turned them into a fundamentally anti-Lutheran attack. The confiscation of their liturgical books and devotional texts prevented the nuns from carrying out their reformed services of worship; instead, only 'forbidden, damned new Lutheran doctrine' was preached to them. For them it was, as the imperial letter put it, the 'banishment, prevention and aberration of their traditional Christian nature, extermination, ruin, disadvantage and harm'.[18]

Particularly revealing for the quarrel with the new faith in Kloster Medingen is the letter of complaint about the Lutheran preacher written by the convent to the ducal governors and councillors in Celle on 1 June 1553, only one year before the official adoption of the Lutheran Reformation. In it the pastor is no longer rejected on principle, but simply because of his own personal ineptitude: for three years Preacher Bierwirt had been 'listened to with diligence but, unfortunately, without much edification', since he had preached some useful things, 'yet always much useless stuff mixed in, diabolical, cursed and given over to Satan with body and soul and many more heinous expressions which we do not even wish to mention'.[19] The nuns cite as witness Captain Franz Enghusen, who had been appointed by the duke and taken over the function of provost. He would be in a position to confirm that listening to Bierwirt's sermons was unbearable and that the nuns all refused to

---

18 *verjagung ... Verhinderungen unnd Irrungen, Ires heerprachten Christenlichen Wesens, außreutten, verderben, nachtail, und schaden*, Urkundenbuch Medingen No. 697/8.
19 *doch jummer vele unnutte sage manckt gemenget, vormaledyet, vordomet und dem sathan mit lyve und zele hennegeven und noch vele gruwelicke wordt, de wee thomale nicht mogen anthen.*

receive the sacrament from him: 'We are, therefore, so upset that we can no longer expose ourselves to his sermons. Nor are any of us willing to receive communion from him'.

The abbess suggested to the duke that he appoint in his place Johann Linde from Uelzen, who had promised to distribute holy communion *under one kind, only in the form of bread, and to act as confessor. They had listened to sermons by him on a trial basis and could become used to him if need be, whereas predicant Bierwirt had 'harassed' (*molestert*) them in his sermons as in everything else. The decisive request concerned their own participation in the services of worship: 'But we ask that you continue to let us sing the mass – introit, kyrie, gloria and preface – in Latin. We do not intend to sing all these hymns in German, for we are used to the Latin hymns'.[20] In other words, they were not willing to exchange the solemnity of Latin for German in the liturgical pieces to which they were accustomed.

In this the nuns were successful: on 6 March 1554 the unpopular preacher was replaced by Johann Linde, as requested, and the chants for the mass remained in Latin. The insistence on these passages from the mass remaining in the familiar wording points to the importance of the liturgy in providing a source of identity as part of the women's convent life, a part which had recently been reinforced in the monastic reform of the fifteenth century. The devotional manuscripts written in Kloster Medingen illustrate how the nuns had practised writing new meditations and spiritual exercises based on the texts of the Latin mass. Some of the prayer books dedicated to the veneration of the personal Apostles (whose importance for the nuns was already apparent in the disappointment of the diarist that on 'her' Apostle day the cardinal did not come) demonstrates vividly how the Medingen nuns wrestled with the representatives of the Lutheran Reformation over every nuance of this spiritual heritage. In the manuscript written by a nun whose personal apostles were the Saints Peter and Paul, now in the Victoria & Albert Museum in London, individual words and phrases have systematically been erased; the erasures concern the notion that the deceased saints intercede with God on behalf of those who invoke them. This is visible,

---

20 *bidden averst missam, introitum, kyrieleyßon, gloria in excelsis, prefationem uns in Latino wyllet singen laten; dat wy scholden dudesch singen alße de senge, wo dusse gedan hefft, denke wy nicht tho donde, denne wy der Lattinschen senge gewonth.*

for example, in a prayer written in Latin and addressed to Christ. In the middle of 'grant me the spirit of wisdom and understanding', the words 'through the intercession of St Peter' have been erased after 'me'. In order to be able to continue using the Latin meditations and prayers written in the convent itself, the nuns were apparently prepared to give way on particularly contested areas of the veneration of saints. The erasures correspond to the points attacked by Luther in his treatise on the intercession of the saints published together with the 'Open Letter on Translation' (*Sendbrief vom Dolmetschen*, 1530). They allowed the nuns to continue the practice of a personal relationship with the Apostles as patron saints, a practice which was of particular personal importance to them. Thus, 95% of the devotional text could remain in existence. A similar intervention is shown in the psalter written by the then *cantrix* Margarete Hopes, who had entered the convent at the same time as Elisabeth Elvers. The Latin prayer addressed to her patron apostle John the Evangelist as intercessor and mediator was cut out and replaced by a prayer in Low German addressed to God the Father and invoking Christ as intercessor and high priest. The scribal hand which added this prayer resembles that of the young Margaret Hopes, but is shakier, so it seems plausible that the *cantrix* herself adapted her personal copy of the psalter to the new situation in order to continue singing the Liturgy of the Hours in the familiar format.

Latin Educational and Low German Vernacular Language

In most convents in the late Middle Ages, there was some form of bilingualism: Latin, which was necessary for the liturgy, and alongside it the vernacular. For this reason, scribal activity in Medingen had also taken place over centuries in both Latin and Low German. It was, therefore, not a fundamental rejection of German as a language of piety that was expressed in the vote for the Latin liturgy. Rather, the women defended the latter because, as *lingua sacra*, Latin was the 'language of wisdom', with whose wording and exegetical traditions they were familiar; and because scholarly Latin distinguished the liturgy from forms of devotion in the lay world. It was precisely this difference between the laity and the religious that the Protestants sought and intended to abolish. The letters from Kloster Lüne make it clear that the other convents in the region also insisted on the familiar Latin. In Kloster Lüne this led to a parallel service: while the Lutheran minister appointed by the duke preached in German for the lay congregation from Lüneburg in the convent church below, the nuns continued their customary Latin prayers in their choir. After the dismissal of the clergy, they also conducted the entire mass on their own, each one silently reading the parts that were otherwise spoken by the clergy.

The Nuns Yield Ground – And Stand Fast

How long a convent's resistance to the Protestant reformation lasted and what shape it took depended on the order to which it belonged, on Catholic church structures, the respective convent's legal status and its composition. The family relationships of the nuns were also decisive. The Medingen convent was composed of members of patrician families with excellent relations to the Lüneburg council, whose stance towards the Reformation was sceptical. Like Willibald Pirckheimer from Nuremberg and his sister, the learned Abbess Caritas Pirckheimer, the fathers, brothers and other relatives of the Medingen nuns engaged in a scholarly exchange with their relatives and discussed controversial theological issues with them in their letters. As *master salters of the Lüneburg saltworks, the nuns' relatives administered the wealth from which the convent was financed and had no interest in surrendering these family foundations to the duke without a fight. Once the attitude towards the Reformation of the Lüneburg families eligible to serve on the council changed, things began to happen in the convent.

In Medingen the public acceptance of the *Confession of Augsburg, i.e. Protestantism, was ultimately due to the abbess's correspondence with her brother Nikolaus Stöterogge. He understood what Willibald Pirckheimer had also written (Chapter IV.1): the women wanted to be persuaded and not forced! In a letter from June 1554 Nikolaus Stöterogge skilfully uses the Latin hymns defended by his sister as a means of persuasion and, citing a stanza by Thomas Aquinas which was sung in the convent at Corpus Christi and during Lent, points out that 'communion under both kinds' had already been praised by the ancient church. He also took further action, sending his sister 'for occasional instruction' (*pro informatiuncula*) the pamphlet by which he himself had been converted who had 'also wandered in darkness and blindness in times past', as well as 'a booklet' (*eyn bokeschen*) on the Lord's Supper by Urbanus Rhegius, who was active as a reformer in Lüneburg.

Four years later, Urbanus Rhegius himself wrote an 'Open Letter to the Entire Convent of Virgins of Kloster Wienhausen against the Unchristian Chant *Salve Regina*'. In it he points out that in the fourth century the Council of Laodicea had explicitly forbidden the singing of chants composed by lay people in church as well as the reading of texts other than the Holy Scriptures. He cites two more church councils and concludes that an unlearned person must have written the *Salve Regina*, since it would contravene the Ten Commandments and the gospels if Mary were thus made into a 'goddess'. Even Mary herself would protest against this. His argument is that none of the church fathers, neither Augustine nor Chrysostom, mentions the *Salve Regina* and this misguided development was set in motion by unlearned bishops. In Kloster Medingen as in Kloster Wienhausen, the theological dispute caused the nuns to surrender and signal their acceptance of the Lutheran Reformation. In Medingen they agreed as late as 1554 to accept the chalice at communion. By accepting, the nuns ensured they could continue their spiritual life largely undisturbed and had a say in the appointment of the parish priest and in the continuation of the Latin hours and liturgy of the mass.

Documentary evidence of convent life after 1556 shows that, in both its spiritual substance and the nuns' everyday experience, it mostly continued the customs of the fifteenth-century convent. Even in the late seventeenth century, a statue of Mary was displayed on high feast days; a Latin inscription beneath praised her as the queen of heaven and asked for intercession. It was not until the tenure of Abbess Catharina Priggen, who presided over the convent from 1681 to 1706, that the inscription was replaced by a text from the epistle to the Hebrews in the translation from Luther's bible. The statue of Mary, however, continued to be displayed in the nuns' choir on feast days, and the feasts of Mary and the convent's patron saints continued to be celebrated. Documents from the Early Modern period speaking of 'traditional customs' refer to the status quo which had prevailed since the monastic reform of the fifteenth century, such communal meals, which continued until 1698. The abbess of Medingen still uses the medieval crozier with the Virgin Mary and St Maurice for ceremonial occasions to this day.

For the Lüneburg convents and a further group of foundations in Lower Saxony, it paid off that during the monastic reform they had built up such a close-knit network of allies and cultivated their theological arsenal. Whilst in many other territories converted to Protestantism, all monastic institutions were indiscriminately dissolved, in Lower Saxony a compromise was found in the continued existence of the convents as Protestant institutions. This permitted the preservation, under changed auspices, of a way of life and of educational establishments for women that were considered important. The modern 'General Convention of Abbesses of Protestant Convents and Collegiate Institutions in Lower Saxony' (*Generalkonvent der Äbtissinnen evangelischer Klöster und Stifte in Niedersachsen*) is a very active group, perpetuating these networks into the present and thus 'tending the hearth', to quote the title of a series of publications jointly published by the convents.

3. A Vision of the Reformation

A visual testimony from Kloster Lüne provides a unique illustration of the upheavals but also the continuities of the Reformation period. The vision of Dorothea von Meding was only painted in the early seventeenth century but illustrates events from 1562. At that time, Kloster Lüne had already officially affiliated itself to the Lutheran Reformation, but the old way of life was still present. The painting is titled 'A consolatory picture of the crucified Jesus Christ, which the venerable, noble, most honourable and virtuous virgin Dorothea von Meding, *Domina of Kloster Lüne, along with several other virgins, saw in the clouds on St Philipp's & St James's Day 1562 in the evening after six, just as it is painted here'.

Fig. 32 Vision of Dorothea von Meding 1562, painted around 1623, on the nuns' choir in Kloster Lüne. Photograph: Sabine Wehking ©Kloster Lüne.

Old Believers and Protestant Nuns in the Picture

A group of women can be seen, largely from the back, standing inside the convent wall. All the women wear black robes, which corresponded to the habit of Benedictine nuns, but their headdresses differ. The two women standing closest to the viewer, who therefore appear taller than the others, wear black veils over which the fabric strips of the nun's crown are clearly recognizable. The other women wear white veils, like those which were also worn by bourgeois women of status and formed part of the clothing of the women until the modern era. The different forms of the veil mark the difference between those who had taken their vows before the Reformation, who retained the nun's crown as a sign of their election as brides of Christ, and the women who had entered later and laid aside the visible sign of their eternal vow, but continued to see themselves as a community with a religious purpose, even if they rejected the meritorious character associated with entering the convent. The smaller figure on the left is probably meant to be the young Dorothea, for she lifts her head to look at the cross hovering above the group so as to be in direct eye contact with Christ, who looks down at them. Apart from her, the two Benedictine nuns and at least two other women look upwards, probably the 'several other virgins' mentioned in the caption, while the rest of the group look down, their hands folded in prayer – either their immersion in prayer has caused them to miss the vision in the clouds, or they are already meditating on it.

The Text of the Painting

The vision, which belongs to a long tradition of medieval spiritual visions, tells us a great deal about the self-image of women after the Reformation. The painting was held in high esteem, as demonstrated on the one hand by the reframing of the canvas and on the other by the fact it had been kept in the nuns' choir since at least the eighteenth century. The long, rhymed inscription under its title functions like a speech scroll for Dorothea von Meding: on it she addresses Christ and asks for an explanation of the vision. She surmises that the presentation of Christ's wounds is intended to dispel any last remaining doubts that Lutheran doctrine correctly represents the word of God, whilst the 'cunning' papacy should be overthrown. She refers to redemption through the blood of Christ and his consolation through word and sacrament on earth and in the last judgement:

> Tell me, O my heart Jesus Christ, if it does not harm my soul, why did you show me your holy wound at the evening hour? I think it happened in order that everyone should see clearly, that because God also wished to give Luther's word and speech to this place that you wished to spread the doctrine early and late with wise counsel, and completely overthrow the papacy with its false, cunning doctrine.[21]

The text is written in Early New High German, which in the course of the sixteenth century replaced Middle Low German in official written documents in northern Germany. This was a consequence of both the gradual decline of the Hanseatic League and the proliferation of religious publications in High German as a result of the Reformation, even if the confusion of dative and accusative in the phrase *an deinen Tod Freude finden* (find joy in your death) betrays the influence of spoken Low German. It is remarkable that the contents of this address to Christ, who appears as a 'consolatory image', could have been found word-for-word in the devotional books written in the course of the fifteenth century monastic reform – except, that is, for the anti-Catholic jibe and the mention of Luther. Dorothea von Meding may no longer have been crowned with the nun's crown, but her direct connection to Christ, his 'rose-coloured' blood and, above all, her markedly visual inner devotion are not an innovation of the Lutheran Reformation, but a continuation of the convent education she had received. Conventual women were prepared to encounter Christ in liturgy and devotion: He showed them his wounds as he had shown them to the apostle Thomas; he entered into conversation with them as he had done with Mary Magdalene and with the bride of the Song of Songs; and he presented himself to the trained eyes of the mind in the sacrament. The Revelations of St Bridget of Sweden played a special role in training the women to travel through meditation with 'the eyes of the mind' to the Holy Land. Bridget had

---

21 *Sag mir O mein Herz Jesu Christ/ wenß meiner Seel nicht schedlich ist,/ Worvmb hastu zur abend stund/ gezeiget mir dein heilig Wund / Jch dencke zwar eß ist geschen/ daß iederman solt klerlich sehn,/ Weil Gott LVTHERI wort vnd red/ auch wolte geben dieser stett/ Du wolst die lehre fru vnd spat/ auß breiten weit mit klugen raht/ Daß Pabsthumb aber stürzen gar,/ mit seiner falschen listign lahr.* DI 76, no. 221, urn:nbn:de:0238-di076g013k0022104.

experienced a detailed vision of the birth of Christ when she had made the journey to Bethlehem in 1373. With her account as a spiritual guide, it was possible, as it were, to raise the Christ child out of the manger when the priest elevated the host. In the nuns' choir, they had, since time immemorial, performed liturgical Easter celebrations in which they approached the altar as if it were the tomb of Christ. Hence the clouds of heaven also became legible to them as signs, allowing them to enter into dialogue with Christ. Whether before or after the Reformation, this dialogue remained the common thread in their prayers, which were performed at the traditional times of prayer.

Beneath the surface of the Lutheran polemic against the 'cunning doctrine' of the papacy, text and image thus speak of the continuity of community life, which continues to move in the rhythm of the saints' days, in which 1 May is noted as the feast of St Walpurga and the Apostles James and Philip. Moreover, everyday life is still marked by group rituals such as communal bloodletting (which a chronicle records as having been performed just prior to the vision) and shared religious experiences. Across the generations and confessions, the two nuns with the black veils and the woman with the white veil standing between them on the left have raised their hands in a parallel gesture of adoration and wonder, testifying that the personal dialogue between Dorothea von Meding and the crucified Christ is part of communal experience which has survived the Reformation.

VII. Illness and Dying

Caring for the poor and accompanying the sick and dying were an integral part of monastic life. The very first convents in the Merovingian Empire in the sixth and seventh centuries were founded together with hospitals where the poor, pilgrims and the sick found shelter. In many cases across the centuries, they were run by women. For example, on the well-known St Gall plan from the early ninth century – the ideal conception of a Benedictine monastery that was never built – a sick room is provided for the monks. That convents should be well equipped to care for the sick was also a concern of the monastic reform. Dealing with death and dying was a natural part of everyday convent life. Last but not least, intercession for the dead and the care of family burial sites were one of the nuns' central tasks, if not their most important, for this was often already stipulated in a convent's foundation documents.

The nuns' networks enabled an exchange about methods of treatment as well as participation in the commemoration of the dead through prayer fraternities. There was a difference between the scholarly medicine practised by doctors, who were summoned to the convent in serious cases, and what we might today refer to as naturopathy, natural healing methods, about which a great deal of knowledge was handed down within the convents.

1. Death in the Community

After a Long Illness

For more than twenty years Prioress Remborg Kalm had managed the internal affairs of the Heilig Kreuz Kloster, overseen discipline in the convent, settled disputes or stood in for the abbess when she was ill or away travelling. Then at the beginning of 1506, she discovered a lump in her left breast as big as a small nut (*nobbeke*), located deep in the flesh. When she asked for advice on what to do about it, she was counselled to treat her breast with hot water. She also asked her relatives, who in turn asked several other women what could be done. One of them advised something, the other something else. In the meantime, her condition worsened. Her breast had swollen, turned hot and red and as hard as a stone. Moreover, the prioress became so weak she could hardly walk or stand, but she kept on walking and standing up as best she could. Then everything happened very quickly.

On 6 January, Epiphany, as the diarist relates, she became so mortally ill that she wanted to make confession and take communion, but because of Lent she postponed both until 16 January, when the convent would eat with the abbess. On the eve of this appointment, friends came and suggested a new treatment for her so that she forgot to make confession. That same evening, her health deteriorated rapidly, and death came swiftly and on quick feet. She was barely able to confess her sins. At the eleventh hour, the father confessor came to administer the last rites, made the sign of the cross over her, and she died. The diarist notes: 'We were so terrified and paralysed by fear that we could not read and pray the liturgy of the dying as is fitting for the last rites and the act of dying. We immediately rang the bells and buried the prioress the next day'.[1] Abbess Mechthild of Vechelde, who was also laid low, got up from her sickbed, joined the chapter meeting the following day and redistributed the offices, as was necessary.

---

1 *nec ciuimus legere, que pertinebant ad unxionem nec ad exitum, quia omnes eramus perterriti et timore percussi. Statym compulsavimus et altera die sepelivimus eam*, fol. 224r.

After a Sudden Accident

The convent was responsible not only for the community of nuns, but also for the whole convent *familia*. Accordingly, the Cistercian nun also relates another event in the convent: a year earlier, the scholar Nicholas, who was always on hand to help with all the work, had wanted to help with the building work in the convent when he was knocked to the ground by a falling beam and lay as if dead. Deeply frightened, they poured cold water over the poor man and took him to the convent as quickly as possible so that the lay sisters could come to him and aid his body and his soul. In the meantime, they laid him out like a corpse in the provost's office. The confessor was summoned, for when cold water had been poured over the scholar, he had regained some consciousness and had responded. Yet when the confessor wished to help him and enquire about his sins, he rebuffed him angrily and shouted at him, remembering an argument he had had with the confessor a few days before. A doctor was summoned, and the lay sisters who had rushed to the poor man's aid returned to the convent. The doctor began to wrap the scholar in bandages so that his limbs could heal, but when he returned the next day and saw that the scholar had suffered an epileptic fit and torn and stripped off the bandages, the doctor refused to treat him further. The poor scholar was so hurt and tormented by the terrible pain that all those present were moved to tears of pity and could hardly bear to look at the poor man in his suffering:

> And so there was no one who could bear to remain in his presence except one old woman, who was our prebend. She alone stood by him in everything during this most terrible time of his illness. In the three days after his fall, he grew worse and worse so that we not only feared for his life, but actually hoped for death as his salvation from his misery.[2]

She goes on to write:

> Our Provost Georg Knochenhauer personally took care of the scholar and sang holy mass for him at Whitsun, cheerfully and with a firm voice,

---

2 *nec erat, qui cum ipso perseveraret excepta una sola vetula, que erat prependaria nostra, illa sola sibi fidelissime astitit omni tempore gravissime huius infirmitatis. Ab illo igitur die, quo casus predictus sibi acciderat [...] languor illius in tantum in eo prevaluit, quod non solum de vita illius omnes desperarent, sed eciam mortem ipsius quasi pre tedio miserie eius optarent*, fol. 207v.

when things suddenly took a turn for the better and it seemed as if the scholar had been touched by the right hand of God. From that day on, he began to improve steadily, and the illness left him so completely that many later said he had never really had epileptic seizures, because these did not disappear completely, but always left aftereffects. Some were of the opinion that those seizures, the spasms in the limbs and the banging of the head, were due to the fact that at the very beginning, when he was lying there lifeless, ice-cold water had been poured over him. Then when the provost visited him on the Monday after Pentecost, he was again stricken by the old illness, from which he later died; and in addition, he was struck by blindness, with the result that he could see nothing, not even with his eyes open. When our abbess learned of this, she visited the scholar the same day and admonished him to submit to God's will, to strengthen himself with the holy sacraments and to call for executors to make his will, which he did willingly. On Friday, he made his confession; the priests came with the last rites and communion, followed by the convent. The ailing Nicholas tearfully asked the convent to forgive him all the careless errors he had made as a scholar. The provost and the priests alternated with the convent in singing the funeral hymns, the litany and the collects at the scholar's bedside. When the convent withdrew, the abbess stayed with him and talked to him about a variety of things that could be of use to the community, but alas, he brought none of these more useful things that he had framed in his mind to fulfilment, after his memory and reason failed together.[3]

---

3   *Prepositus noster Georgius eo tempore adhuc aliquantulum valuit et vices suas personaliter per se ipsum implebat et in die sancto Pentekosten celebrando summam missam hilarior et forcior in cantu et ceteris agentis, quasi per omnia convaluisset, videbatur, sed protinus affuit mutacio dextere dei. Scolaris sepefatus ab illo die cepit habere melius et languor eius ita perfecte deseruit eum, quod plurimi dicerent eum caduco morbo numquam fuisse gravatum, quia ille non posset hominem tam perfecte deserere, quin aliquod signum in eo remaneret; et dicebant quedam, quod omnis illa afflictio et concussio membrorum et agitacio capitis accidisset ei ex hoc, quod in principio, quando iacuit exanimis, aqua frigida perfusus fuisset. Igitur feria II^a in Penthekosten media nocte visitavit pius dominus prepositum et tetigit eum infirmitate, qua prius eum tetigerat, qua et posmodum mortuus est; percussit insuper eum cecitate, ita ut apertis oculis nichil videret. Quod cum domina nostra intellexisset, visitavit die eadem et premonuit, ut conformaret se divine voluntati et faceret se muniri ecclesiasticis sacramentis disponeretque prepositure eligendo testamentarios et ponendo testamentum, cui per omnia libens obtempperabat sicque fecit. Feria 5^a eiusdem septimane mane, cum fecisset suam confessionem, omnes sacerdotes cum unctione conventu sequente portabant unxionem et corpus dominicum, rogabat totum conventum cum lacrimis ei ignoscere negliencias suas circa suum officium. Post percepcionem sacramenti et unctione peracta legebant septenas alternatym cum conventu, post letanias et adiuctas collectas redibant ad ecclesiam et, cum conventus recederet, mansit ibi domina abbatissa, tractare cepit de hiis, que communitati expedire videri potuissent; sed, proch dolor, nichil horum, que aliquando utiliora in animo conceperat, memoria simul et racione deficiente ad effectum perduxit,* fol. 208r.

That is why, to their distress, the community of nuns with whom he had lived was not included in his will.

The sick boy was now given a widow as a companion, who assisted him day and night and made sure that he wanted for nothing. She stayed by his side until his death, but when he had died, she refused to leave his room until she had received adequate remuneration. A doctor was also called again. He could do nothing but was nevertheless paid after the scholar's death. The diarist observes:

> Our provost Georg Knochenhauer counted amongst his scholars and priests some very rich and influential men who had been relatives of the scholar Nicholas so that he would have become a priest and in the course of time could have taken over the parish of St Michael and then our provostry, which is why they were always happy to oblige him. They visited him frequently when he was still healthy and then when he fell ill and stood by him in word and deed. Now, when he was ill, the scholar chose these men as his executors and made his will according to their will. Without the knowledge and consent of the abbess and our convent, he bequeathed and promised many things to them and to others, all of which they would demand and receive from us after his death, down to the very last farthing.[4]

Medicine has made enormous progress in modern society, especially during the last 200 years, with the result that today, dying and death have been pushed into the background. Previously, death had been an integral part of everyday life. The nuns had generations of experience in dealing with illness and the death of individuals. Convents had developed rituals of mourning and dying that closely involved the living in the process of dying. It was hoped that death could be overcome by means of common commemoration, creating a community of the quick and the dead. People did not die alone; this explains why there was always someone keeping watch at the scholar's bedside, while

---

4   *Habebat namque predictus prepositus quosdam familia sibi divites et potentes viros, quorum parentes sibi fuerant, ut ad gradum sacerdocii pervenisset et processu temporis ad porrochiam Sancti Michaelis, deinde ad preposituram nostram promotus fuisset, quapropter libenter eorum voluntatem morem gerebat. Ipsi eciam eum adhuc sanum et iam infirnum frequenter visitabant, concilium et auxilium, ut aliqui dicere consueverunt, afferebant. Hos ergo in sua infirmitate testamentarios elegit et ad voluntatem eorum testamentum suum fecit. Absque scitu et conscensu domine nostre et conventu fecit, multa illis et aliis donando in rebus et precio promisit et in testamenta scrlbi fecit, que omnia post mortem a nobis usque ad ultimum quadrantem exigerunt et receperunt*, fol. 210r.

all the others sang funeral hymns, litanies and so forth. In this way, it becomes clear how holding fast to life (administering medicine) and letting go (administering the Last Sacraments) went hand-in-hand. It was well known that death was not in human hands. The nuns had an exceptionally developed understanding of the art of consolation. The collection of letters from Lüne contains hundreds of letters of consolation on the death of loved ones; and the replies sometimes show that they did not fail to have an effect. This was not contradicted by the concomitant wish for the convent to be acknowledged financially after the death of the person concerned. There were also situations in which such ritual accompaniment was no longer possible, such as epidemics and pandemics, and especially the plague that repeatedly raged through Europe.

The Plague Comes to Braunschweig

During outbreaks of epidemics and plagues, communities were particularly vulnerable since people lived together in confined spaces, whether in a convent or in a city. Ignorance of the pathogens that caused the Black Death, which had become endemic in Europe after the great outbreak of 1346, but also of the causes of other contagious diseases, meant that people were almost helpless in the face of this deadly phenomenon. While the prosperous citizens in the cities could flee to the countryside and save themselves from the recurrent onslaught of the plague, a community of nuns living in isolation stood barely a chance when an epidemic hit them.

The first years of the sixteenth century were thus a difficult time for the community in the Heilig Kreuz Kloster: at the beginning of 1507, canine parvovirus broke out and their best dogs fell ill. The nuns wrote prayers such as 'The word became flesh' or 'Thou preservest man and beast', as well as other prayers, on slips of paper. The lay sisters gave these slips of paper to the dogs to eat with bread and butter – whereupon, so legend has it, the epidemic actually subsided.[5] In spring 1507, the diarist jotted

---

5   *Anno domini M° CCCCC° VII° in Carnisprivio habuimus novam plagam, quia optimi cani fiebant insani. Tunc scripsimus versus 'Verbum caro'* (John 1:14) *cetera, 'Homines et iumenta'* (Psalm 35:7) *et cetera; hoc dederunt eis converse cum pane et buttiro, et cessavit plaga*, fol. 235v.

down her last lines on the parchment of her former prayer book; at the same time, the plague began to rage through the town of Braunschweig. Since the first great waves of the plague, the disease had broken out time and again at longer or shorter intervals, especially in the cities. Personal testimonies concerning the outbreak of the plague, especially in monasteries and convents, are very rare. The diarist obviously did not have much time left either:

> Several girls, and male and female servants died of it; very many fell ill, some of whom recovered. At this time the *suffragan of the bishop of Hildesheim consecrated the cemetery of St Martin's in the town, so our abbess had sent him the cross above the chapel by the choir with which to consecrate it. He granted a major indulgence to the cross and, out of affection, visited us personally, doubling our indulgence by both his own and the bishop's authority and granting absolution and blessing to the convent in the nuns' choir. At this time our procurators, Gerd Hollen and Cord Broysem, were removed from office without the knowledge and consent of the provost and our abbess, and we were given two new ones, namely Werner Lafferdes and Cord Breyer, both of whom died of the plague a few weeks later.[6]

It would be interesting to know what happened next. The diary of the Cistercian nun of the Heilig Kreuz Kloster breaks off abruptly in midsentence. Her last words are:

> At Whitsun in 1507, our baker died of the plague. A few days later, Elisabeth Kalm fell so badly ill with the plague that she made confession that very evening. The next day, she took communion, received the last rites and died the same evening, on the eve of Corpus Christi, before vespers. After vespers, she was carried into the church, and the next morning we buried her at the fifth hour.[7]

---

6 *puelle, servi et ancille multi obierunt, et plurimi infirmaverunt; aliqui convaluerunt. Eodem tempore dominus suffraganeus consecravit cimiterium Sancti Martini, quod domina nostra misit I crucem consecrare super capellam apud chorum, ad quam dedit multam indulgenciam. Et ipse personaliter visitavit locum nostrum pre dilexionem et duplicavit omnem nostram indulgenciam de sua et episcopo potestate et absolvit conventum in choro et benedixit simpliciter, quantum potuit, et recessit. Item ipso tempore deposuerunt nostri procuratores asque scitu et consensu prepositi et domine nostre viros Gerden Hollen et alter Coer Broysem, qua de causa ignoravimus, et posuerunt nobis Werneken Lafferdes et Coer Breyger, et circa festum Iohannis Baptiste obierunt ambe in pestilencia*, fol. 236v.

7 *Item in festo Pentekosten obiit pistor noster feria quarta in pestilencia. Item feria Va fiebat infirma Elisabeth Kalm in pestilencia ita fortiter, quod ipso sero confit. Altera die communicavit et fiebat inuncta et obiit in vigilia Corporis ante vesperas. Et post vesperas*

A little later, Katharina Kampe fell ill with the plague; she was sixteen years old and had already been crowned a nun.

> In the evening, she fell into such a deep sleep that we were unable to wake her. Three days later, she woke again, opened her eyes and made a sign that she was thirsty, but she was barely in her right senses and was not able to speak much. The confessor entered alone, elicited her confession, made a sign of penance, and gave her the final blessing. She could hardly drink and died the following Saturday during the night. Then our under-baker John and the scholar Hermann died in the night...[8]

Then the diarist fell ill and died. Only she was no longer able to inform us of it.

Fig. 33 End of the diary, HAB Wolfenbüttel, Cod. 1159 Novi, fol. 238r. Photograph: Henrike Lähnemann ©HAB Wolfenbüttel.

---

portatur in ecclesia, in mane ad horam quintam sepelivimus eam, fol. 237r.

8 *ipso sero cecidit in sompnum sic graviter, quod nequivimus eam excitare. Feria tercia revixit a sompno, aperuit oculos et requisivit per signum bibere, sed modicum erat racionalis, quod vix potuit loqui. Confessor intravit solus ad eam et requisivit confessionem et signum penitencie, post hec benedixit; potuit sumere potum, obiit sabbato in nocte hora quasi; obierunt Iohannis subpistor noster. Item scolar Hermanus in nocte...*, fol. 237v.

2. Medicinal Knowledge and the Rituals of Dying

As we have seen from the medical and spiritual care given to the prioress with cancer and the scholar who died in an accident, illness and death challenged nuns in two ways: the practical treatment of the illness and the spiritual accompaniment of the sufferer. Both required specialized training. While only the doctors who were called to the convents in serious cases had academic medical knowledge, some knowledge of the arts of healing formed part of the syllabus taught in convent schools and of the established knowledge in the convents. This knowledge is evident in the countless collections in their libraries which deal with medicine and recipes for medication, containing short Latin treatises on topics such as the examination of urine, information on the symptoms of the plague or pharmacopoeias. This knowledge was then put to use by the convent infirmary, where the infirmarian was responsible for prevention, medication, and nutrition for the sick, who were cared for with the help of the lay sisters.

The Doctrine of the Four Humours in Application

Treatment in the convent predominantly followed the *doctrine of the four humours and its diagnosis of people's temperaments. The appearance and behaviour of a person indicated the dominance of a certain 'humour' – namely, whether there was an excess of blood, phlegm, yellow or black bile. Sanguine people, for example, had too much blood and were characterized by dry heat, i.e. they were 'hot-blooded'; melancholic people, on the other hand, had too much cool, moist black bile, leading to depression. It was, therefore, necessary to analyse the patients' respective symptoms in terms of their dampness and warmth in order to ascertain which herb could be used in their cure. For stomach aches, for example, the Low German 'Storehouse of Medical Knowledge' (*Promptuarium Medicine*), printed by Bartholomäus Ghotan in Lübeck in 1483 and copied in Kloster Wienhausen in the fifteenth century, recommended administering nutmeg, galangal, sweet flag, cloves, or ginger. True galangal, a plant related to ginger, contains pungent essential oils which can have a digestive, anti-spasmodic, anti-bacterial and anti-inflammatory effect and was therefore counted among the 'dry-hot' spices, just like cloves or normal ginger. Accordingly, it was, and still is, used in both Asian and medieval medicine to treat 'damp-cold' complaints such as stomach aches. Conversely, damp-cold elderberry water is meant to be good against any kind of heat in the human body.

An astonishing variety of ingredients can be found in the prescriptions and instructions for preparing medicines. Some of their applications for everyday ailments live on as home remedies, whether it be a simple salt solution or spices, some of which are still grown in the herb beds of convents today. One formula, for example, names violet leaves, maidenhair fern, hart's tongue fern, and oregano, ingredients that are still made into cough syrup today. Another combines field, forest and meadow herbs with other ingredients and calls for mallow, two *lots of finely chopped marshmallow, two lots of finely chopped liquorice, two lots of finely chopped male fern, eighteen finely chopped figs, one lot of mallow seeds, a small handful of winter barley, two quarts of water, and one lot of raisins. The more precious ingredients such as figs, nutmeg, and ginger, which had to be imported, were sometimes baked in order to preserve them for longer and be able to ship them. The whole life of the convent was determined by a rhythm of fasting and feasting which was set by the church year, as is also shown by the specifications of food for Lent from Kloster Wienhausen (Chapter V.2). The boundary between dietetics and medicine was fluid; and the letters from the convents frequently mention spiced baked goods, for example in the form of gingerbread (*Lebkuchen*), as New Year greetings, or other *pastries baked in special shapes as gifts. Nonetheless, a medical manuscript from the Dominican convent of Lemgo, written in 1350, around the time of the Black Death, informs its readers in rhymed hexameters: 'Know this: against love no medicinal herb can be grown'.[9]

The medicine books or prescription slips, like those preserved in the find from the nuns' choir in Wienhausen, albeit often in fragmentary condition, give instructions for the preparation of remedies. The following is typical: 'Strain this through a linen cloth until it is pure. Then put the purified liquid back on the fire and add two egg whites.

---

9   *Scito quod nullis amor est medicabilis herbis,* Staatsarchiv Detmold, L 110, no. 19, fol. 22v.

Let it all come to the boil again so that it produces a great deal of foam'. The subsequent use of the remedy is also specified: 'Those who suffer from a dislocated lower jaw should finely crush cinnamon and put it in a small bag. Boil the sachet in sweet milk and then place it on the lower jaw'.[10] For headaches 'one should finely crush juniper berries and hemp and then add two egg whites. Boil this mixture together with wine and bind it on the head and forehead of the sufferer'. Calendula, spearmint (sweeter than peppermint), lavender and common liverwort are said to help against consumption: 'These four medicinal herbs should be put into fresh beer and left to ferment in it'.[11] Another recipe instructs us: 'Take chamomile, honey, rosehip, wood sanicle, and agrimony. This is to be boiled up in old beer mixed with bean stalks that have been burnt to ashes and then this beer is to be strained. Then add red ointment to the beer and drink it with your lunch'.[12] To improve one's memory, wine should be poured onto finely chopped parsley and then this mixture should be drunk.

While some of the herbal remedies were indeed calming, anti-inflammatory, or possessed other healing properties, even in cases when a pharmacological effect was doubtful, the awareness of having been looked after and given medical treatment in the convent helped just as much – or at least as much as placebos work in modern medicine. The medieval concept of illness assumed that the soul could make the body sick and, similarly, healthy. In this sense, nursing was always as much about caring for the soul as about caring for the body, an approach that today seems really indeed modern. Of course, a modicum of miraculous healing was also part of the mix. For example, another Wienhausen

---

10 *Sigget dat denne reyne dorch eyn lynen dok, dar na settet dat so reyne gesegen wedder by dat vur unde slat daryn dat wytte van twen eyggeren unde sedet dat to hope wedder upp, so wert dat eyn groff schume denne so sigget dat ouer. Item we de heft enen kunnerbeken in loca, de schal stoten simynum vnde don in enen budelken, unde seden in suter melk, unde legghen darup...*, Kloster Wienhausen, Hs 116_7.

11 *Item to der swinden suke: hintlope, cruseminten, lafundel, lunghenkrut; dusse veryleye schal me legghen in varsk bery vnde laten dar mede geren*, Kloster Wienhausen, Hs 116_7.

12 *steynblomen, honrig, haghen, seneckel, borwort, dat schalme tho seden in oldem bere unde born aschen van bonenstro, unde dut beyr dar dore le[...]en, so don in dat ber rode saluen vnde drink dat to deme brot*, Kloster Wienhausen, Hs 116_7. The name *seneckel* derived from Latin *sanare*, meaning 'to heal', because it was considered a cure for 'hot' wounds and a universal panacea and as such also appears in the manuscripts of the *Physica* attributed to Hildegard of Bingen.

prescription, one for stopping nosebleeds, states that the sign of the cross was to be made over the nostrils and the following incantation recited: 'Through the mediation of Mary, hell is closed, the gates of heaven are opened'. Then the prologue of the Gospel according to St John was recited, from 'In the beginning was the word' to 'and without him was not anything made that was made'; this was considered the most effective incantation of all. That the help from the saints invoked in prayers also extended to animals is demonstrated by the use of the verse 'The word became flesh' from the prologue of St John's gospel when dealing with the sick dogs in the Heilig Kreuz Kloster. The scribe adds: 'If you wish, you may substitute the missing name of the sick person in: "Lord be nearer to your servant / maid N"'. Then the carer was to make another sign of the cross and 'say: from her nostrils let not a drop of blood come forth. Thus may it please the Son of God and the holy mother of God, Mary. In the name of the Father, let the blood cease, in the name of the Son'.

Plasters and ointments were made for the sick room. For example, we know from the Lüne letter books that there was a lively exchange about the preparation of a lavender ointment supposed to help against the chest complaints of an old nun. Amongst the Wienhausen fragments is the formula for an ointment that contained a mixture of herbs made both spreadable and preservable by lard: 'As long as the poppy is in flower, add poppies, henbane, violet leaves, caper spurge, blackberry leaves, mandrake leaves, black nightshade, houseleek, greater burdock and common houseleek. These medicinal herbs should all be crushed beforehand and then boiled with the lard until everything has turned green. Then strain everything through a cloth. Put everything in a tin. This is black poplar ointment'.

Spiritual Care

If none of this helped, it was the task of the community to ensure that a dying member of the convent received last rites from the provost and an opportunity for confession and penance. The convent was at all times a community of both the living and the dead. The rituals which accompanied dying and death were one of the few occasions on which the door to enclosure was opened. This was true both for the nuns who, when the provost died, took in his body and for the provost, who sought out dying nuns and then buried them in the cemetery within the cloister. The convent was present at extreme unction as well as at the funeral ceremony itself and returned to the church together with the provost. Back in the church after the procession from the interment in the cloister courtyard, in some convents known as 'paradise', the nuns sang in answer to the responsory sung by the provost. It was also the provost who, in front of the altar in the church, sang 'In the midst of life we are in death' (*Media vita in morte sumus*) as the final chant. A Medingen nun's account of the death of the provost Tilemann notes a range of sequences and rituals performed by the nuns, some of them analogous to the rites for a deceased sister. Throughout the whole of the Tilemann's illness, readings, prayers and chanting took place at his bedside, in the cloisters and in the nuns' choir.

Of Vigil, Mass and Burial

The psalms were read individually and collectively by the nuns at the vigil for Tilemann; the prioress arranged matters so that people alternated in groups of ten at a time and then went back to the nuns' choir for the choir service, as the report says: 'In the convent one psalter was read with the nuns taking turns. It was arranged so that some people remained during vespers and some went to the choir so that everyone might go to the sick chamber once. Our abbess saw to it that after the meal ten or more people read the psalter there; after compline they went in again and others came; whoever wished to stayed there throughout the night; and so it was properly and fittingly arranged that it would not be too onerous for any one person'.[13]

For the reception of the body the nuns sang in the provostry the responsory 'Deliver me Lord' with the accompanying verse from 'Day of wrath' (*Dies irae*), the hymn about the last judgement. The convent

---

13   *in dem Clostere laß men enen Psalter sub choro, Chorus contra chorum, vnd dat wart so ordineret, dat etlike Personen vnder Vesper dar bleuen, vnde welke to Chore ghingen, des jelik schüde ok vp der kemnade. Vnse Dompna vorbade post cenam x vel vltra Personen de lesen dar den Psalter post completorium gingen se wedder in, vnd quemen andere, wede wolde, de blef de Nacht auer dar, Süs wart dat schikkelken, vnd matelken ordineret dat dat deme ene nicht to vele worde*, Landesbibliothek Hannover, Sign.: MS XXIII, Nr. 975, fol. 80v.

then moved into the church with the corpse carried by the clergy, and from there to the nuns' choir, where a rich liturgy unfolded: 'When he had been taken into the church, they sang "May the angels lead you into paradise". This was followed immediately by the convent singing the requiem mass. After the mass we held a meeting of the chapter, then sang the mass "I am risen".' During these three masses the convent sang 'sacred sequences'.[14]

Women and clergy then took turns during the vigil. The abbess personally supervised the lay sisters, who were in the church during the day, while the deputy provost was supposed to stand watch at night. He fell asleep during this task – something which led the nun writing the account to compare him to the guards sleeping at Christ's tomb, before she added by way of an excuse that it was probably due to his old age. On Monday the commemoration of the dead man continued. At all three masses the nuns singing in their choir must have been clearly audible to the assembled congregation of secular visitors in the part of the church reserved for the parish. The account emphasizes that at the funeral itself the nuns held their own customary memorial service but entrusted the performance of the funeral service, in accordance with Tilemann von Bavenstedt's rank, to Abbot Johannes of the Benedictine monastery of Oldenstadt as the celebrant and to other high-ranking visitors. From their point of view, however, its performance left much to be desired, since the visitors did not observe the established customs for the interment of a provost:

> On Monday, he was buried. Therefore in the morning the whole convent wore white robes because of the funeral. We stood in the choir, read during the procession out of the church and sang 'Maker of all things' and 'Deliver me'. However, we relied on the many people present who had more experience of burying lords and prelates than we did. For that reason, we gave no instructions regarding how they should hold the service as befits a prelate, but unfortunately the Abbot of Oldenstadt buried him in accordance with his own order and did not say the formula of abjuration, nor did he place a chalice on his body as is the custom,

---

14 *Also ene in de kerken brocht hadden, sungen see In paradysum perducant te angeli* (Cantus 003266). *Statim post hec Conuentus cantauit Missam Requiem. Post Missam tenuimus Capitulum, deinde sacram Missam: Resurrexi. Summa Missa fuit Jubilate, et Conuentus cantavit. Vnder dessen dren Missen sacra cantavit*, Landesbibliothek Hannover, Sign.: MS XXIII, Nr. 975, fol. 81r.

nor did he sing 'I receive the chalice of salvation' three times. May God forgive him.[15]

3. This World and the Next in the Wienhausen Nuns' Choir

Bloodletting as Prevention

One particularly important area, which fell into the realm of prophylaxis as well as healing, was bloodletting. This was regularly carried out for the entire convent, even in the sixteenth century, as is clear from the account of the vision of Dorothea von Meding (Chapter V.3): the vision is said to have occurred after the women had just been gathered in the calefactory for bleeding. The fact that the procedure was carried out in the only heated communal room was intended to prevent attacks of weakness after the blood had been taken. On the monastery plan of St Gall, the warming house is located next to the dormitory for the sick, the bloodletting house, the bath house for the sick and a separate kitchen for the sick and those who had been bled. Their sojourn in the calefactory was certainly also one reason why the nuns positively looked forward to the dates for their bloodletting, which came round two or three times a year. Bloodletting was closely linked to the calendar, to a complex set of rules specifying 'good' and 'evil' days. Each sign of the zodiac was allotted to a particular part of the body, which was good to cup at that time. In the prayer book of Abbess Odilie von Ahlden of Mariensee, for example, a section has been inserted at the end of the prayers with the remark that the best time for bloodletting is from mid-April to mid-June, because 'the blood then grows and increases'. A depiction of how bloodletting was conducted in the convent can be found on one of the arches in the nuns' choir in Wienhausen (Figure 35).

---

15 *En Mandage wart he grauen, vnd totus Conuentus hadde den Morgen auer wyt ane propter sepulturam. Men we deden dar nicht sunderkes to, sunder we stunden sub coro vnd lesen 'In Exitu' vnd sungen 'Creator omnium', vnd 'Libera'. Men we verleten vns to deme vele volke dat dar was, dede mer myt Heren vnd Prelaten bygraf vmme gan hadden wan we. So bode we nenerleye aff wo se dat scolden holden sicut decet Prelatum, men leyder Abbas Van der Oldenstad grof ene secundum ordinem suum, nicht omnino renunciauit, eciam non posuit calicem super corpus, sicut mos est, et non cantans. calicem tribus vicibus. Dominus ei ignoscat*, Landesbibliothek Hannover, Sign.: MS XXIII, Nr. 975, fol. 80r–81v.

A Colourful Array of Pictures

For 1488, the Wienhausen Chronicle mentions the renewal of the wall painting in the nuns' choir, dating from the early fourteenth century, 'by three sisters called Gertrud'. The nub of the entry clearly lies in the similarity of the names, whereas it was obviously not at all surprising that women were active as church painters. The nuns' choir in Wienhausen displays one of the richest and most sophisticated iconographic programmes in medieval architecture to have survived in its entirety. The images cover the ceiling and walls of the choir, which has the dimensions of a sizeable church. Starting with Adam and Eve, biblical events are depicted on the walls in two strips which run all round the choir from the south- to the west- to the north-wall. The strip above these shows scenes from the legends of the saints. On the vaulting, divided into various fields intersected by the ribs, the most important stations in Jesus's life are depicted.

Fig. 34 Wienhausen nuns' choir. Photograph: Ulrich Loeper ©Kloster Wienhausen.

Certainly, this richly coloured array of pictures – for example, the Red Sea into which Pharaoh sinks in his pursuit of the Israelites is actually shot through with red waves – not only provided a welcoming viewing material for the girls who, sitting on a low bench in front of the nuns, took part in divine office at certain times, but also functioned as a theological commentary on the nuns' singing and praying. This is reinforced by the interplay of the images with the other furnishings, such as the Holy Sepulchre which must have been in a place such as a chapel accessible to the nuns; and in the placement of the individual pictorial themes next to and above one another and in relation to the architecture of the chapel. The nuns sat in the choir stalls, which were divided according to the two choirs (cf. Chapter V.2). The space, protected by stained-glass windows and well lit, was used not only for divine office but also for needlework and other convent activities. This becomes clear from the variety of objects found underneath the floorboards, which have already been mentioned several times as evidence of everyday culture in the convents. There were small weaving discs, fabric remnants, strips of embroidered cloth, appliqué work, stencils, figurines, a variety of small and very small written texts such as recipes, invoices, devotional sheets, bookmarks, and duty rotas; as well as material evidence of education, above all the oldest preserved spectacles in the world, pointer sticks, small wax tablets, and writing pens. For the nuns, the choir was a space for both working and devotion.

On the east side, it allowed access to the east choir of the parish church, meaning there was no space for paintings there. Instead, the vaulted arch between the nuns' choir and the parish space is decorated with its own cycle of paintings combining spiritual and secular interests, namely, the depiction of characteristic activities for the twelve months of the year, known as the 'monthly works'. Bloodletting is pictured in the first circular painting on the south side of the arch above a depiction of Luna as a woman with a moon.

A woman hands a white bandage to a seated man after she has cupped him – he still holds the bowl in his right hand in which the blood was collected. The event is not depicted as a convent act: both persons are dressed in secular clothes. Yet the nuns, as the accounts from the convents show, were very familiar with the procedure.

Fig. 35 Bloodletting among the pictures representing each month in the Wienhausen nuns' choir. Photograph: Ulrich Loeper ©Kloster Wienhausen.

Between the Transcendent and the Temporal

The depictions of the months formed the appropriate interface between the nuns' choir and the parish church. Here the sequence of the calendar with its practical activities met the transcendence of temporal order as represented in the nuns' choir. The nuns were part of both worlds: that of the history of salvation, its structure transcending time, in which they already participated as brides of Christ; and the seasonally recurrent structure of sowing and harvesting, pruning and healing. This is particularly clear in the picture that can still be found today above the door in the north-east corner of the nuns' choir, through which the nuns left the sacred space again after divine office.

In the transverse rectangular field, two six-winged cherubs on the left and right stand sentinel over an architectural ensemble which looks as if it were projected onto a wall fortified by crenelations. A blank speech scroll hovers above the gables. The group of buildings displays a characteristic profile: above the lower buildings at the front rises a storehouse with numerous door and window hatches in the triangular stepped gable. It boasts a small, round staircase tower and stands at right angles to another building complex marked by a ridge turret as a church building. The tracts of high Gothic windows in the upper section indicate that this is a more modern building than the lower part with the round windows which adjoins it on the right. This description also accurately reflects the view of Kloster Wienhausen from the south today, right down to the relationship between the Gothic nuns' choir, which towers over everything else, sits above the parish church and rises far above the older east section.

Fig. 36 Wall painting in the Wienhausen nuns' choir. Photograph: Wolfgang Brandis ©Kloster Wienhausen.

Fig. 37 View of Wienhausen from the south. Photograph: Wolfgang Brandis ©Kloster Wienhausen.

The painting from the 1330s is thus not only the oldest depiction of Wienhausen, but above all a multilayered and highly symbolic interpretation of the meaning and purpose of convent life. When they were in the nuns' choir with its tracts of high Gothic windows, the nuns saw themselves already absorbed into the future joy of heavenly Jerusalem, which had been promised to them when they were crowned as nuns. Convent life is shut off from the world by the enclosure walls, but open towards heaven.

The nuns knew full well that illness and death formed an inseparable part of life because they constantly reflected on them in meditation and in song. Unlike in modern society, illness and death were not pushed to the margins: dealing and coping with death and grief were a communal task to which nuns devoted a great deal of their energy. Communal singing played a decisive role in this, connecting them with both the living and the dead in their invocation in the liturgy of the divine sphere and the closeness to Christ. In this spiritual understanding, knowledge of the connection between life and death opened up deeper aspects of what it is to be human, which – as not least the Lüne letters reveal – were experienced as very comforting, with the result that many lay people sought proximity to the nuns and their community. In this respect, the nuns constituted an entirely independent force and strong voice within medieval society. Even though history has often overwritten or erased their cloistered lives and we barely seem to hear their voices today, in their own time they were by no means invisible or inaudible; and when they had to defend their own cause they could also become outrageously obstreperous. By their heavenly bridegroom Christ – of this they were firmly convinced – they were heard and exalted.

VIII. Appendix

1. Convent Histories

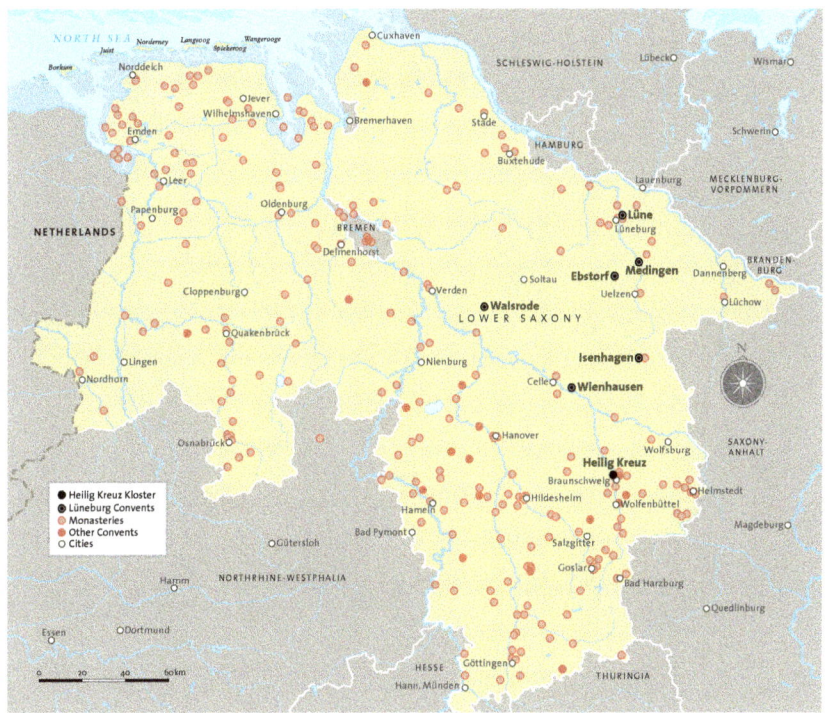

Fig. 38 Map of the Convents in Lower Saxony. ©Peter Palm.

1.1 Heilig Kreuz Kloster near Braunschweig

The Heilig Kreuz Kloster near Braunschweig is a Cistercian convent founded around 1230, presumably as an act of atonement after a feud between the Guelph nobility and the town of Braunschweig. It was located outside the gates of the town on the Rennelberg, the nobility's former tournament ground. Until 1532 the convent existed as a Roman Catholic community which followed the rules of the Cistercian Order, but was not incorporated into the Order; then the first Lutheran abbess was appointed under pressure from Braunschweig Council. The nuns' main tasks were the care of the sick and the girls' school established in the convent. After 700 years the buildings of the Heilig Kreuz Kloster were completely destroyed during a heavy bombing raid on Braunschweig in 1944; only a small portion of the early modern convent cemetery was spared.

1.2 Lüneburg Convents

The six convents of Kloster Ebstorf, Kloster Isenhagen, Kloster Lüne, Kloster Medingen, Kloster Walsrode and Kloster Wienhausen are located in the territory of the former Principality of Braunschweig-Lüneburg. They share the same fate: they underwent monastic reform in the late fifteenth century; continued as women's religious communities after the Lutheran Reformation. Together with the former women's foundations and convents of the Duchy of Calenberg, but in contrast with them still as independent institutions under public law, they now belong to the administrative province of the Klosterkammer Hannover, the state institution responsible for looking after former monastic estates, buildings and communities.

Kloster Ebstorf is a former Benedictine convent near Uelzen. The Gothic complex, almost completely preserved with its cloister (Figure 1), stained-glass windows, keystones (Figures 21 and 25), the chests on display in the corridors there and the layout of the convent church, still conveys a good impression of medieval convent culture. The extensive library, which has been preserved, is an important source for the history of education (Figures 27 and 28; Chapter II.2), as is the Ebstorf World Map (Figures 8 and 9; Chapter I.3). Its works of art also include *horti conclusi* (Gardens of Paradise), which contain fragments of saints' relics and were made by the nuns, as well as a larger-than-life statue of St Maurice.

Kloster Lüne is a former Benedictine convent in Lüneburg, which celebrated its 850th anniversary in 2022. The three books of letters from the convent (*see* Sources and Literature) provide information about the nuns' networks in the late Middle Ages, as does the depiction of the convent in the painting of Dorothea von Meding's vision (Figure 32). The late-medieval dormitory with the wing containing the nuns' cells has been impressively well preserved here. The convent is now also known for its tapestry museum, exhibiting examples of whitework embroidery and large-scale pieces from the reform period in the late-fifteenth and early-sixteenth centuries (Figure 15). The museum also houses the textile restoration department of the Klosterkammer Hannover.

Kloster Medingen is a former Cistercian convent near Bad Bevensen dedicated to St Maurice (Panel 8). Information about the early history of Medingen is provided by the panels depicting its history in sixteen pictures, starting with its foundation and ending in the 1490s (Figures 3, 6, 8, 10). In the fifteenth and sixteenth centuries, numerous illuminated devotional books were produced in the convent, which also contain a rich body of songs (Panel 12 and Figure 12). The convent burnt down almost completely in 1781 and was rebuilt in the neo-classical style.

Kloster Wienhausen is a former Cistercian convent near Celle (Figure 37). The late-medieval complex has been preserved almost in its entirety, including the sculptures, tapestries and stained-glass windows. A particular treasure is the 'nuns' dust' found under the floorboards of the richly painted nuns' choir in the 1970s (Figures 5, 35, and 36; Chapter VII.3). It includes the oldest pairs of spectacles in the world, fragments of manuscripts, slips of paper and tools for writing and handicrafts.

2. Schematic Representations of Convent Life

2.1 Overview of the Daily Routine in a Convent

The times and sequence of the individual elements can vary in the different congregations and from convent to convent. In contrast to the custom described here, there are convents where the nuns' rest is interrupted at midnight to sing matins together with lauds in the convent church. Afterwards, the nuns return to their beds and get up again at 6:30 for prime (this 'division of the night' is the original Benedictine custom and reflects the standard way in which most people slept in the premodern period). In some convents it is not customary to work before terce. The first meal of the day always comes after the conventual mass, in some convents before, in others after sext; in Lent possibly only in the afternoon, after none, or after vespers.

4:00	Matins and Lauds	Divine office in the convent church, with possible votive offices (Marian psalter)
6:30	Prime	Divine office in the convent church, followed by private masses of the priest-monks spread across the morning.
7:00	Chapter Office	In the chapter house, reading of a chapter from the rule of Benedict, martyrology, remembrance of the dead, blessing over the day's work (possible debates).
7:30	*Lectio divina*	If applicable in the cells, Bible reading and personal prayer.
8:00	Handwork/Study	In the areas of the convent set aside for these functions or in the cells.
10:00	Terce, followed by the conventual mass and sext	Divine office in the convent church.
12:00	Lunch	In the refectory.
12:30	*Recreatio*	Midday break, to sleep or go for a walk.
14:00	None	Divine office in the convent church
14:20	Handwork/Study	In the areas of the convent set aside for these functions or in the cells
16:00	Vespers	Divine office in the convent church, with possible votive offices (Marian psalter)
16:30	Amongst other things, reading/lecture, followed by dinner and free time	Dinner in the refectory (no dinner during Lent)
18:45	Compline	Divine office in the convent church
19:30	Night's rest	If applicable in the cells, otherwise in the dormitory

3. Glossary of Terms

A detailed German glossary of terms used in the monastic history of Lower Saxony, as well as the basis for the map above, can be found on the Göttingen Regional History website at http://www.landesgeschichte.uni-goettingen.de/kloester.

Abbess	Head of a convent.
Antependium	Curtain or attachment for an altar which could change in the course of the church year.
Antiphon	Alternating chant or counter-chant in which several voices or instruments 'answer' one another, i.e. sing or play alternately.
Augustinian canonesses	Religious women who lived on the basis of the Rule of St Augustine and pursued a free way of life.
Benedictine nuns	Nuns who live according to the Rule of St Benedict of Nursia (died 547). The Cistercian nuns also followed the Benedictine Rule, but in the stricter interpretation of the Cistercian Order. To a certain extent, they were considered reformed Benedictine nuns.
Bursfelde Reform Congregation	Association of West and Central German, but also Dutch, Belgian, Danish and Luxembourgian Benedictine convents and monasteries that interpreted the Benedictine Rule strictly.
Canon	Priest who is part of a community of clerics, e.g., of a cathedral chapter; also canon of a chapter.
Canonical hours	→ Hours
Cantrix	→ *Precentrix*.
Cellar mistress	Nun with responsibility for managing the convent stores and the provisioning of the community.
Celleraria	→ Cellar Mistress.

Chapter (house) A room distinguished by particularly ornate architecture and usually located in the east wing near the choir. It opened onto the cloister and was a central part of the → enclosure. A chapter of the Rule of Benedict was read out there every day; the business of the convent was discussed; and violations of the rules were punished in 'chapters of fault'.

Cistercian nuns Nuns who follow the Cistercian Rule, → Benedictine nuns. Only some of the Cistercian nuns were legally full members of the order (incorporation), i.e. the order had the duty of supervising their spiritual life (*cura animarum*) and their goods (*cura temporalium*). They were then exempt, i.e. freed from the bishop's duty to supervise them. The Cistercian nuns of the Heilig Kreuz Kloster near Braunschweig were not incorporated, i.e. they followed the Cistercian rule and also shared in the privileges of the order, but continued to be subject to the bishop and, with regard to the administration of their property, to a secular cleric, the provost.

Cloister In the narrow sense the roofed rectangular walkway enclosing the cloister courtyard and connecting the east, south and west wings of the convent buildings. The north wing is usually directly connected to the south wall of the convent church. In a wider sense, the enclosed area reserved for the nuns, comprising the nuns' choir, the cloister with dormitory, refectory, workrooms, garden and cemetery

Compline Last time for prayer before the night's rest.

Convent The entire community of nuns, novices and servants; more narrowly, the community of choir nuns.

Corporal Linen cloth on the altar as an underlay for the communion vessels.

Confession of Augsburg → Protestantism.

Divine office → Hours

Domina Designation for the abbess of a religious women's community.

Dormitory Common dormitory in the convent, which could consist of a single room with small partitions or of a cell wing.

Enclosure The concept of the separation of women from the world.

Familia The secular servants of a religious community.

Flax-breaking A stage in the process of extracting linen from flax.

Four Humours Classical medical doctrine (humoral pathology) of the four bodily fluids: yellow and black bile, blood and phlegm.

Gradual Book collecting all the musical items of the mass.

Guild master Head of a guild or fraternity.

Habit Clerical garments that differ in colour, fabric and cut depending on the monastic order and consist of a cowl and various outer garments such as the scapular; in addition, nuns wore veils and possibly a → nun's crown.

Hours The seven times of day at which a religious community sings prayers and psalms, structuring everyday life, also the divine office or horary prayer.

Hymn Form of Latin strophic congregational singing attributed to Ambrose of Milan (died 397). Certain hymns were sung during the → Hours, as well as on feast days.

Interdict A church punishment that applies to a geographical area, e.g., a city, whereby all sacraments and religious acts, i.e. also baptism and burial, are temporarily forbidden. By contrast, the ecclesiastical ban (excommunication) affects individuals, who, when excommunicated, are temporarily excluded from the Christian community.

Lay brothers → Lay sisters.

Lay sisters Women who were part of the community but had fewer obligations to prayer and did manual work for the nuns.

Liturgy	Sequence and entirety of the religious ceremonies and rites of Jewish and Christian worship.
Liturgy of the Hours	→ Hours
Lot	Unit of measurement roughly equivalent to a spoonful.
Magistra	→ Schoolmistress.
Master salter	Overseer of the boiling pans for salt production, an office that was usually held by patricians and carried considerable political weight.
Middle Low German	Medieval variety of German spoken in Northern Germany and used as business language in the Hanseatic League, forerunner to *Plattdeutsch*.
Ministeriales	Lower nobility which from the 13th century formed the core of the German knightly class (*Ritterstand*).
Nuns' choir	Area of the church reserved for the choir nuns, from the twelfth century onwards often a gallery at the west end of the convent church. Before that the nuns' choir was often located in the northern or southern part of the transept, as was still the case in many convents in the late Middle Ages.
Nun's crown	Cloth crown given to nuns by a bishop as the sign of the church's official recognition of their status as virgins; it symbolized the nuns' future coronation by Christ following the model of the coronation of Mary.
Oblation	Handing over of a child to the convent, during which ceremony the parents take the vows on behalf of their child.
Old Believers	After the Reformation the term for those who remained Catholic.
Pastries and biscuits	were Produced in special shapes, such as Spekulatius baked in moulds, decorated gingerbread or wreaths made out of bread, and were often sent as gifts by the convents at New Year or other feast days. They were known as *Gebildbrot*.
Paten	Plate for the bread at the celebration of the Eucharist.
Paternoster	The Latin title for the Lord's Prayer, composed of the first two Latin words 'Our Father'.

Patriciate	Urban upper class.
Prebend	Income for priests, also benefice: material foundation for a male or female religious which either belonged to the initial provision of a parish or was the result of a later endowment.
Prebendary	Secular woman who, often in old age, is cared for in the convent.
Precentrix or *Cantrix*	Nun who led the choral singing and often taught the girls = precentor in a men's community.
Prioress	Highest office within a women's community after the abbess, who bore the responsibility for the community. If there was no abbess in a convent, the prioress was its head.
Procuratrix	Convent office, bursar, representative of the convent to the external world.
Profession	Legally valid act of entering holy orders at the age of majority.
Procurator	Office held by a member of the patriciate, similar to a church warden.
Provost	Cleric who supervises the affairs of a convent.
Psalter, Psalteries	The biblical book in which the psalms of David are collected; also the compilation of the psalms and other prayer texts used by the nuns for the Liturgy of the Hours.
Religious	Men and women who have committed themselves to a spiritual life.
Responsory	Singing alternating between a precentor and the choir.
Sacrista	Sexton, nun in charge of the service, church and sacristy.
Scapular	Liturgical outer garment.
Scholastica	→ Schoolmistress.
Schoolmistress	Nun responsible for the education of girls in a convent school destined for the religious life.
Sequence	Latin chant in pairs of stanzas.

Subprioress Deputy for the → Prioress.

Succentrix Deputy for the → *Precentrix*. While the *precentrix* (*cantrix*) leads one choir in the alternate chant, the *succentrix* presides over the other choir.

Suffragan Bishop subordinate to an archbishop.

Under one kind / under both kinds Form of distributing the Lord's Supper to the laity either only as the host (bread) or also with wine. The Lord's Supper under both kinds became the distinguishing feature of the acceptance of Protestantism, but also of the Utraquists, one of the first denominations to form in Bohemia; it goes back to Jan Hus (died 1415).

Vicarius Priest who is the deputy for the provost among the clergy of the convent.

4. List of Illustrations

Fig. 1	Floor plan of the monastic buildings at Ebstorf.	page 9
Fig. 2	Map of Braunschweig around 1400.	page 11
Fig. 3	Map view of the Grauer Hof in Braunschweig. Albrecht Heinrich Carl Conradi *c.* 1755.	page 15
Fig. 4	Wichmannsburg Antependium, Kloster Medingen, late 15th century.	page 22
Fig. 5	Nuns' choir at Wienhausen, looking towards west.	page 23
Fig. 6	Plan of St Gall, Reichenau, early 9th century. Stiftsbibliothek St. Gallen, Ms. 1092.	page 25
Fig. 7	Candelabrum from the nuns' choir.	page 29
Fig. 8	The Ebstorf World Map, 14th century.	page 31
Fig. 9	Lower Saxony on the Ebstorf World Map.	page 34
Fig. 10	History of Kloster Medingen, Panel 4. Lyßmann (1772) after paintings from 1499.	page 46
Fig. 11	Benedictine nun with nun's crown (detail from Fig. 27)	page 50
Fig. 12	Nun's crown from the twelfth century.	page 51
Fig. 13	Heiningen Philosophy Tapestry.	page 53
Fig. 14	Philosophy enthroned and surrounded by personifications (detail from Fig. 13)	page 56
Fig. 15	Bartholomew tapestry of 1492.	page 66
Fig. 16	Procession to the new convent in Medingen. Lyßmann (1772) after Medingen 1499.	page 71
Fig. 17	Wienhausen Tristan Tapestry.	page 73
Fig. 18	Bathing scene from the Wienhausen Tristan tapestry.	page 75
Fig. 19	St Maurice threatens Provost Dietrich Brandt. Lyßmann (1772) after Medingen 1499.	page 76
Fig. 20	St Maurice. Lüneburg: Hermann Worm 1506.	page 79
Fig. 21	Two nuns wearing crowns, the initials GLM und GF on a capital in the cloisters of Kloster Ebstorf.	page 91
Fig. 22	Heiligkreuztal: Christ embracing John.	page 98
Fig. 23	The Resurrected Christ, Kloster Wienhausen.	page 100
Fig. 24	Holy Sepulchre, Kloster Wienhausen	page 101
Fig. 25	Keystone, Kloster Ebstorf, 2nd half of the 14th century.	page 109
Fig. 26	Communal meal after the reform. Lyßmann (1772) after Medingen 1499.	page 113
Fig. 27	Guidonian Hand. Klosterarchiv Ebstorf V 3, 15th century, fols 200v–201r.	page 118
Fig. 28	Owl and monkey looking in the mirror (detail from Fig. 27).	page 119
Fig. 29	SUB Göttingen 8º Cod. Ms. Theol. 243, fols. 1v–2r, *c.* 1500.	page 121
Fig. 30	Dombibliothek Hildesheim Ms J 29, fol. 119r.	page 123

Fig. 31 Dombibliothek Hildesheim Ms J 29, fol. 52r.	page 125
Fig. 32 Vision of Dorothea von Meding 1562, painted around 1623, on the nuns' choir in Kloster Lüne.	page 150
Fig. 33 End of the diary, HAB Wolfenbüttel, Cod. 1159 Novi, fol. 238r.	page 162
Fig. 34 Wienhausen nuns' choir.	page 170
Fig. 35 Bloodletting among the pictures representing each month in the Wienhausen nuns' choir.	page 172
Fig. 36 Wall painting in the Wienhausen nuns' choir.	page 174
Fig. 37 View of Wienhausen from the south.	page 174
Fig. 38 Map of the Convents in Lower Saxony.	page 177

5. Sources and Secondary Literature

The titles of the secondary literature provide chapter-by-chapter references to the sources and research results used for and cited in this volume. They are also intended as recommended reading for greater in-depth study.

The introductory stories are taken from Eva Schlotheuber, *Klostereintritt und Bildung. Die Lebenswelt der Nonnen im späten Mittelalter. Mit einer Edition des "Konventstagebuchs" einer Zisterzienserin von Heilig Kreuz bei Braunschweig (1484–1507)* (= Spätmittelalter, Humanismus, Reformation 24), Tübingen 2004.

The letters of the Lüne nuns can be viewed online, including short English summaries of each letter, a detailed introduction on the historical background to their creation in German and English and a bibliography, at: http://diglib.hab.de/edoc/ed000248/start.htm. Book: *Networks of the Nuns. Edition und Erschließung der Briefsammlung aus Kloster Lüne (ca. 1460–1555)*, ed. by Eva Schlotheuber, Henrike Lähnemann et al. (= Late Middle Ages, Humanism, Reformation 24), Tübingen 2024.

Brief descriptions of all medieval women's monasteries in the region of present-day Lower Saxony, with lists of all office-holders and historical treasures, architectural descriptions and a bibliography can be found in the four-volume reference work *Niedersächsisches Klosterbuch. Verzeichnis der Klöster, Stifte, Kommenden und Beginenhäuser in Niedersachsen und Bremen von den Anfängen bis 1810*, ed. by Josef Dolle, Bielefeld 2012, 2nd edition 2022. Abstracts of the articles exist on the website of Landesgeschichte Göttingen: http://www.landesgeschichte.uni-goettingen.de/kloester/.

Many of the pictorial documents can be found in the exhibition catalogue *Schatzhüterin. 200 Jahre Klosterkammer Hannover*, ed. by Katja Lembke and Jens Reiche, Dresden 2018. The Medingen panel paintings and the reform movement in the convents are discussed in Ulrike Hascher-Burger and Henrike Lähnemann, *Liturgie und Reform im Kloster Medingen. Edition und Untersuchung des Propst-Handbuchs*, Oxford, Bodleian Library, MS. Lat. liturg. e. 18 (= Spätmittelalter, Humanismus, Reformation 76), Tübingen 2013. Much of the material can be accessed (largely in English) on the Medingen Manuscripts blog: medingen.seh.ox.ac.uk. Medieval visual evidence with inscriptions, such as the tapestries, can also be viewed online on the website of the Inscriptions Commission: inschriften.net. The volumes on the Lüneburg Convents, from which much of the visual material is taken, are Volume 24 (1984, Kloster Lüne) and Volume 76 (2009, including Kloster Ebstorf, Kloster Medingen and Kloster Wienhausen). For manuscripts, the web portal handschriftenportal.de provides up-to-date coverage, even more detailed for German manuscripts in https://www.handschriftencensus.de/.

Special literature on individual chapters (many of the publications by Henrike Lähnemann and Eva Schlotheuber mentioned are freely accessible via their publication directories on their university homepages in Oxford and Düsseldorf).

Chapter I: *Die Ebstorfer Weltkarte. Kommentierte Neuausgabe in zwei Bänden*. Annotated edition of the Ebstorf World Map in two volumes, ed. by Hartmut Kugler, Berlin 2007; Henrike Lähnemann, *Eine imaginäre Reise nach Jerusalem. Der Geographische Traktat des Erhart Groß*, in: Sehen und Sichtbarkeit in der deutschen Literatur des Mittelalters, ed. by Ricarda Bauschke, Sebastian Coxon and Martin Jones, Berlin 2011, pp. 408–424.

Chapter II: Eva Schlotheuber, *Ebstorf und seine Schülerinnen in der zweiten Hälfte des 15. Jahrhunderts*, in: Studien und Texte zur literarischen und materiellen Kultur der Frauenklöster im späten Mittelalter (= Studies in Medieval and Reformation Thought 99), ed. by Falk Eisermann et al., Leiden/Boston 2004, pp. 169–221. The primary texts are edited by Conrad Borchling, 'Litterarisches und geistiges Leben im Kloster Ebstorf am Ausgang des Mittelalters', *Zeitschrift des Historischen Vereins für Niedersachsens* 4 (1905), pp. 361–407. Philipp Stenzig, *Die Chronik des Klosters Lüne über die Jahre 1481–1530: Hs. Lüne 13*, Tübingen 2019. Falk Eisermann, 'Die Inschriften auf den Textilien des Augustiner-Chorfrauenstifts Heiningen', in: *Nachrichten der Akademie der Wissenschaften in Göttingen, phil.-hist. Klasse*, 6 (1996) pp. 227–285.

Chapter IV: Eva Schlotheuber, *Willibald und die Klosterfrauen von Sankt Klara – eine wechselhafte Beziehung*, in: *Pirckheimer Jahrbuch für Renaissance- und Humanismusforschung* 28/2014, pp. 57–75; *Willibald Pirckheimers Briefwechsel*, vol. 5, ed. by Helga Scheible, Munich 2001. Wilhelm Nyssen (ed.), *Aelred von Rieval, Über die geistliche Freundschaft. Lateinisch–deutsch*, Trier 1978. *Amicitia: Friendship in Medieval Culture*, Essays in Honour of Nigel Palmer ed. by Almut Suerbaum and Annette Volfing, Oxford German Studies 36/2 (2007). *Companion to Mysticism and Devotion in Northern Germany in the Late Middle Ages*, ed. by Elizabeth Andersen et al. (Brill's Companions to the Christian Tradition 44), Leiden 2013.

Chapter V: Henrike Lähnemann, 'Per organa. Musikalische Unterweisung in Handschriften der Lüneburger Klöster', in: *Dichtung und Didaxe. Lehrhaftes Sprechen in der deutschen Literatur des Mittelalters*, ed. by Henrike Lähnemann and Sandra Linden, Berlin/New York 2009, pp. 397–412; Eva Schlotheuber, 'Wir, die wir von Kindheit an wie in einem Rosengarten erzogen worden sind ... Klostereintritt und Ausbildung in den spätmittelalterlichen Frauenklöstern', in: *Damals* 7/2003, pp. 30–36; Henrike Lähnemann, 'Armbrust und Apfelbaum. Eine lateinisch-niederdeutsche Hoheliedauslegung' (Mscr.Dresd.A.323), in: *Auf den Schwingen des Pelikans*, ed. by Ralf Plate et al. (= ZfdA-Beiheft 40/2022), pp. 403–429. Conrad Borchling, 'Litterarisches Leben in Kloster Ebstorf'.

Chapter VI: Henrike Lähnemann, 'Der Medinger "Nonnenkrieg" aus der Perspektive der Klosterreform. Geistliche Selbstbehauptung 1479–1554', in: *1517–1545: The Northern Experience. Mysticism, Art and Devotion between Late Medieval and Early Modern (Ons Geestelijk Erf* 87/2016), ed. by Kees Scheepers et al, pp. 91–116; Martin Luther, *Sendbrief vom Dolmetschen und Fürbitte der Heiligen*, ed. by Howard Jones and Henrike Lähnemann, Oxford 2022 (online at editions.mml.ox.ac.uk). Beth Plummer, *Stripping the Veil*, Oxford 2022.

Chapter VII: Generally on the significance of food and dietetics in convents see Caroline Walker Bynum, *Holy Feast and Holy Fast: The Religious Significance of Food to Medieval Women* (1988). The recipes from Kloster Wienhausen in Chapter VII.2 are taken from an essay by Timo Bülters which appeared in 2017 and can be viewed online: https://doi.org/10.11588/artdok.00005030. The library catalogue of the Dominican convent in Lemgo and a description of the medical manuscripts can be found in Jeffrey Hamburger, Eva Schlotheuber, Margot Fassler, Susan Marti, *Liturgical Life and Latin Learning at Paradies bei Soest, 1300–1425: Inscription and Illumination in the Choir Books of a North German Dominican Convent*, Münster 2017, 2 vols. The magazines *Das Feuer hüten* (first volume translated by Anne Simon as Tending the Hearth) published by the General Convention of Abbesses of Protestant Convents in Northern Germany http://generalkonvent.de/), provide a vivid and tasty introduction to the North German monastic landscape. The magazines present the convents in the area of the Klosterkammer Hannover by means of photos and recipes from the regional cuisine selected by the women who currently live there. The magazines are available in the convents.

Index

abbess, role of 27, 68
Aelred of Rievaux 94–95
   De spiritali amicitia 94–95
animals 36, 119–120, 123, 166
   medical care of 166
   symbolism 36, 119–120
antiquity, authors of 54
Apostles, the 44, 80, 145–146, 153
   personal 145–146
architecture, monastic 6, 22, 24, 26, 170–171, 182
Aristotle 54–55
Bavenstedt, Tilemann von (Provost) 167–168
bells 13–14, 71, 123–124, 143, 156
Benedictines, the 9, 21, 31, 44–45, 47, 50, 65, 67, 85, 97, 114, 129, 142, 151, 155, 168, 178–179, 181–182
Bierwirt, preacher 144–145
bilingualism 146
Black Death. *See* plague, the
bloodletting 153, 169, 171–172
Braunschweig 2–3, 6, 10–12, 14–16, 18, 20, 24, 35, 37, 44, 48, 59–60, 63–64, 70, 74, 82–83, 105–106, 115, 128–131, 133–135, 138–139, 141, 144, 160–161, 177–178, 182
   civic feud 10–14
   Heilig Kreuz Kloster. *See* Kloster Heilig Kreuz
   patriciate 12
   town council 10, 12, 16, 59, 63, 129
Busch, Johannes 38, 41
calefactory 42, 169

cantrix. See precentrix
cellar mistress 17, 68, 181
Celtis, Konrad 88–90
chant 30, 41, 88, 107, 115, 117–119, 124, 130, 132, 135, 145, 148, 167
chapter 16, 27, 37, 39–40, 47–48, 64, 70, 111, 156, 168
   of fault 111, 182
chapter house 9, 16, 22, 24, 27
choirs 3, 5, 9, 14, 22–24, 27–29, 33, 37, 41, 43, 47, 52, 55, 57, 59–60, 68, 80, 96, 102, 106, 108, 111, 117–118, 121–124, 132, 143, 147–148, 150–151, 153, 161, 164, 167–175, 179, 182, 184–186
Christ 1, 6, 21, 26, 28, 30, 33, 44, 51–52, 59, 66–68, 70, 78, 80–81, 90–91, 94–102, 107, 124, 132, 139–140, 146, 149, 151–153, 168, 173, 175, 184
   and John the Evangelist 96
   as heavenly bridegroom 1, 21, 44, 51, 59, 67, 81, 91, 99, 107, 139, 151, 173, 175
   depictions of 80, 95–102, 149
   love for 6, 91, 94, 96
   physical closeness to 99, 143, 175
Christmas 26–28, 30, 76–77, 80, 86
Christoph, Bishop of Bremen 143–144
church 9–10, 14, 16, 19–22, 24, 26–30, 47, 49, 57, 64, 71–72, 77–78, 83, 93, 95–96, 100, 107, 117, 124, 129–133, 135, 137,

139–140, 147–148, 161, 164, 167–168, 170–171, 173, 178–185
convent 9, 14, 19, 22, 30, 72, 77–78, 124, 133, 147, 178–179
parish 21, 64, 117, 171, 173
Church, Catholic 84, 127, 139, 147, 178
structure of year 27–28, 30
Cicero 94
Laelius de Amicitia 94
Cistercians, the 2–3, 5–6, 10, 12–14, 16–17, 21, 26, 37–38, 44, 47–48, 60, 65, 70, 76, 82, 94, 97, 104–105, 107, 111–115, 129, 131–136, 138, 157, 161
monks in Braunschweig 14, 129
commemoration 30, 57, 59, 66, 155, 158–159, 168
communion 15, 78, 123, 145, 147–148, 156, 158, 161, 182
under both kinds 147
community 1–6, 16–21, 24, 26–28, 30, 38–39, 43–45, 47, 52, 54–55, 57, 59–61, 64–65, 67–71, 76, 78, 80–82, 85, 87, 91–92, 95, 98, 103, 110–114, 117–118, 121, 129–130, 133, 140–142, 151, 153, 156–160, 166, 175, 178, 181–183, 185
convent 1, 4, 21, 27, 39, 44–45, 59, 61, 64–65, 69, 82, 92, 103, 114, 117, 121, 140, 142, 157, 159, 166
secular 68–70
Compline 15, 27, 111, 167
Confession 15, 71, 111, 127, 139, 147, 153, 156, 158, 161–162, 166
convents 1–7, 9–10, 12–14, 16, 18–22, 24, 26–31, 33, 35, 37–49, 52, 54–55, 57, 59–65, 67–72, 74, 76–78, 80–85, 87, 91–92, 96–97, 99–108, 110–117, 120–124, 127, 129–130, 132–149, 151–152, 155–161, 163–169, 171, 175, 177–186
admission to 44–45, 49, 61

contact with outside world 22, 69, 107, 111, 143
daily life 13, 15–16, 26–27, 30, 41, 110, 117
economy of 38, 110, 112
education in 37–40, 43–45, 48, 103, 112, 152
festivals in 106
furnishings of 78, 80, 171
guests in 26, 37, 60, 105, 117, 129, 136
music in 37, 49, 102, 106, 117, 120, 122, 131, 142
size of 57, 67–68
coronation, nuns' 44, 47, 49, 51, 184
correspondence 81, 83, 88, 117, 142, 144, 147
Damman, Dorte 39–41
Dankwarderode Castle 35
death 5, 30, 61, 66, 70–71, 74–75, 81–82, 85, 90, 92–93, 95, 152, 155–157, 159–160, 163, 166–167, 175
rituals 159–160, 163, 166–167
Derneburg, Cistercian convent 37–40, 115–116
diarist, Cistercian 3, 16–19, 40, 60–62, 82, 104–106, 129–130, 132, 134, 137, 145, 156, 159–162
diary, of Cistercian nun 2–4, 6, 10, 12–13, 42, 81, 135, 161–162
diet 42, 164
Divine Office 15–16, 41, 171, 173, 183
Dorothea von Meding 149–153, 169, 179
vision 149–151, 169, 179
dying. *See* death
Easter 28, 86, 90, 100, 117, 123–124, 127, 130–131, 153
Elisabeth of Braunschweig-Lüneburg (Prioress of Steterburg) 129
Elvers, Elisabeth (Abbess of Medingen) 141–143, 146

enclosure, monastic 5, 9–11, 13, 16–17, 19–21, 24, 27–28, 31, 36, 38, 41, 43, 47–48, 54, 67–69, 72, 81, 91, 96, 103–104, 106, 110–111, 117, 120, 124, 129, 134–135, 139, 143, 166, 175, 182
   attitudes to 143
   observance of 104, 106, 129, 143
   physical 19–21
   protection of 17, 143
Ernst, Duke of Braunschweig-Lüneburg 141, 143–144
family
   convent 43, 59, 64, 69, 143
   secular 45, 47, 59–62, 65, 67–69, 142, 147, 155
      influence of 59, 65
      relations to 59, 61, 67, 69
famine 18, 38
festivals/festivities 62, 74, 77, 100, 103–107
festivities 110
flax-breaking 103–106, 108, 110
   songs 103–104, 108, 110
Four Humours, the 163
friendship 5, 64, 81–83, 85, 91–96, 116
   cultivation of 67, 81, 95–96
   exploitation of 64, 95
   external 81, 83, 91
   models of 93–95
   role of 81–83, 91, 95–96
funerals 71, 158, 160, 167–168
   rituals 71
Gertrude the Great 101–102
Herald of Divine Love 101
gifts 48, 51, 56, 64, 67, 81, 83–84, 92, 95–96, 105, 132, 164, 184
   culture of 67, 84, 96
Gisela von Damme, abbess of Heilig Kreuz 81
Glümer, Bodo, Braunschweig councillor 63–64
God 5, 14, 17, 27–28, 35–36, 47, 50, 54, 57, 65–66, 72, 81–82, 90, 92–94, 102–103, 107, 117, 124, 128, 134–135, 139–140, 143–146, 151–152, 158, 166, 169
Grauer Hof, the 14–15
Guidonian Hand, the 118–119
Hanseatic League 35, 152, 184
Heiningen Philosophy Tapestry 52–55, 57, 110
Henry IV (the Elder), Duke of Braunschweig-Lüneburg 129–131
Henry V (the Younger), Duke of Braunschweig-Lüneburg 10
High German 152
Hildegard of Bingen 1, 6, 50–51, 165
Hours, Liturgy of 28, 60, 70, 93, 110, 117, 146
Humanists 54, 83, 87–88, 90, 127
humour 83–84, 86
Indulgences 36, 128, 133–134, 138–139
investiture 37, 44, 47–48, 52, 117, 130
   ritual of 47
Jerusalem, Heavenly 33, 129, 175
Jonathan, son of King Saul 92–93
Kalm, Remborg, Prioress of Kloster Heilig Kreuz 14, 156
Karstens, Heinrich, Provost of Heilig Kreuz 63–64
Kerkhove, van dem, family of 59
Kerkhove, van dem, Margarete 60
King David 50, 108
Kloster Ebstorf 24, 31, 33–34, 41, 43, 49, 91, 109, 114, 118, 120–123, 178
   education in 49, 114, 118, 120–121, 123
   saltworks 35
   World Map 28, 31–32, 37, 74, 178
Kloster Heilig Kreuz 1–4, 6, 10, 12, 16, 18, 21, 24, 35, 37–41, 48, 59–61, 63–65, 71, 81–83,

104–106, 129–134, 136, 156, 160–161, 166, 177–178, 182, 189
diarist in. *See* diarist, Cistercian
education in 39–40
flight from 10–14
visit by papal legate 129–131, 134
Kloster Lüne 1–3, 7, 21, 24, 26, 29, 35, 44–48, 51, 65–67, 69–70, 72, 82, 91–93, 96, 142, 146–147, 149–150, 160, 166, 175, 178, 188
architecture 26
layout of 26, 179
letters from 67, 146, 178
painting of vision 3, 149–150, 179
Kloster Marienberg, education at 41
Kloster Mariensee 115
Kloster Medingen 2, 21–22, 24, 27, 46, 67–68, 70, 75, 78–80, 110, 115–117, 121, 141, 144–145, 148, 178–179
acceptance of Lutheran Reformation 144–145, 148
conflict with Duke Ernst of Braunschweig-Lüneburg 141, 143–144
education in 121
furnishings of 78, 80
pictorial panels 14, 24, 46, 70, 75–77, 113, 123, 179
Provost's Manual 2, 124
reform in 24, 70, 110, 115–116, 140, 144, 148
St Maurice 78
Kloster Wienhausen 23, 28, 73, 75, 80, 100–101, 115–117, 148, 163–165, 170, 172–174, 178–179
nuns' choir 164, 169–170, 172–174, 179
painting in 170–171, 173, 175
Tristan tapestry. *See* Tristan tapestry

Kloster Wöltingerode 38, 48–49, 105, 110
Knochenhauer, Georg, Provost of Heilig Kreuz 106, 130, 132, 157, 159
Last Judgement 49, 139, 152, 167
last rites 71, 156, 158, 161, 166
Latin, use of 4, 37–38, 40–41, 43, 57, 67, 87, 115, 133, 141–142, 145–147, 163
lay brothers 68, 71, 117
lay sisters 14, 16–19, 24, 27, 45, 52, 55, 60, 67–68, 71, 91, 104–105, 112, 115, 121, 132, 137, 157, 160, 163, 168
Lent 115, 147, 156, 164, 180
liturgy 2, 16–17, 24, 27–28, 30, 40, 43, 60, 70–71, 88, 93, 102, 106–107, 109–110, 114, 117, 120–121, 124, 145–146, 148, 152, 156, 168, 175, 184–185
Latin 43, 145–146, 148
love 5–6, 53, 72, 74–75, 81, 89, 91–96, 99, 101–102, 107–108, 164
cultivation of 81
for Christ 6, 81, 91, 94, 96
for family 83, 88
for God 92, 94, 102
of God 82, 107
role of 82, 91–92, 96
Low German, use of 4, 10, 21, 48–49, 67, 72, 74, 77, 121, 141, 146, 152, 163
Lüneburg 3, 7, 9, 35, 67, 72, 76, 78–79, 99, 110, 115–116, 129, 141–143, 147–149, 178
town council 72, 116, 143, 147
Luther, Martin 2, 140, 146
Ninety-Five Theses 2, 54
manuscripts 2–3, 7, 30, 68, 78, 97, 115, 118, 120–121, 140, 143, 145, 164–165, 179
devotional 68, 145
illustration of 78, 97, 115, 118, 120

medical 164
production of 120
structure of 3, 30, 120
Mass 16–17, 27, 29, 42, 47–48, 70, 76–77, 127, 129–130, 140, 145, 147–148, 157, 167–168, 180, 183
  banning of 127
  celebration of 17, 47, 70, 77
  investiture during 47–48
Matins 24, 27, 102, 179
Maurice, Saint 71, 77–78, 80, 149, 178–179
  portrayals of 77–78, 80
  role of 80
meals, communal 24, 27, 48, 105, 111, 114–116, 149
Mechthild of Magdeburg 1, 101
medicine 37, 55, 155, 159–160, 163–165
  books on 163–164
memoria. See commemoration
music 5, 37, 49, 56, 102–103, 106, 108, 115, 118–120, 123–124, 129
  depiction of theory 118–120
  in manuscripts 118
  instruction in 49, 118
  notation of 118, 120
  role of 5, 106
naturopathy 155
networks, monastic 38–39, 64, 80, 96, 110, 115–116, 149, 155, 179
Nicholas, scholar at Heilig Kreuz 157, 159
Nocturnes 27
nuns
  as Brides of Christ 1, 44, 91, 99
  coronation of 44, 47, 49, 51
  correspondence of 81, 83, 142, 144, 147
  crowns of 47, 49–51
  dowry of 61, 65
  friendship between 81–83, 89, 95–96
  image of 86–87
  investiture of 37, 44, 47–48, 52, 117, 130
  networks of 80, 110, 115, 155, 179
  profession 27, 37, 44, 46–48
  relationship to families. *See* family
  vestments 45, 47, 151
nuns' choir 3, 9, 22, 24, 27–29, 33, 47, 52, 57, 80, 96, 102, 117, 143, 148, 150–151, 153, 161, 164, 167–175, 179, 182, 184
Nuremberg 6, 35–36, 45, 83–85, 87–88, 90, 114, 127, 147
  Convent of Poor Clares 84–85, 127
  Convent of St Katherine 36, 114
  Lutheran Reformation in 127
oblation 47, 62
ointments 74, 165–166
organ 49, 71, 120, 122–124
Ovid 54
patriciate, the 12, 61, 65, 81, 85
Pawel, Elisabeth, Abbess of Heilig Kreuz 38–40, 63
Pawes, Ulrich, Confessor at Heilig Kreuz 132, 134–135
Peraudi, Raymond, Cardinal 128–134
pilgrimage, spiritual 28, 33, 36, 139, 155
Pirckheimer, Caritas 84–90, 127, 147
  correspondence with brother Willibald 85, 87–89
Pirckheimer, Eufemia 83–85
Pirckheimer, Juliane 45
Pirckheimer, Katharina 84–85, 128
Pirckheimer, Klara 84, 86–87
  correspondence with brother Willibald 86–87
Pirckheimer, Sabina 83–85
Pirckheimer, Willibald 45, 83–88, 127–128, 147

plague, the 3, 18, 38, 45, 82, 160–164
precentrix 29, 68, 186
Prime 27, 111, 179
processi 130
processions 13–14, 16, 68, 71, 80, 129, 135, 137, 167
profession 27, 37, 44, 46–47, 144
  tacit 47
provost, role of 14–17, 24, 45, 47, 59, 63, 69–71, 112, 116, 166–167
Provost's Manual 2, 124
Psalms, the 26, 28, 30, 88, 117, 122, 167
Psalter, the 30, 146, 167, 180, 185
Puffen, Margarete, abbess of Medingen 70, 78, 116, 142
refectory 9, 15, 22, 24, 27, 111–112, 114, 180, 182
Reformation, the 2, 5–6, 29, 57, 84, 87, 102, 127–128, 130, 139–141, 143–145, 147–149, 151–153, 178, 184
reform, monastic 6, 24, 38–40, 42, 45, 47, 55, 70, 103, 105–107, 110–118, 121–124, 140–143, 145, 148–149, 152, 155, 178–179
  introduction of 2, 110, 115
relics 83, 99, 101, 130, 132, 135, 137, 139, 178
remedies, herbal 163–166
  formulas for 164, 166
Rennelberg, the 5, 10, 12, 60, 178
Resurrection, the 28, 33, 100
Riddagshausen, Cistercian monastery 14–16, 82, 129, 132
routine, monastic 13, 15, 26–27, 110
saints 1–2, 25–27, 30, 36, 47–48, 52, 61–63, 65–66, 71, 74, 76–80, 83–86, 92, 96–97, 99, 102, 107, 114, 129, 131–132, 134, 137–138, 140, 145–146, 148–149, 152–153, 155, 159, 161, 166, 169–170, 178–179, 181

feast days 13, 30, 44, 48, 57, 59, 67, 71, 97, 107, 134, 148, 153
intercession by 81, 83, 140, 145–146, 148, 155
patron saints 30, 47, 52, 65, 71, 76–77, 80, 107, 146, 148
  role of 80, 140
veneration of 36, 145–146
Schaper, Dietrich, provost of Kloster Lüne 72
Scheurl, Christoph, advisor to Nuremberg council 87, 89
scholastica. See schoolmistress
Schomaker, Nikolaus, provost of Lüne 92
schoolmistress 40, 68, 113
Schulenburg, Sophie von, abbess of Derneburg 37, 39
Sext 27, 180
sick room 155, 166
singing 28, 41, 104–107, 117, 121–122, 124, 132, 140, 146, 148, 158, 168, 171, 175, 183, 185
songbooks 104, 108
Song of Songs 21, 81, 99, 101, 107, 152
songs, secular 103–104, 107–108, 110
space, monastic 15–16, 19, 21–22, 24, 26, 28, 59, 124, 160, 171, 173
Steterburg, Augustinian convent 129–130
St Gallen Monastery Plan 25
Stöterogge, Margarete (Abbess of Medingen) 141–143
Stöterogge, Nikolaus 147
symbolism 74
  of animals. See animals: symbolism
table readings 27, 112–113
tapestries 5–6, 52–54, 57, 65–66, 72–75, 110, 131–132, 179
  function of 52, 54
  Heiningen. See Heiningen Philosophy Tapestry

Wienhausen. *See* Tristan tapestry
time 26–30, 33, 36, 173
transcendence 30
transcendence of 36, 173
transcendence 30, 36, 88–89, 107, 173
Tristan tapestry 57, 72–75
Vechelde, Albrecht von, Braunschweig town councillor 63–64
Vechelde, Carl Friedrich von 3
Vechelde, Mechthild von, abbess of Kloster Heilig-Kreuz 13–14, 60, 103, 156
Vespers 16, 27, 161, 167, 180
vestments, nuns' 100, 114
virginity 11, 19, 33, 44, 46–47, 49, 51–52, 88, 97, 99, 102, 107, 129, 137, 149, 151

Virgin Mary, the 17, 28, 76, 80, 97, 107, 133, 149
Virgins, Wise and Foolish, the 52
visions 51, 101, 149, 151, 153, 169
vows 20, 44, 46–47, 60, 62, 68, 128, 140, 151, 184
profession of 46
rejection by Martin Luther 140
significance of 62, 140
Weferlingen, Elisabeth von 61
Weferlingen, Fia von 62
Weferlingen, Katharina von 61–62
Weferlingen, Ulrich von 61–62
Wienhausen Liederbuch 108
Wilde, Mechthild, Prioress of Lüne 47, 142
writing materials 2–4, 6, 26, 31–32, 78, 117, 120, 161
Zodiac, the 169

About the Team

Alessandra Tosi was the managing editor for this book.

The German text was translated by Anne Simon; Andrew Dunning, Cecilia Thon, and Charlotte Pattenden proof-read the manuscript.

Hannah Shakespeare indexed the book.

The authors created the descriptive text for images.

Jeevanjot Kaur Nagpal designed the cover. The cover was produced in InDesign using the Fontin font.

Jeremy Bowman typeset the book in InDesign. The main text font is Tex Gyre Pagella. The heading font is Californian FB.

Cameron Craig produced the paperback and hardback editions, as well as the PDF and HTML editions. The conversion was performed with open-source software and other tools freely available on our GitHub page at https://github.com/OpenBookPublishers.

Jeremy Bowman created the EPUB.

This book need not end here...

Share

All our books — including the one you have just read — are free to access online so that students, researchers and members of the public who can't afford a printed edition will have access to the same ideas. This title will be accessed online by hundreds of readers each month across the globe: why not share the link so that someone you know is one of them?

This book and additional content is available at:
https://doi.org/10.11647/OBP.0397

Donate

Open Book Publishers is an award-winning, scholar-led, not-for-profit press making knowledge freely available one book at a time. We don't charge authors to publish with us: instead, our work is supported by our library members and by donations from people who believe that research shouldn't be locked behind paywalls.

Why not join them in freeing knowledge by supporting us:
https://www.openbookpublishers.com/support-us

Follow @OpenBookPublish

Read more at the Open Book Publishers BLOG

You may also be interested in...

The Sword of Judith
Judith Studies Across the Disciplines
Kevin R. Brine, Elena Ciletti, & Henrike Lähnemann (eds)

https://doi.org/10.11647/OBP.0009

Touching Parchment: How Medieval Users Rubbed, Handled, and Kissed Their Manuscripts
Volume 1: Officials and Their Books
Kathryn M. Rudy

https://doi.org/10.11647/OBP.0337

 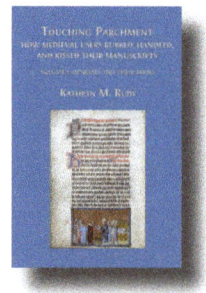

Piety in Pieces
How Medieval Readers Customized their Manuscripts
Kathryn M. Rudy

https://doi.org/10.11647/OBP.0094

 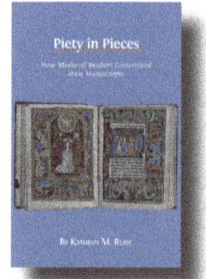

The Juggler of Notre Dame and the Medievalizing of Modernity
Volume 1: The Middle Ages
Jan M. Ziolkowski

https://doi.org/10.11647/OBP.0132

www.ingramcontent.com/pod-product-compliance
Lightning Source LLC
Chambersburg PA
CBHW042043240426
43667CB00048B/2971